ENTERTAINING DETOURS

Unique Tales from My Journey Along the Road Less Traveled

By Michael J. Hawron

ENTERTAINING DETOURS
Copyright © 2015 by Michael J. Hawron.

Cover Art by Chris Works

Special thanks to Jacob Cuthbertson for his patient and invaluable assistance with formatting and design.

Cover Photo by Nathanael Hawron

All photos by members of the Hawron family or Ark Eden

Foreword

"A spry debut memoir charting the adventuresome life of a well-traveled, nature-loving family man. 'I have had the privilege of living a full life,' writes Hawron, who spent time on five continents in about 30 countries and fathered 12 children. In this book, he generously shares stories of his life, accompanied by photographs of locations, family members, and cherished friends. Spurred on to complete his memoir by his daughter Suzy, who passed away prior to its publication, Hawron narrates a rich, hardy memoir filled with harmless escapades, unconventional follies, and familial love. Unsurprisingly, his childhood in New York State's Hudson River Valley was spent hiking; later, he attended college at the Massachusetts Institute of Technology, and he later indulged his wanderlust.

"Among the more colorfully depicted places he visited was Lantau, Hong Kong's largest outlying island, where he lived for years with his wife and kids; it's a locale that he ponders extensively with an engaging amalgam of adoration and trepidation. With that same diligence, the author educates readers on what he considers the 'major Hong Kong fear factors,' including typhoons, noise, the city's 'olfactory tapestry,' and traffic (Hawron's chapter on Hong Kong taxicabs is riveting).

"He also reveals the origins of his surname and the wonderment he harbors for his children, tells of his time spent in New Zealand, and reflects on the strangeness of life in China. Certainly, the writing is splendidly detailed, and Hawron's skill as an engaging raconteur is evident throughout... the memoir's wholesome core and genuine verve for all things wild and worldly remain: 'Actually, my real purpose is to entertain,' the author writes...A...diligently chronicled travelogue featuring tales that are illuminating and effortlessly entertaining..."

– Kirkus Reviews

Dedication

To my daughter Suzy

December 15, 1975 - December 26, 2014

"Dad, you really need to finish this book! I will never get around to writing a book myself. But this is brilliant! Promise me you will finish the book!"

–From the last conversation I had with Suzy just days before her passing.

*****

I also wish to extend my sincere gratitude to the visionary leadership and fine staff of the Ark Eden Foundation in Hong Kong, whose unique and vital environmental mission and whose help and encouragement were a great inspiration during this book's creation.

Table of Contents

INTRODUCTION

"**Y**ou should write a book!" I have lost track of how many times I have heard this gentle curse uttered over the decades by well-meaning friends, family and associates after they were regaled by one of my entertaining tales. Over the years I have pretty much determined that if I ever did so, that would be the working title: "You Should Write a Book!" Perhaps if each of those well-wishers had also chipped in a couple dollars each time they said "you should write a book!" I would already have a tidy publisher's advance in hand. But alas, here I am, hoping that you will buy my book so I can retire in peace. Actually, my real purpose is to entertain: I enjoy making people happy. As 'they' say, "laughter is good for the soul" and these stressful times do seem to require an extra dose of good cheer, which I am happy to provide at my own expense. I also hope these stories will stimulate your own innate imagination and creativity, as we all occasionally need to think and dream outside the box, for our own well-being.

Who am I that you should have to read my book? Even the great Russian author Dostoevsky grappled with this same thorny question, in the foreward to his masterpiece *The Brothers Karamazov*. As for me, I consider myself to be an average, intelligent, healthy person who has had the good fortune to experience an above–average amount of unusual adventures and experiences. I've lived on five continents in about thirty or so countries—some for a few days, some for years. Whether I was being attacked by baboons, pummeled by typhoons, caught in a war zone, accosted by strange and mysterious individuals, or surviving several close brushes with the afterlife, I have had the privilege of living a full life. If that weren't fun enough, I have a quiver full of children and grandchildren—twelve and fourteen respectively, at last count. The myriad of stories I tell are indeed all true: there really is no need for fiction.

I have often started on this project but alas, it has never happened: perhaps in part because my life's travels, work and large family have all kept me very busy. Or maybe it was just pure laziness on my part. Writing is hard work after all; otherwise everyone would be doing it and giving it away. That was, until Monday the 18th of August, 2014. I will tell you more about that amazing day in just a moment. So here I am as my sunset approaches, reflecting on my travels and adventures (perhaps not unlike Tolkien's Hobbit, albeit minus the hairy feet).

At one point I toyed with calling this book "Tales from Lantau"—the beautiful island west of Hong Kong that was once my home. Many of these tales, such as "Primate Bullying" are indeed set in that amazing commercial and cultural stew called Hong Kong, where I lived for eleven years. Other stories, such as "Wounded Knee and Naughty Nurses" tell of my numerous adventures in the lands Down Under—Australia and New Zealand—where I had the pleasure of living for six years. Still other anecdotes occurred while I was crisscrossing the globe, such as "The Cost of Free Champagne!" And yet other chapters such as "Why I Now Love Goats" detail adventures I have experienced since finally settling down on my little farm in rural Texas with my second family where I now write this book.

Most of these stories hail from another time and another place: I was younger then, in my twenties and thirties. Many of the people who are now very important in my life—family and friends alike—had either not been born or met at this stage of my life.

Regardless of the stories' origins and the public's reception of same, at least my many children and grandchildren will have a good supply of stories from my younger days to enjoy and later pass on to their children and maybe thereby remember me as well. If this book becomes a best seller, thanks in part to your purchase today, then maybe my family will remember me even the more fondly.

There are some other compelling reasons why you should buy this book, now that I have finally written it. Firstly the book is a collection of short stories. The uniqueness of this book is that there is no firm chronology. You can start reading anyplace you want! Pick any chapter where the title arouses your curiosity and you only have to read a few pages to get to the punch line or the end of the story. If I refer to something described in greater detail elsewhere in the book, I try to always put the chapter title in brackets for your easy reference, like this: [read the chapter about all my detours in "Primate Bullying."] While on the subject, Chapter 14, "Primate Bullying" probably best contains the central theme of this book: how my adventurous penchant for detours has led to some of my life's most rewarding experiences. Had I stuck to the road most travelled that was suggested for me by well-meaning individuals, I would never have had the amazing material for this book.

Each chapter is complete on its own and thus you don't have to wade through hundreds of pages before you find out what happens, all the while wondering if it is indeed worth the bother. Just pick up my book when you have a few spare moments in your busy day to relax. Read a few pages and enjoy the journey along the detour until a smile or a chuckle arrives at your heart. Then I will have done my job for the day and accomplished my purpose.

Perhaps the psychoanalysts among you will conjecture that my writing this book represents a long-suppressed career move. When I was in fourth grade at St. Joseph's, our class was chosen to put on a Christmas show for a local nursing home. I had never been to such a place in all my sheltered young years, so I soon discovered that "nursing home" was a euphemism for a crowded building filled with old people and strange smells. (Come to think of it, the strange smells may have been good preparation for my days in Hong Kong.)

I was chosen as the emcee, probably because I was always in trouble with the Sisters of Mercy nuns for talking in class. I guess they could say I had a habit as well. [Puns like this will be scattered throughout the text for those who appreciate such; the balance of my readers will be unaware that anything untoward has happened.] I always got that one glaring "I" which meant "needs improvement" on the behavior side of the report card for my grade in the virtue of "practices self-control." But I always had all "A's" on the academic grade side of the card, so I guess that is why they put up with me.

But let's get back to the folks in the nursing home! This was a tough first audience to play to, and I now understand why stand-up comics complained about "dead crowds." This crowd was literally half-dead. But with a little determination and perseverance, aided by my best jokes and continuous banter, I soon had the crowd smiling and laughing as much as they could under their circumstances. I was hooked! I was going to be a comedian!

Years later, after apparently telling one too many jokes at a leadership training seminar I was co-conducting in Japan, my senior partner confronted me about my delivery. I explained that my earliest life-long ambition, even before architecture, was to become a comic. I went on to explain how starting at ten years old I began collecting and indexing joke material after my first successful engagement—the one mentioned above. He eyed me coldly and simply advised that I seriously reconsider my ambitions. Maybe if this humorless chap is still alive and reads this book he will change his mind. I was undaunted, by the way.

In any event, in these tales you will find neither bothersome boastings nor author self-aggrandizement. There are plenty of people in the world already trying to tell you how wonderful and special they are. Likewise, I don't need you to cry or feel pain on my behalf: we all have heartbreaks and trials enough, so I will not burden you with details about darker and less happy days. A few of my chapters might have a touch of the bitter-sweet, but nothing requiring excessive sympathy. For me it is no sacrifice to forgo the sympathy.

I have no regrets for all the detours I have chosen to entertain throughout my life's journey. Instead I am quite grateful for the wonderful gift of life and all the resulting opportunities, challenges and rewards that I have experienced. In this book I have attempted to walk a middle path, willingly using self-deprecation as a comfortable vehicle to transport my reader through this assortment of short stories. I hope you find my many detours entertaining. Enjoy! And Thanks!

1. How This Book Began: August 18th, 2014

There are no coincidences.
Each step in our journey was meant to be.

On an otherwise un-extraordinary Monday I was quite unaware that my life was about to be significantly altered and enhanced. It was August 18, 2014 to be precise. During an ordinary hot summer in Texas my oldest son and daughter and I had recently discussed our oft-mentioned intentions to re-visit Hong Kong; only this time, we had finally committed to doing so. Plans were set in motion. Once again I studied the map of where the Pearl River met the South China Sea, attempting to conjure up a clear image of a very unique piece of real estate from a distant past.

It had been twenty-nine years. We had spent several happy years living in the former British colony of Hong Kong on mountainous outlying Lantau Island. Nestled in a lush green valley surrounded by towering granite hillsides lay the tiny remote Tung Hang Mei village, where a half-dozen houses clung to a winding footpath along the mountain stream. It was almost at the end of the earth—8,000 miles from my birthplace. Over the past three decades, I had often thought about that special isolated acre in a tucked-away corner of this vast planet. We had just decided to visit Hong Kong and see if the old remote mountain house we once lived in was still standing. There were of course mixed emotions about the proposed search, since the old place might have fallen into disrepair, or been bulldozed over by forces of commercial progress: thus our happily anticipated reunion would instead become a disappointing let-down.

From Google Earth views of Hong Kong I could make out the narrow walking trail that led up the thickly forested mountainside, but the property itself was obscured from view. [I would later discover the very special reason for this.] When I switched instead to Google Map view, as I often had done over the years, this time a logo "Ark Eden" suddenly appeared in the approximate location of our former happy home. I felt the twinge of excitement that was harbinger to a discovery; serendipity soon took over. I clicked on the little Ark Eden logo and happily a website sprung open. I excitedly plunged ahead and clicked on the "contact" tab which led me to an email link. Perhaps you yourself are familiar with that uncertain, hesitant feeling which accompanies a conversation you tentatively start with: "you don't know me, but…" You can only brace yourself so much against all the possible unfavorable reactions such as rejection, apathy or silence. Following are excerpts from the ensuing emails. On Monday August 18, 2014 at 11:25 a.m., I tentatively wrote:

"Dear Ark Eden folks: I stumbled across your wonderful project and website quite by accident. I am planning a trip to Hong Kong and in particular, to Lantau Island next year. I was looking at a Google Map view of the area where I once lived for six years on that island, and your logo popped up. My home was a two-story concrete structure (painted green at the time), up a narrow winding path, NNE of Mui Wo village proper and it had a swimming pool of sorts dug into the hillside above it. Is this the property where you are now based? Or are

you aware of the place I am describing? My family and I hiked the trails and paths and mountains all over Lantau Island when the kids were little. My two oldest children and I plan a return visit this next fall after being away nearly thirty years. Needless to say, we are excited! I was so excited to learn about your vital, unique conservation and local permaculture mission. Anyways, if you receive this and have time to respond, I would love hearing from you. Perhaps we can visit with you when we come to Hong Kong next year. Sincerely, Mike Hawron."

Twelve hours later, at 11:05 p.m. an unknown Ms. Jenny Quinton replied: *"Dear Mike, I am so excited to get your email. Were you the family that lived in the house before us? And you have lots of children? - Who will be very big now, like mine are. We moved in 25 years ago this December - so 1989. It would be great to meet you and hear some of your stories. Please come and visit us. There will still be some people here that you will know as well I think. I started the Ark Eden project nine years ago and it is doing so well. A few years ago we also started operating out of # 13 as well. We have a really big mission underway now to buy the valley and thus save it from commercial development. The house is still green - and in need of painting. The pool was just repaired THIS spring - and is a natural swimming pool. All the best, Jenny."*

Perhaps the thrill a gold prospector experiences when the pickaxe he has just thrust into the barren earth uncovers a shiny nugget best described my emotions. I eagerly wrote back the next morning:

"Dear Jenny, You have no idea how happy and excited I was to receive your email! Over the years since I left Hong Kong in 1989 (the year of your arrival at my old home!) I have had a recurring dream / nightmare where I struggled against many obstacles to return to that old beloved place, only to find it derelict and badly in need of saving but I couldn't find the people to help me. Hearing from you gives me wonderful, peaceful closure! Your Ark Eden project is beyond my wildest hopes and dreams for what could be done with that (then) sleepy valley: as we were moving out we could hear the roar of distant bulldozers tearing up the landscape to make the new golf course on the opposite mountain ridge…

"Yes, my first wife and I raised and home-schooled six young children there – they were ages fourteen years to six months then. I think we were the only Westerners ever to live in that valley up until that point, so we were quite the novelty, to say the least. However, eventually we won the locals' trust and hearts by our hard work and honesty. I was very sad to have to leave there. It was my tiny private Shangri-la. It will be lovely to sit and chat with you. In the meantime, I would love to keep up a correspondence until we come. I wish you the best of success with your upcoming project to save that beautiful, special valley! –All the best, Mike."

The next morning an email from Ark Eden awaited me: *"Dear Mike, Oh my goodness! We are so blessed to be sharing the same intention to care so much for this incredible treasure of a valley and a home. Your fire stories are the same as mine and your list of stories are a bit similar too! It was the experience of the first fire I fought with my two babies and the constant battle to save the house (I saved it four times in total) that just about forced me to become what we are today. I am so happy that you have found us and connected. When you and your children (I know not so much "children" any more) come back next year I am more than happy to have you stay at Eden Rock across the valley so you can re-connect with Hong Kong from your source- as it were). I would love them to meet my children too! –Jenny"*

Later that day when I replied, the seed of an idea was taking root in my subconscious as I wrote: "Dear Jenny, This is all so very fascinating and inspirational, and more incredible than a fictional movie could ever be! I hope you don't mind, but I have decided to start collecting our emails about Lantau into a Word document – who knows, it may make a great story someday, or at least be a means for our children to remember the place.

"That is most generous and gracious of you to offer us a place to stay when we visit next year. I gratefully accept your kind offer. I very much look forward to hearing from you again. I do so look forward to meeting you and your children Adele and Angus. I can tell you are very proud of them. They must indeed be very special individuals.

"About your place – I am curious as to how you found the property? I left Hong Kong in October of 1989, just a couple months before you moved in there. I went back for one last look at the property before I left, but it seemed vacant at the time. You weren't there yet. There used to be a funky gate at the entrance to the property. I believe the Chinese characters meant something like "10,000 Victories Garden." There was no fence of course, just the bamboo "wall" that joined the gate. My daughter Suzanne asked if the gate was still there. How we found out about the place was through the landlords we rented a small flat from in another area of MuiWo. [See the chapter: "Hong Kong Culture Shocks."]

"One day they asked if we wanted to rent a house with a pool – certainly a royal rarity for Hong Kong—I thought they were joking! We were told by our landlords that the previous owner, after building and tending to that place, decided to move back to Mainland China. We never learned any more about him. We thought the place was like the Garden of Eden (or Heaven on Earth!) after having lived in high-rise apartments in the likes of the Wan Chai and Causeway Bay neighborhoods, and on the 21st floor at that!

Our Eden/Heaven hunch was strengthened by the "12 manner of trees that each bore fruit in their own time" – it seemed there were indeed twelve different fruits we got, and they each had individual months of harvest, much as is written in Revelations Chapter 22, verse 2. The trees were peach, lemon, mandarin, orange, guava, lychee, longan, star fruit, kumquat, mango and of course the banana plantation fertilized by our bathroom runoff. It has been a long time but it is all coming back to me now, thanks to my fortuitous contact with you. So interesting that you named the place "Eden" as well! Take care! Bye for now, Mike."

The next day that little seed I just mentioned got watered when Jenny wrote: *"Mike - I can tell you are a writer. Because you write! I have so much to say about this place and how much I love it, so it is so GOOD to find you and your family, who say it all too. Adele has just cried with the connection and Angus has been very happy and said - "I want to meet those 'kids'." All of us feel this. It is really wonderful. We found the place as we were helping serve the old people vegetarian lunch at the temple and one day Mrs. Sai So there asked us if we wanted to see a house with a pool! Sound familiar? - And yes - we moved in, mostly based on that! The gate is still there - but it got mistakenly painted green - I plan to fix that some time*

very soon and the water supply is still mountain spring water and we drink it - we have no other source. Thank you for telling me about James and Suzanne and all your interesting life. Keep writing! - Jenny."

And so I stepped out onto the water and wrote: "Dear Jenny, I wish you all the best with the various irons you all have in the fire right now. I was so impressed by the YouTube video to see how you have really transformed that place into a veritable Garden of Eden. We so look forward to seeing you and your two children as well. Thanks so very much for answering about the gate, the water source and how you found the place – it sounds so much like my past life there that it is eerie, but in a good way. I love hearing the details and getting my curiosity satisfied.

"Perhaps I'm being over-dramatic, but I think I may have just had an epiphany and it is a wonderful turn in my life! Over the many years, when I told one of the many tales of my many travel detours, folks would often remark "you should write a book!" I have pretty much determined that if I ever do so, that will be the working title: "Mike: You Should Write a Book!" Well, sadly, up until now it has never happened, I think partly because I couldn't clearly visualize my reading audience. That was, until I stumbled across your wonderful family and the Ark Eden project. Jenny, you "put a burr under my saddle"—as they say in these parts—when you wrote today: "I can tell you are a writer. Because you write! Keep writing!" Suddenly it all seemed so sparklingly clear to me: who could ask for a more understanding & empathetic audience than you!? I fully understand if you don't quite share my enthusiasm for this project, so be honest with me, OK?

"The thought of writing a book seems daunting. But writing you folks a page or two every now and then when something in our email communications stirs my memory would be fun and perhaps inspiring work. I can imagine us all sitting in the shade on your front patio, sipping tea and chatting. I will of course welcome any feedback, ideas and constructive criticism, since I could not ask for more knowledgeable 'editors' than you. Some 'chapters' will be humorous, others sad or serious. Let me know if you are interested – if so, the first tale I send you will be 'The Dangers of Discounted Chicks!' Have a wonderful day! It's a wonderful life, isn't it?! –Mike."

And I held my breath! Surely my idea was over the top and Jenny is politely trying to find ways to word it gently for me. But instead, the little seed that had been watered now received a healthy dose of sunshine and fertilizer when Jenny soon replied: *"Hi Mike, I was so excited by your email that I had to dance around the living room and then tell all the people who were here at the time and they all got so excited too (but didn't dance around.) I wanted by return to write you my 'tree story'. I too love to write, so definitely yes, yes I would love to do this!!!! Thank you! Let's just keep swapping stories and see where the path leads... -Jenny."*

And thus it all began. Seven months later, on March 13th, 2015 I revisited the Google Earth Maps of Hong Kong and the icon for Ark Eden was not visible! Apparently, had I not viewed this map back on that particular fateful August 18th, perhaps this story might never have begun! As I said, there are no coincidences.

2. A Survivor's Guide to Cantonese!

Since many of my stories take place in the crowded, savory, smelly, noisy, exciting, clever and frenetic non-stop city of Hong Kong, I thought it only fair to offer you, the reader, a brief orientation, as it were, and give you a little primer to the local language. If you have ever been to a Chinatown anywhere in the world, you may have heard the amazing Cantonese dialect of the Chinese language. I spent eleven years surrounded by the cacophony of six million people all speaking it loudly at the same time: I grew to love, and fear it! I want you to be prepared!

Public transport is the smart way to get around Hong Kong. So, picture yourself on a very crowded public bus or subway car. Two men are shouting at each other, their noses barely inches apart. Their speaking volume steadily rises, while the pitch varies erratically, like a world-class roller coaster ride. There's lots of gesturing as well. You begin to fearfully surmise, like in Olivia Newton John's song, that the couple is about to "get physical". So you nervously begin looking for a handy escape route, in case the fighting spills over into your personal space.

Suddenly, without warning, one of the shouting combatants stands up, displays a mouthful of gold-capped teeth, and then just waves goodbye while alighting from the bus, all in good nature. Where are you? Was this a drug-induced nightmare? No, you are wide awake, and in Hong Kong, the "Fragrant Harbor", the land of "a thousand distinct stinks".

Can you sing? I mean can you really sing, like on-key and with perfect pitch? Do you know the difference between a sharp and flat? If not, you might want to consider mastering another less challenging language, such as French, instead of this challenging Chinese dialect. Anyways, French is easier because you only have to pronounce about half the letters, ha!

Not discouraged yet? Consider this: Cantonese has 9 -- count them nine – distinct tones. That's correct: there are eight different ways to mispronounce <u>each syllable</u>. Thus a Cantonese sentence with only five two-syllable words would offer you about 1,073,741,824 opportunities to have egg foo young in your face. That's over a billion, with a "B". And if you tried each possible combination at the lightning-fast rate of one per second, you could be at it for 34 years before you got it right!

For example, please consider the following little phrase: 'da fo je'. (which means = cigarette lighter). The two most common mispronunciations translate to either: "beat up the waiter" or, "go $#@* yourself," neither of which would really be safe to utter in public. Do you really think you can clearly distinguish between a high-falling tone and a mid-rising one? It's not too late to try the "parlez-vous" stuff instead....

As you will witness in the next chapter, my wife's failure to properly negotiate all of these tones unknowingly sent a very wrong message to some local farmers, much to their amusement, and her embarrassment.

"Perhaps I'll try the written language instead!" you conjecture. Good choice! It is claimed that in all their variations, there are over 100,000 Chinese written characters! There are about 7,000 generally recognized Chinese characters. But fear not: modern Chinese has only about 3,500 characters! Easier still, you will only need knowledge of about a mere 2,500 characters to pass the exam.

I posit that the wonderful Chinese people are not "inscrutable:" It is their incredibly complex language that is nearly inscrutable!

3. Hong Kong Culture Shocks

Sometimes life's collective experience cannot adequately prepare you for what lurks ahead. My first wife Erica and I and our three small children lived for several years on crowded Hong Kong Island in a variety of flats (British = apartments)—in various high-rise neighborhoods called Wan Chai, Causeway Bay, Happy Valley (not to be confused with Frankie & the Four Seasons) and finally we moved on up to the pricier Mid-Levels district. Regardless of where we lived, three factors did not vary much: the size (small), price (big) and location (high). Raising very young children in a home 100-200 feet above the ground is for the birds!—or other unfortunate creatures born at such dizzying heights.

More people there live and work above the 14th floor than in any other place on earth, making Hong Kong the world's most vertical city. With over 6500 skyscrapers, it has a third of the world's tallest housing towers. Tiny apartments go for outrageous prices. The one I'm describing in this tale today goes for $4 million. Large, more reasonably-sized accommodations were, of course, much more unreasonably-priced. Hong Kong is, after all, capitalism in its purest laissez-faire form. But the real terror was not financial; it was in the view. Granted, the view was romantic if you were single, or high [pun intended], but if you have small children about whom you care

14

greatly, then the daily fear of your offspring falling out one of the windows to the pavement far below was unsettling, at the very least.

If you dared to look down, pedestrians on the distant sidewalk far below looked no larger than ants. Various shattered items that had fallen out of the thousands of windows littered the rooftops and awnings below. Laundry was hung out the windows on bamboo poles coated in brightly-colored plastic. You hooked the far end of the pole into one of a series of three-inch metal loops that were welded onto the frame, which jutted out about three meters from the building's exterior.

If you made the mistake [once was usually enough] of hanging a heavy wet item at the far end of the pole, then the item's weight multiplied by the distance was enough to suck you and the laundry, pole and all, out the window. In such a scenario the safe choice was to let go of the pole and buy new replacement items. It was apparent that many folks had made that wise decision over the years and thus there were lots of abandoned laundry items on the floors below. And, of course, unless you were lucky enough to live on the top floor, stuff—liquid or otherwise—was always falling onto your freshly washed laundry.

Lucky us! One time we did get to live on the top floor, and that was our very first day in Hong Kong and that was on the 21st floor of a very narrow new building in upper Wan Chai, named Tonnochy Towers. We had been space-spoiled, and were thus totally unprepared for the high life: we just arrived from Australia, a vast continent filled with open spaces. My wife grew up in the Outback, with acres of not much of anything except the dirt between her bare toes. Even in big-city Sydney our growing little family usually had a lovely back yard with grass and trees and plenty of space for the kids to safely run around. After our two-day flight from Sydney via Bangkok, we arrived at our new 254 square foot [23 square meters] home in the clouds and for the next 24 hours my wife could not bring herself to look out the window.

Kids are kids however, and our little ones were especially unaware of the gravity of the situation, so to speak. They ran around happily and energetically bounced off the walls, which were very close together, as this tiny place was dubbed a "bachelor flat." With bedroom, living room, bathroom and kitchen combined, it was just about the size of an average closet in Texas. Imagine a young, unprepared married couple with three small children and all their life's possessions together 168 feet above the ground in this space! Claustrophobia, anyone? Little did we know the "fun" was just beginning!

Next day came the real hard-core initiation to Hong Kong living: a typhoon. A typhoon is like a hurricane on steroids. Typhoons seemed to show up about once every two or three weeks during the summer months. The reinforced concrete skyscrapers of Hong Kong are built to withstand sustained winds of 200 mph. The architectural secret is: the buildings sway a bit. In a big typhoon, like the one that welcomed us to the territory, the buildings sway a lot. You get the picture: lots of panicky screaming. And just our luck; we seemed to be on a roll, as this was a "two-fer": a rarity among typhoons—one that goes away and then loops back to play havoc yet another day. We had about three days hunkered down in our cozy little concrete cocoon of a home.

But I really am being self-centered talking about the fears of living at such heights. Consider the daily work place of the Hong Kong construction worker. Like a giant spider weaving a coarse web, scaffolding is made of bamboo poles, passed up from the ground by hand from worker to worker, higher and higher up the thin air surrounding the construction site. These poles are deftly lashed together by hand with reed-like strips. The worker wraps one leg around the scaffolding as he reaches down to grab the pole being hoisted up to him. All the way up twenty-one stories, in the case of our building, which was about the tallest around back in the 70's.

Now days these buildings can be as tall as 75 floors! That is quite a different story indeed. The process is really something to behold, a combination of kamikaze and ballet. When the project is completed, the scaffolding is dismantled by the same workers and it all goes back into huge flatbed trucks and off to the next adventure—which is never very far away. The Flying Wallendas had nothing compared to these guys! What makes this feat all the more incredible is that these same construction workers consume more Remy Martin cognac on their lunch breaks in Hong Kong than all the snifters in France!

After the height and the typhoons, the two other major Hong Kong fear factors include the noise and the traffic. [We'll talk about the all-pervasive smells elsewhere in "The Fragrant Harbor"] First, let's consider the noise: by comparison, things were pretty quiet in

Australia. People work, but not too much. People shop, but only on Thursday nights are the shops open "late"—till about 9 pm. People make noise, but not too much, and only at designated times. Once I had a workshop in the backyard of our home in the southern Sydney suburb of Allawah. I was happily hammering away when a neighbor objected, "Stop that hammering! It is 5 o'clock!" Sure enough, it was exactly 5:00—he must have been watching the second hand on his watch. I was young and defiant and painfully close to being finished with the project, so I took another loud whack at the board. "I'm coming over there!!!" was the instant, angry response. Feeling playful, I yelled back through the wall, "Go ahead, but remember: I've got the hammer!" He stopped yelling after that and I stopped hammering. After all, one must respect the peace.

In Hong Kong however, people yell and hammer away at all hours. When Erica finally worked up the courage to look out the window and saw the crowds milling below, she wondered if it was Thursday, because folks below were shopping late that night. However, we soon learned that every night in Hong Kong was late night shopping, and usually busily so until around midnight. It was only relatively quiet on the streets during those afore-mentioned terrifying typhoons. What is that cryptic Shakespearean expression? "It is an ill-wind that blows nobody any good?" That means a mixed blessing of such sorts, I believe.

And the traffic: all manner of transportation—double-decker buses and taxis, trams and 16-passenger mini-buses (officially PLB's—Public Light Bus—possibly so named because you felt light-headed after the frenetic ride), rickshaws and carts, little old ladies dressed in black armed with pointy umbrellas and laborers carrying baskets balanced on bamboo poles over their shoulders: all these raced pell-mell along narrow twisting streets with scant regard for safety. [Hong Kong taxis merit special mention in the chapter "Little Green Pacifier".]

Navigating our little flock of fair-haired toddlers along very narrow sidewalks through this racing flood of activity was nerve-wracking at the best of times. And we haven't talked enough about construction yet which was ever-present, ubiquitous, noisy and dangerous. So, as I was saying, Hong Kong can be dangerous. Amazingly however, there are also beautiful, peaceful outlying islands with idyllic rural settings to which we escaped weekly for family outings.

Once child number four and son number two—Philip—was born, we began to look for a quieter nest for our ever-growing brood. We found a cute, roomy three bedroom apartment for rent located on the middle floor of an unimposing three story building on Lantau Island, a twenty minute walk along a serpentine cement pathway leading from the Mui Wo ferry pier. One floor up was much more reasonably close to terra firma for us and it was so quiet out there! No noisy vehicles – only push carts.

Our landlord lived downstairs, Mr. Wong. We later discovered that he was a retired police sergeant—as every now and then a column of uniformed patrolmen would come to pay their respects. Sergeant Wong was kindly and patient and often amused by our "gweilo" ways and he was quite taken by our cute children. In time, I think Mr. Wong even grew to appreciate us, being foreigners and all, in preference to the noisy groups of Hong Kong city kids who rented the top floor for loud weekend getaways.

Well, by now I have set the scene for you. We loved our new-found freedom from uber-crowded metropolitan Hong Kong and we reveled in exploring the myriad pathways which wound between vegetable plots, rice paddies, waterfalls and water buffalo stomping grounds. The noisiest noise we had to endure was the enormous shrieks from the enormous pigs that protested enormously about being transported—on push carts—to the nearby market in enormous metal cages.

The word "market" here is your clue to today's title feature adventure. There was no hopping a bus, or tram or PLB (remember what those are?) or taxi to go shopping here in our paradise found. Everyone walked. When we joined the ranks of the wealthy we acquired our very own bright green push cart. It was a real beauty, with hard rubber tires that never went flat. And so when I was off on business or working in the office, my wife "drove" the family cart to the local markets. While there were thousands of western folks to be found in the cosmopolitan parts of Hong Kong – tourists and business people and British government civil servants and the wives and children of same - there were no Westerners in the little village where we had taken up residence, except for the six of us Hawrons.

Westerners are perhaps rightly viewed with suspicion and some hostility. Remember the Opium Wars and the Unequal Treaties, for example. "Gweilo" (鬼佬) was the term we often heard as we passed by. "Ghost chap" would be a passable literal translation, but more often the phrase translates just as handily to "white devil" or "foreign devil." Many Cantonese speakers will claim it is a non-derogatory term. Rural older Chinese folks would more likely still hold the less-cosmopolitan view regarding foreigners and thus here in this tiny village we really stuck out. Besides our funny looks and weird language, we did everything so differently too. We ate with forks, wore white clothes when it wasn't even a funeral and so on. But we were honest and hard-working and as polite and as respectful as our language barrier would allow. Eventually we won their trust. Or at least we kept their mistrust at bay.

My uprooted Aussie wife was a hard worker, an intrepid shopper and a devoted mother to our young kids, but she was in no way a skilled linguist. She went shopping for produce each morning at the tiny local rural market on our remote island in the South China Sea. Once they warmed up to her, the friendly but ever-inquisitive older women in the rice paddies along the path way would begin the daily routine by asking her: "Mei mat yeh eh?" (= Where are you going?) The foreign devil lady (my wife) would innocently reply "Mei seng!" (= go shopping, or at least that is what my dear wife thought she had said.)

At that, the boney old women would slap their boney old hands against their boney old knees and laugh uncontrollably. My wife suspected nothing and this daily routine was repeated for months on end without much variation. Except that sometimes one or more of the children would ride along on the cart, which as you will discover, made the whole scenario that much more absurd. My wife suspected nothing under foot, nothing more than some good humor amongst neighbors, the similar sort of conclusion TV's Lisa Douglas in "Green Acres" might come to while assessing the unfamiliar ways of "Hooterville."

Many moons later, when we were able, we employed the help of an "amah" – a local domestic servant. We learned quite a lot from her in a short amount of time: more efficient and less expensive ways of going about managing a household in southern China. More importantly perhaps, we learned what we had wrongly concluded or were clumsily doing wrong. Thus was spectacularly the case the first time my wife was accompanied to market by her newly-hired Cantonese amah. There was the usual daily question and answer

19

session with local old ladies in the vegetable fields and the usual resultant knee slapping and laughter.

Our amah was suddenly ashen-faced and became rather edgy and quiet. After an uncomfortable time together in the market, the shopping duo returned home in silence. Once inside the confines of our little apartment the amah excitedly confronted my wife: "Do you know what you are saying to those little old ladies?" "Sure," Erica replied; "they always ask me where I am going and what am I doing and I always say that I am going shopping." Amah Fung Yee clarified: "They are indeed asking you where you are going but every day you tell them that you are going to buy sex!"

Well, it wasn't really an intentional off-color remark my wife was making, more a case of an unintentional off-tone remark. Nevertheless our dear amah insisted that remedial Cantonese language classes begin in earnest post haste. Somehow I think the local village ladies preferred the good old days when they had their fun morning routine at my gweilo wife's unwitting expense.

4. The Dangers of Discounted Chicks!

Alternatively: "The Yolks on You"

Back in the Dark Ages – that is, before Color TV, Facebook and Google searches – there was "The Egg and I:" a movie starring Fred MacMurray and Claudette Colbert about a young couple's misguided attempts to become successful chicken farmers. Back then, the family farm was an entrenched feature in American culture revered almost as holy ground—the epitome of all that was decent, noble, courageous and productive.

Three decades-plus later, and still before the days of two out of three of the above-mentioned technologies (every little tar-paper hut on our remote Lantau Island had a color TV if nothing else), there was another such misguided attempt—this time not in the safe confines of the American Midwest but rather on the wild hillsides of an Island in the South China Sea. There would be nothing noble or productive about this second venture.

As you perhaps remember from the chapter "August 18th, 2014", I had lucked upon a house with an acre of land available for rent on the sparsely populated outlying island of Lantau, twelve miles west of Hong Kong's otherwise crowded, frenetic metropolis. Like the fictitious MacDonald family of that above-mentioned 1947 film, my own little family bravely and loyally followed me up the narrow winding footpath to our new home in the secluded Tung Hang Mei valley. It was peaceful and, as real estate agents are wont to say, "The place had potential".

Having studied electrical engineering at MIT for a while and then spending the next ten years of my adult life living exclusively in crowded metropolitan areas—Auckland, Sydney, Melbourne, Brisbane and now Hong Kong—somehow I considered myself fully qualified to raise chickens! The glorious prospect of free fresh eggs to feed my vast and growing family beckoned me into the poultry enterprise.

First I cut down local bamboo with my machete to build the pen and the run, and situated the structures to the right side of the front yard, just past the fragrant and deliciously-fruited guava trees. Next I headed down the path to the local MuiWo market to deal in livestock. Mind you, I was about the only non-Chinese shopper around and as such, understandably, the concept of bi-lingual signage had not yet reached this particular village.

If you are unfamiliar with written Chinese characters, imagine an explosion in an old-timey typeset room. There are thousands of Chinese characters, some of which have dozens of individual brush strokes. I had mastered a grand total of about seven of these. Further complicating matters, Cantonese is a tonal language, with nine distinct possible pronunciations for each sound. Being left-brained and somewhat tone-deaf I had not yet mastered this linguistic challenge. I elaborated on this tonal issue in the little chapter "A Survivor's Guide to Cantonese". In spite of not being able to read or write Cantonese, I soldiered on.

Having caught Asian Bartering Fever my first summer in Hong Kong, [see "Close Encounters"] I was ever the intrepid bargain-hunter. Needless to say, I was excited to discover that some of the chicks for sale were only HK$4 per dozen, compared to the neighboring basket containing an exotic HK$5 per dozen variety. Using my growing arsenal of self-taught conversational Cantonese, I attempted to extract from the vendor an explanation as to the price difference. The specimens in both baskets looked the same to my untrained eye. He just shrugged his shoulders and cracked a wry smile which betrayed his two remaining gold teeth. Those two teeth were whispering "you'll see."

Undaunted, I selected a dozen of what I ascertained to be the best-looking of the $4/dozen chicks available, then procured a big sack of feed and headed triumphantly back to my future poultry empire. I had already shaved HK$1 off my expenses! (For a clearer perspective as to the scale of this triumph, please note that HK$1 converts to about twelve cents US.) This triumph would later prove to be a pyrrhic victory...

The chicks grew fast and hardy under my watchful, caring eye. Their growth was aided by the abundance of crawling life forms available for snacking upon. Curiously enough, this particular variety of hens developed what closely resembled combs and wattles. They also grew to be enormous – at least two feet tall or about 60 cm—with frighteningly powerful huge feet. The first day I went to gather eggs I learned why ranchers don't raise bulls for their milk. The dual-price market mystery that had puzzled me was now unraveled: hens cost more than roosters. Well, those twelve roosters penned up together were no happier with this latest development than I was and they took turns attacking me to vent their frustration. Soon I would learn the origins of football.

There were snakes and huge centipedes and lots of mud everywhere in my little Shangri-la, so I usually sported a pair of industrial-strength Chinese black rubber boots whenever I was out of bed. On this particular fine morning, one of those non-hens raced at me, became airborne and aimed its bony claws at my scrawny abdomen. Not being exceptionally athletic, it must have been my purely defensive reflexes that kicked in (pun unintentional) and my size nine Double Happiness right boot landed smartly between those threatening claws. Gravity took over: our front yard overlooked a tar-papered shack in the fields far below at the bottom the steep slope, inhabited by a friendly but ultra-thin farmer we affectionately referred to as "Stretch Jr." (His dad, of course, was "Stretch Sr.")

Stretch had just emerged from his shack to go replenish the supply of fertilizer in the ceramic pot at the edge of his vegetable plot when he saw the airborne fowl rocketing his way. I'll explain about the pot in a moment. Stretch made a perfect catch from my perfect kick. We mainly communicated with sign language at this point in our relationship* and so with his hands he did a great Marcel Marceau impression. (You see, he was already wearing black pajamas.) First he gave a thumbs-up, then with two hands wrung an imaginary neck, and finally used his index and middle fingers to mimic a busy pair of chop sticks.

Perhaps there is space here to interject an explanation in way of local color. In this case, the color was mainly some shade of brown. The crops proliferated throughout this valley, in part due to the abundant rainfall. However, the real secret of local agricultural success was the miracle-grow: those large glazed ceramic pots dotting the corners of all the vegetable patches were not there for decoration. These pots were where farmers such as Stretch "did their business," as it were, each day.

If you are still uncertain as to their contents, let me give you another clue: There was no need for an indoor toilet in the farmers' little abodes. [If you walked by those pots on a warm day, your nose would give you a clue as to their contents, and you would have no further need of explanation.] My oldest son James reminded me the other day of how his mom was clueless as to the origins of this liquid fertilizer and went to ask one of the field workers if she could have some of the stuff for her garden. The bewildered farmer looked curiously at her, as if to ponder: "surely you white folks must have bowel movements of your own!"

Back to the flying chicken story! That night we enjoyed a meal featuring a basketful of fresh greens from Stretch's well-fertilized garden. This bartering process continued until all twelve of those roosters of mine were gone. My poultry farming experiment came to a screeching halt: I did not have the courage or humility to revisit that chick-vendor in the local market. I was certain the notoriety of my rooster-raising skills by now had reached his ears and been spread far and wide throughout the marketplace.

As my Cantonese vocabulary was growing painfully slowly compared to speed of all that I hoped to accomplish while developing my homestead, I came to embrace the centuries-old adage "A Picture is Worth a Thousand Words", especially when it came to words in Cantonese! So, for example, if I needed a new 5/8" rubber washer to replace the one on my leaky faucet, all I had to do was bring the old item with me to the little dry goods shop, point to the item saying "yaht-goh, ng goi." [= "One Please"]

*Note: Years later when we had to leave our happy home there in the Tung Hang Mei Valley, Stretch waved goodbye and then put both fists to his eyes and gently rubbed them back and forth to show his unabashed display of sorrow at our departure. Despite our somewhat limited ability to communicate, over the years we had grown to become good neighbors and friends. He dearly loved the children and thoroughly enjoyed all their playful antics.

5. Happy Ending's Unhappy Ending

In life, not all endings are happy. Some are. The ending to the path in peaceful Tung Hang Mei Valley on Lantau Island led to our happy little slice of paradise, tucked around the mountains and across the West Lamma Channel portion of the South China Sea, far away from the noisy concrete jungle of the Hong Kong "mainland." This is another animal story from our farm, this time a four-legged variety. The ending—of our dog's tail—was always wagging with happiness. But I am getting ahead of myself.

It was a "long and winding road" (foot / cart path actually) that led up from the Mui Wo ferry pier to our gated home in the mountain valley. When you are well-conditioned, it takes about a half-hour to walk up the hilly path. Out-of-shape novices will require at least 45 minutes. Downhill on bicycle is only ten minutes if there is no "traffic" – like a cart load of pigs on their way to market, or a huge spider web stretched across the path.

During the approximately 363 days of the year when it is humid in Hong Kong, it was a relief at the half-way point up our path to reach the "bus stop" for a break before ascending the steepest part of the journey. We humorously called it the "bus stop" because there were no buses or cars of any type; there were only people, bicycles, and push carts on this path.

The "bus stop" was a sturdy concrete structure with benches under its welcoming shade. Most permanent structures were made of concrete or else they will not survive the typhoons' blasts. [See more about typhoons in "Ellen's Nasty Visit!"] I saw on a GoPro video done on a mountain bike by Angus Quinton-Page (Jenny's son), that this ancient shelter is still standing and in apparently fine condition, some 30 years since I last rested there.

Right next to the bus stop was a ramshackle dwelling where a most unpleasant gentleman lived. From the yellow of his eyes, it seemed he lived mostly on a liquid diet of a near-fatal brew of some vile concoction. The place was filthy and a total mess. Except for this gorgeous copper-haired little dog with the waggiest white-tipped tail you have ever seen. The dog seemed greatly cheered every time he saw us. His tail wagged furiously when he spotted us! The dear creature must have sensed a touch of kindness that was lacking in his life. His owner did not seem to be the personality you would want working at an animal shelter for example.

One day the kids excitedly noticed that there was a cute dog at our gate happily wagging its tail. Thus they dubbed him "Happy Ending." He was trailing a leash of sorts and had obviously broken free and followed our scent up the mile-long stretch from the bus stop. I sadly told the kids that the dog had an owner and I walked the poor dog back to that salty character, albeit not without serious misgivings. I did have respect for property rights, such as they were; and I was the new kid in town, a "gweilo" at that. The next day the dog was happily at our gate again. Again I returned the dog to the owner, who simply grunted.

That dog and I made that pilgrimage up and down that steep path countless times, each time with a thicker and heavier leash attached which Happy Ending had managed to break. It seemed that Happy Ending was very unhappy with his master. I know you can hear my children's voices in the background "can we keep him, daddy?!" One of those unthankful chores of a parent is trying to convincingly explain to them why we couldn't, when I wasn't all that convinced myself. The phenomenon of dogs taking an instant liking to me is something I've come to accept, as happened in "The Return".

As they say, "don't leave school until the bell rings". We had a little bicycle bell attached to our gate so visitors could signal us. One morning the bell rang. It was Happy Ending, carried by his grumpy, disheveled owner. When we opened the gate, he handed the dog to us without a word and walked off. I guess he decided it was too expensive to keep buying stouter leashes to restrain his dog. The kids were ecstatic. Me too – I was 32 at the time and this was my first dog!

Up until now my only two brief experiences with pets had been a tiny turtle that was stepped on by my younger sister during the excitement of a turtle race, and a parakeet that flew off one day when my mom hung the cage outside ("for fresh air").

Happy Ending was so beautiful and so very happy. We all had lots of fun chasing each other around the yard and being amused by how fast and furiously Happy Ending could wag that tail of his! He slept right outside the front double doors, guarding his new home at night and waiting for us to wake up and play each day.

Every day we seemed to have a different snake pass through our yard, often a new variety. [See "Snakes and Shakes."] The fateful night came when a cobra slithered into our front yard and faithful Happy Ending barked furiously to warn us before bravely attacking the intruder. Alas, the cobra prevailed. Happy Ending died that night defending his little family. We found him the next morning on the front patio under the big beautiful Flame of the Forest tree, stiff as a board, the early sunlight reflecting off his copper coat for the last time. The kids had a farewell ceremony for Happy Ending on the hillside to the north of the house. I asked a friend to go in my stead. I wasn't up to saying goodbye quite yet. Happy Ending was the first loved one larger than a parakeet that I had ever lost, and I wasn't handling it very well. It would be twenty-odd years and 8000 miles away before the next happy dog wandered into my life, one day showing up as a puppy in our back yard. Happily, Zoey is still wagging her white-tipped tail every night when I return from work.

Introducing the series: "Echoes from Eden."

As incredible as you may find some of my tales, what is even more incredible to me is that when I sent Jenny Quinton drafts of these tales, she would often reply with similar stories of her own. Where available, I will include these "echoes" from her Ark Eden home at the end of the chapter. Here is the first of many echoes from Jenny to resound in this book:

"Hi Mike! Thank you for the "Happy Ending" story! That story certainly reverberates with us! We remember well that man you mentioned! In fact I kicked him once! When I was pregnant and a

bit emotional/sick, I came around the corner at the "bus stop" only to see him kicking one of his two little dogs. Needless to say we ended up with both of them too! And we have many, many dog stories. And snake stories. I have seven dogs right now living out their stories, here at Ark Eden."

Meet "Belle", the leader of the pack at "Ark Eden", aka "PermaPug".

6. The Little Green Pacifier!

Or: Peace at What Price?

"Taxi 4 seats" states that innocuous green half-circle metal plaque mounted at the front grill. What is not stated is that there are only two hand grips available.

Those who have prior Hong Kong taxi travel experience understand all too well the subtle significance of this equipment limitation. All Hong Kong's 18,000-some taxis come with two standard items: a powerful horn and an extremely powerful air-conditioning system.

Little else is needed, as I will explain. I never missed roller coasters or other scary things when I traveled in Hong Kong. Like most people there, I did not own a private car, so when public transport proved inadequate for the need, I availed myself of the ubiquitous red cabs. They run day and night, everywhere and every day, except perhaps when a full typhoon blows. But there are <u>no</u> taxis at 4 p.m., as I learned the hard way. Well <u>most</u> of the cabs are red; but those in the new territories are green and the few on Lantau Island are a pretty shade of blue.

Cautious types are probably wondering about the brakes as they read this. The fact is I do not believe I have ever witnessed a Hong Kong taxi coming to a complete stop. For example, in most other countries, you line up and wait your turn for the next taxi; in Hong Kong there is a sport not unlike bull-fighting where the contestants chase after the approaching taxi. Those clever enough to guess the exact stopping (or slowing-down) point hop in as the alighting passenger exits.

I eventually acquired the skill of jogging alongside the slowing taxi while clutching one of the available door handles; admittedly it was a little over-the-top, albeit an effective technique. Little crooked old ladies, usually clad in black or gray, who have long since lost the speed of their youth, have evolved an effective survival adaption: a long, sturdy umbrella with a sharpened point. Only the foolhardy or the uninitiated dare compete with them. I don't know; I imagine by now they may have even developed some umbrellas with tips of depleted uranium.

Our little family's first experience with the never-stopping taxi law was on Day One upon our arrival from Australia, back on a sweltering June afternoon. I was such a babe in the woods! [Jungle, more appropriately.] Someone was supposed to meet my wife and I and our three little ones upon our arrival at busy Kai Tak airport. But they didn't, so we were on our own.

My first sensation upon exiting the air-conditioned arrival lounge was that I couldn't breathe! It felt like a stinky old wet blanket had been wrapped around me, cutting off my supply of fresh air. "Air you can wear" is the expression. "Oh, this is humidity, I've read about this!" I then guessed that perhaps it was simply due the closeness of the traffic in the confined space. I thought perhaps this was just an anomaly—a rare day of some atmospheric disturbance. I thought "This can't be for real! No one could live in this air!" Well, I thought wrong! As I would soon learn, it turned out that humidity at exceptionally high levels was quite normal in Hong Kong for a majority of the year, whether it was hot or cold.

In Australia we were pretty much used to no one being in too great a hurry. I'll have a story about that later. [See: "Things Learned the Hard Way!"] So I parked my young bride, the three young Hawron children and our mountain of luggage at the curb (I guess it was a "kerb" there at the time since Hong Kong was then a British colony) while I went in to phone our contact. In those days if you were at Kai Tak Airport, that was area code "3" for Kowloon, so if you dialed to the new territories you had to dial "12" first, or "5" for Hong Kong Island numbers. If you were already in the area you were calling, you dropped the prefix and so on. I obviously had not yet mastered the system and so instead I learned what a wrong number sounds like in Cantonese.

By the time I gave up dialing and went back outside to break the unpleasant news to my family that we were, for all intents and purposes, completely alone in Hong Kong—they were gone! No wife, no children, no pile of luggage! In just a few minutes they had completely vanished. I had lost my family in my first hour in this strange place. The high humidity of Hong Kong was such an unfathomable shock after years of living in a desert continent Down Under that I thought maybe I just wasn't seeing straight. Still, my mouth went dry with panic.

Suddenly I heard a familiar voice in the distance. It was my wife, yelling for all she was worth, hanging out of the window of a taxi that was driving away. Apparently she, the kids and the luggage had been scooped up, much like pieces on a never-ending conveyor belt. She was unsuccessful in communicating to the driver that I was missing. He was convinced that he had successfully collected a fare. In his mind it was time to move on. Somehow I caught up with them, and my pounding heart caught up with me later on. Hong Kong Valuable Lesson Number One learned: never leave anything or anyone unattended for even a fraction of a second in this busy, crowded, impatient place!

At this point in the story I will interject that another great Hong Kong Olympic Taxi sport is maneuvering to get the last available taxi before they all mysteriously disappear at 4 pm. Equally challenging is trying to catch the first of the new batch of taxis that reappear. I suspect this has something to do with a shift change: time to fuel up and so forth. The seasoned Hong Kongese knows never to plan on grabbing a taxi at 4 pm for a 4:15 appointment. It just won't happen. So now let's get back to my arriving in Hong Kong story.

Since our hosts did not pick us up and we could not contact them—this was before the days of cell phones—we now needed a place to stay for the night. "Well, there must be a YWCA or something we can afford to stay at" I reasoned and tried to tell the driver where to go. Hong Kong drivers are not required by law to know their way around. And they certainly are not required to negotiate in English to frantic silly foreigners. When our driver felt he had driven us far enough to collect a good fare, he let us off. It was 3:59 pm. We were about to learn about 4 p.m. It was time for that shift change for all taxis: A perfect storm!

It took the driver just seconds to get rid of us and our luggage and be on his way with a small bundle of our money, in time to go wherever the taxis go when they disappear. It also only took us seconds to realize that we had been dumped in the middle of nowhere. We were not at the "Y". We certainly didn't know why, or how, or where, or what was next. It was four o'clock. The red sea of taxis had parted, leaving all the desperate, anxious fares waiting for the first ones to reappear with fresh drivers. And we soon learned you cannot successfully compete for a taxi with three children and a pile of luggage. We were rank amateurs, as it were.

It had been two long days for us, travelling with three small children, complete with a stopover in Bangkok at some over-heated student hostel. We were tired. We were dirty and sweaty and badly in need of a shower. We needed to find a bathroom. And we were completely lost, and clueless. The kids were hungry. And we were all very thirsty. This was like one of those impossible-to-answer science questions they ask on college entrance exams – there were far too many variables and unknowns and no constants, it seemed. But I learned (adapted?) fast: nearby was a five-star hotel complete with a liveried doorman.

I was desperate and no longer concerned with ethics by this point; my animal survival instincts had kicked in. I knew I was never going to get a taxi myself at this rate; I feared we'd spend the rest of our lives trying unsuccessfully to get out of that spot. So I begged this hotel doorman to get us a taxi. Turns out these chaps do have a certain amount of clout. Quickly improvising, I lied that my baby was sick and we had to get to the hospital. I guess that was a little "white lie": we would indeed all get sick eventually standing alongside that busy, dangerous, smoggy street.

Anyways—either out of universal compassion or an intensely practical desire to get the unsightly crew away from his beautiful hotel entrance—the doorman helpfully commandeered us a taxi and away we went. After a block or two, we convinced the driver not to go to the hospital but to the YWCA. We got a room for the night and finally figured out the phone system after we were showered and fed and in our right minds again.

In Hong Kong another favorite taxi-related sport resembles bowling; except that the taxi is the ball and the pedestrians are the pins. The trick is to blow the horn loud enough to scatter the crowd so you can drive through without slowing down in the least. Since jaywalking is a way of life in this city, and you are talking about a world-class population density of thousands of people in any given block, the result is not unlike the parting of the red sea. Seeing this unfold from the rear passenger seat is quite awe-inspiring. (One only makes the mistake once of sitting in the front seat of a Hong Kong taxi.)

It's great fun to pick up an acquaintance or business associate at the airport for a taxi ride on their first visit. You can time it precisely: it's usually five seconds after the taxi peels away from the curb until the visitor's hand clutches the overhead grip. If you are feeling particularly evil, you can suggest the newbie rides in the front seat, so "they can see the view better." That way you can better see when their knuckles turn white, usually at the first power swerve, or roughly about ten seconds into the journey.

Most of the HK taxis are Toyotas, made in Japan with special 4-speed transmissions: (fast; faster; extremely fast & insane). The number of licensed taxis is kept fairly constant, while the demand for rides escalates; thus the coveted ownership of an operator's license will nowadays run a cool HK$5 million (about US $625,000). Since a car only lasts just so many years in the sub-tropical salt air, logic dictates that the taxis must move rapidly in order to garner enough cash to pay back this sizeable investment. Everyone (alive) in Hong Kong is in a hurry of some sort, so this haste suits the local clientele just fine.

Taxi drivers themselves must be a very unique breed. Although I don't know their exact genetic makeup, they must possess some blend of Kamikaze pilot, Hun warrior, outlawed NASCAR driver and flying Wallenda. They are fearless. [Except of the parking police; more on that later.] Fares are quite reasonable, given the amount of entertainment provided and speed of delivery to destination, albeit the journey in actual physical distance is very short since you can't really go very far in compact Hong Kong.

Wherever these drivers originated from, it was cold there, very cold in their home land. Hong Kong is humid 363 days of the year, so air conditioning is a welcome relief. But there is still something called "too much of a good thing." These drivers must have lived in the arctic. The air blowing from the vents approaches absolute zero. This is another good reason why you have the new arrival take the front seat in the taxi: it is fun to watch them shiver uncontrollably in the middle of an otherwise torrid summer day.

You can almost tell the time of the year by the length of the icicles forming from the condensation: in summer they grow to about 10 cm (four inches) but closer to 15 cm in winter. I wear eyeglasses so when I get out of one of those red four-wheel freezer boxes, visibility is near zero from the sudden fogging of my lenses which is not unlike what Hong Kong is like everywhere for the gloomy six weeks before spring. [See: "Hong Kong's Four Seasons."]

One particularly self-important visitor to Hong Kong whom I had the displeasure to guide around the city imperiously took exception to this frenetic pace and unreasonably demanded a slow taxi ride. I explained to him that over the years I had used every phrase I knew in Cantonese and none of them had ever been the least bit effective at reducing the taxi speed. Instead, I just got in the habit of saying a little mantra to myself "this is not my day to die" whenever I got into a taxi. "Offer him money!" the tourist stubbornly suggested. Back then you could zip around Central for about HK$5. Fares were cheap. So was life, it seemed! He said: "try $10!"

Back then, before the recently-minted Hong Kong Monetary Authority had begun producing their own new gaudy purple version, the Mercantile, the Chartered and the Hong Kong Shanghai Banks each produced their own version of the cool-green $10 note. [Very logically, each denomination is a different size and color. Thus a "big bill" is indeed bigger than a lesser note.]

Yes, and that's right: in the true spirit of laissez-faire capitalism, three Hong Kong banks are allowed to print their own version of Hong Kong currency, so you have somewhat of a choice in how you spend your money. The Mercantile bank was gobbled up by the Hong Kong Shanghai bank, which brought the issuing banks down to two, but now the Bank of China is churning out notes as well, so we are back up to three choices. [On my recent visit to Hong Kong in July 2015 I discovered that the $10 bill now also comes in a plastic, red-hued variety, much like Australia's currency.]

With an exasperated sigh, sensing the uselessness of the enterprise, I passed a $10 note up to the driver and apologetically explained that the gweilo passenger wanted a slow ride. To my surprise I discovered that Hong Kong taxis do indeed have brakes! The driver gratefully snatched the proffered tip and rapidly decelerated from the customary warp speed. "Was this slow enough?" he asked with a grin. "Go slow and get more money"—only a gweilo would come up with such a crazy idea! But slow our chauffeur did go.

Soon the buses were zipping past us, instead of vice versa. Then the double-decker trams began overtaking us, clanging their warning bells. When the laborers carrying their shoulder-pole basket loads appeared to whiz by, I knew we had achieved celebrity status, something like in "The Day the Earth Stood Still." I had to endure my guest's smug "I-told-you-so" grin, but the experience was well worth it. Seeing even the little old ladies with their umbrellas zip by was quite surrealistic.

Our driver was so giddy with this extra cash that he unwittingly pulled over exactly where we requested, in an illegal zone, sandwiched cleverly between two legal stopping zones. The dread traffic police pounced on him like vultures on a fresh carcass. The fine was a steep HK$200, or about a day's take in fares. Our usually fierce warrior was reduced to a puddle of silent defeat.

My guest was feeling so good about himself and his little triumph that he tossed me two red ($100) notes, pronouncing magnanimously, "It was worth it! Pay the fine for the driver." This turn of events caused the hapless driver to run the gauntlet of emotions back and forth in an eye's blink. Wordlessly shaking his head incredulously at his rescue—at the hand of the two foreigners who got him into this mess in the first place, no less—he gratefully accepted the humongous tip. I'm not sure, but I could swear I saw a tear escape the corner of his steely left eye as he drove away. He certainly had a story to tell that evening as well!

7. The Big Family Tree That Almost Wasn't

Or My Mysterious Grandpa Iwan

This chapter should answer a lot of questions, including the burning question: "what kind of a name is 'Hawron'?" This book chronicles some highlights from my wanderings around the globe, beginning at the tender age of nineteen. None of this would have been possible if it were not for another brave teenager who also left everything behind to start a new life in a strange new world a century ago. In other words: I almost wasn't.

I only really fully learned this story at middle age while doing research for my Master's degree in Higher Education at Texas A&M, so in some ways, the belated revelation is that much the sweeter. My information came not from my family members, but from a perfect stranger who suddenly felt inspired to help me search for a particular genealogical needle in the giant haystack of Eastern Europe: my search for the family roots of my paternal grandfather. I was a very inquisitive young chap back in the heady era of the McCarthy investigations of the 50's, which was a time when folks with Russian-ish heritage kept their heads down and waved the American flag.

When I tried prodding my elders and ancients about our family history I was usually met with the same stone wall: "we are just Americans now." End of story! I didn't really even get the <u>beginning</u> of the story about my grandpa Hawron. I just knew that he was a retired D&H railroad worker who always sat in the same ivory-color recliner when I came to visit his home. No more details emerged until many years later, when I was already a grandfather in my own right.

I'd like to put your mind at ease by telling you it's alright if you can't figure out how to pronounce "Hawron." Seems no one ever does. I have heard all types of variations over the decades, so nothing offends me anymore. Actually you just pronounce it exactly as it is spelled: haw-ron. I automatically spell it out, and as I do, I hear the familiar refrain: "what kind of name is 'Hawron'?"

By way of emphasis, my own sister Jude has shrewdly kept her married name decades after her divorce. She was tired of people misspelling or mispronouncing "Hawron" and since she had married one of those fortunate people who have names that everyone can spell and pronounce—like, "Smith," "Jones," "Miller," or "Brown"—

she hung on to it! Some days I can't say I blame her. Chances are if you look up "Hawron" in your local phonebook you won't find any. I'll bet you big money, unless you live in my town, that is! I happen to know all the Hawron's; every one is a relative. Ha!—Spell check just asked me "what kind of a word is 'Hawron'?" Jude is so smart.

Sometimes tiny things or little individuals end up making a disproportionate difference in the world. I'd like to think of Iwan Havran as a classic case in point. Iwan was a teen when war, revolution and ethnic cleansing broke out in his ethnic Ukrainian-Lemko mountain village of Floryuka on the shifting borders of Poland and Austria during a time when byzantine alliances were tumbling at the outbreak of WWI. Somehow young Iwan made his way to Hamburg, Germany where he caught the steamship "Imperator" to Ellis Island, New York. Through the various immigration, census and draft registration documents—as clerks struggled to spell and pronounce new arrivals' names—"Iwan Havran" evolved to the John Hawron I knew as "grandpa". So to answer your question: "Hawron" is a new, "Americanized" name.

This neat discovery came to me via serendipity, not unlike the Ark Eden story I told you about in chapter one. I was typing in various permutations of the word Hawron in Google search, and when nearing exhaustion, I tried "Havran." Up popped a web site with contact info and I made another of those tentative "you don't know me but I'm looking for..." email overtures and was electrified by the promptness and quality of the response:

"Mike, I'm not the Hawron/Havran that we have on our website but rather one of the editors of the site. I know a lot about the Havrans we have listed on the site since they hailed from the village of my Father's birthplace in former Austro-Hungary. I did a quick search for you on my ancestry.com account and I believe located your grandfather's World War One Draft Registration.

"John Havran was born March 1892 Galicia, Austria. Galicia was in the former Austro-Hungary Empire in present day Poland. There were many Rusyns (called Lemkos) in this region of Poland. An excellent source of data on this region can be found at http://lemko.org/. I never knew that Eastern Europeans settled in that part of New York State! I will keep it referenced as perhaps a future page to add to our site.

"This 1920 Census may also be of assistance to you. It actually has the village of origin listed for your grandparents, a bit difficult to make out but it may provide you with some leads. I see that Pol (Poland) and Austria are listed along with the village name: Austria for the fact that when they were born their area of Poland was part of Austro-Hungary and Poland for the fact of what was as of 1920 after WWI. It's a real find to have the village name as that was not usual in the census records. Also note the immigration date 1913. - Steven"

A real find indeed! Steven must have been an angel making one of those temporary helpful guest appearances on earth, as I never heard from him again. But I learned more about my heritage in those two paragraphs from him than I had in fifty years of searching. I was over the moon! The mystery surrounding my family history had finally cleared away. Below is my one surviving photo of grandpa Hawron, or "Didi" as he was known to us children; there's me at five years old sporting my nifty suspenders.

So now there was one brave young Hawron in the New World in 1913 and when Olga became his wife then there were two. Three daughters followed and now there were five. But the newly minted Hawron name wouldn't see another generation without a son. Then finally my dad, John Philip, was born, but just barely it seems. His mother died in childbirth or soon after, I believe. My dad grew up in a Ukrainian enclave on an island in the Mohawk River in upstate New York, and was schooled in Ukrainian at the village Orthodox church-school.

Now there was at least one male Hawron for the following generation. My dad married at age 22 and shortly thereafter I became "number one son." Now we had a second generation Hawron and there was finally a branch on the family tree. For what it is worth, that made me the first-ever native English-speaking Hawron. I must have been a quick study, because I later won the Brown University Alumni Association award for English proficiency. At that time I was young and intent on becoming an electrical engineer at MIT so the significance of the English award was lost on me then.

Up front I want to get this confession off my chest: I have been very guilty of contributing to the world's overpopulation. In my defense: (a.) there is the issue of quality trumping concerns over quantity and (b.) an endangered species was at stake. And then there is personal pride. Few things will sting worse for the overly self-conscious pre-pubescent over-achieving middle-school pupil than to have the school nurse/doctor gravely tell you that their diagnosis suggests your future ability to procreate is in question. Don't 'they' say that "living well is the best revenge?" Aren't 'they' are also credited with the old chestnut, "he who laughs last, laughs best!"

Apparently, I did more than just laugh and—while it has taken me two families and forty years—to date I have ended up being blessed with twelve children and fourteen grandchildren. I have seven sons to safely ensure that the Hawron name carries on in the next generation and four grandsons surnamed Hawron to further ensure the future forking of the family tree.

And for good measure, five years after my dad was born, grandpa had another son with his new bride: my Uncle Mike, who later in life abandoned his long-standing bachelorhood to produce two sons of his own who have since gone on to have some grandson Hawrons as well. So now it appears that one lone transplanted refugee boy from a village destroyed in a century-old conflict will leave behind an entire forest in his memory.

Echoes from Eden:

After receiving my draft chapter, Jenny wrote: *"Hi Mike, What a wonderful story about your family tree. That was quite extra-ordinary about your 'angel' who guided you there in that only exchange. So magical! It was such a profound reminder of how important and real the family is that came before us and shaped our lives.*

39

"I had to really stop and think about that as I read your story this morning: about how they remain with us - in us. And how we are moved and polished by all the people around us - like little potatoes rubbing together and cleaned in a bag - and how we are inextricably linked to them and connected to place and time in unbelievable ways. Your friend, – Jenny"

Part of the Hawron family forest, with four generations represented is shown in the photo below: My parents John and Shirley (extreme right); Me (striped shirt, left); Four of my oldest kids: Suzy (top), James (right of Suzy), Joanne (center, sunglasses) and Andy (front); and Grandson #1, Javan (up the tree). This picture was taken in front of the huge ancient Chinaberry tree in my backyard, circa 1999.

8. Which Way War?

Or: Lost Patrol with Labor Pains

To my knowledge throughout history—making exception for the Stone Age—most coins have always had two sides. In a more recent geological era, all 45-rpm phonograph records also had a "B side" - the side the radio station didn't usually play. You know where this is going: the old adage about two sides to every situation. The upside to my family's little paradise at in the Tung Hang Mei Valley on Lantau Island, Hong Kong was the near complete isolation and peaceful quiet, up a mostly hidden mountain path and thus tucked safely around the corner from busy civilization.

There I lived like a little king on my little acre of fruit trees and greenery with fantastic vistas of waterfalls, banana groves and vegetable fields. My realm was that much the sweeter since my rent was only HK $4000, or about US$512 per month which, for the 99% of the housing available elsewhere in the colony, would only get me a plain vanilla 350 square foot apartment on the 13th floor of a concrete needle in the concrete haystack where the other six million lived.

The "flip" side was that this isolation meant just that: there were just a handful of houses and a dozen or so farmers living in this remote valley and we were pretty much off the grid. This segues nicely as there were no lights along our pathway at night, so you needed to remember to carry a reliable flashlight to avoid bumping into the locals - snakes, spiders, huge centipedes and so on. When my phone line—a true royal luxury in those parts—went down after Ellen's nasty visit [see the eponymous chapter for details] virtually no one in the outside world knew and probably no one cared. I certainly couldn't call the repair center. This was still a decade before the days of the most rudimentary of digital cell phones.

So I did the next best thing - I shimmied up the poles, clutching my phone set while tapping into the tangle of shredded wires until I found a live one which I then connected to my house. Here I am duty-bound to point out that I discovered that while the voltage and current levels on phone lines are considerably less than those of household electric supply lines, said levels are still sufficient to get your attention, especially on rainy days. I have no "selfie" as evidence—remember this was pre-cellular times—but I imagine I sported an afro for that brief moment of illumination. I digress, as Ellen would not actually arrive for another eight months after the lost patrol—the subject of this story.

Anyways, I think I've made my point about the isolation. Our isolation was so complete that one chilly morning in early January the British colonial military powers decided that our valley would be a great venue for war games. My fifth child, Andy, would be born during this war, which thankfully was even shorter than the skirmish on the Falkland Islands the year prior. The day began with a loud boom and a ringing bell. The loud boom was the sound of mortar rounds being lobbed at the hillside above and just to the north of our happy home. The bell was—you guessed it—the lost patrol had arrived.

Over the years, I was regularly reminded that I was merely a lowly visitor to this part of the planet, neither a native Chinese nor a privileged British colonial civil servant, and that my stay was temporary and tenuous at the whim and good graces of both co-hosts. I cautiously peered out my bedroom window at the gate below, over which Chinese characters proclaimed 萬勝利花園 – which loosely

 translates to "10,000 Victories Garden."

There stood a grim-faced platoon in full battle gear, automatic weapons drawn. The one who appeared to be the lead officer was furiously ringing the little bicycle bell that I had helpfully attached to the old gate so that visitors could announce their arrival. As I surveyed the scene, I was fairly certain that they had come to announce my imminent departure.

Chinese gates being what they were—there was no attached wall or fence, just the gate with adjoining bamboo thickets—I realized instantly that resistance was futile. I dressed quickly and padded down the path to the gate and my awaiting fate, trying hard to give my best impression of someone who was cordially unconcerned. My very-pregnant wife very nervously watched the proceedings from the

42

upstairs bedroom window. Resignation does wonders for one's composure, I soon learned, and my wobbly legs firmed up nicely in timely fashion as I approached the dawn firing squad. Nevertheless, the ground still shook each time a mortar landed.

What my wife could see from the window was a flurry of arm waving and finger pointing from both sides of the gate. She could not yet realize these were all quite benign motions. The Chinese platoon was apparently, simply lost and therefore late for their war and respectfully asked if I could point them in the right direction. Realizing I had been granted a new lease on life, I was suddenly cautiously cavalier as I provided the necessary directions and bid the warriors farewell. [Relief is really too small a word to express the overwhelming sensation that swept over me.]

Now having successfully dispensed with the firing squad, it was time to deal with the mortar fire. A dilemma is akin to scheduling a reunion for hermits. How do you do it? Making the phone call to the British military headquarters was another dilemma. My call would thus end my cherished anonymity; on the other hand, my failure to do so might prematurely end my family's status—visitor or otherwise—if another mortar fell closer to home, as it were. How do you look up the number for "trouble" in the phone directory? It is at the beginning, under the section marked "government." Soon I was being asked annoying questions such as who I was and where I lived and what was I doing there. Mustering my best bluster I insisted that the shelling of my family cease forthwith and unconditionally.

Now came the second of three surprising developments that morning of January 5th. The commander was mildly apologetic and severely perplexed: he had been advised that the valley was vacant. Well, so much for "military intelligence!" Or maybe this was forward-thinking, self-fulfilling prophecy, as a few more mortar rounds and that assessment might have proven correct. In any event, the military chap on the other end of the line explained that—"terribly sorry"—while they could not entirely call off the war games, he would instruct those assembled on the opposite hillside to aim their fire farther afield of our little Eden. It was a diplomatic victory of sorts, I felt.

Attentive readers will now be expecting me to detail the third surprise. Never fear, as even though these are true stories, they remain entertaining till the end. My wife had a history of relatively (no pun

43

planned) long labors with our first four children: so, in my great wisdom, the master birthing plan allowed for the thirty minute walk to the ferry pier, the hour-long ferry ride and the short high-speed taxi ride to the hospital where we were booked. The Great Birthing Plan did not make allowances for the labor-inducing effect of war games, nor the muscle-toning effect of climbing up and down our hilly pathway to and from the village each day.

Nevertheless, my brave wife and I set out arm in arm down the narrow path, ducking fearfully while the projectiles screamed overhead. Off to catch the early morning ferry we went. It would be a peaceful and scenic ride across the harbor at least, I thought to myself. But we never made it. The labor contractions came on very fast, hard and strong and we only made it as far down the path as the little clinic on the outskirts of the main village market. In a dollop of good fortune, a school girl passed by early that morning on her way to catch the ferry to school. She could have been an angel, as she spoke excellent English and ran to wake up the local nurse / sister. Help arrived a few minutes later.

The Chinese local nurse proved to be much more formidable than the military authority I had earlier encountered. Correctly, she proceeded to forcefully lecture me about how foolish we were to have our fifth child there in that rural village, as complications could arise. I acquiesced, reassuring her that I agreed entirely, and even promised that she could yell at me all she wanted; but could it please be after the birth, as with all the excitement of the war games and then hiking down the mountain trail, my wife's cervical dilation was now complete. That bit of anatomical news silenced my accuser, who quickly changed tone as she allowed us into the examination room, and not a moment too soon, as a few seconds and a couple of pushes later, out popped little Andrew David, healthy, hungry and happily oblivious to the morning's drama.

Next day, after mother and newborn son had enjoyed a short stay in the little clinic out of the war zone, we fashioned an "ambulance" for the journey home – by securing a small mattress to our faithful little push cart. With help from Andy's older siblings I pushed mom and baby back up the hill. I think we were the talk of the town for a while after that. I doubt you will find many stories like this in the average Lamaze manual.

My daughter Joanne added the following after reading the above: *"The thing I remember most from Andy's birth is carrot cake— freshly baked to celebrate his arrival and homecoming! Smells are the strongest trigger of memory for me so every time I smell carrot cake my whole life I think of Andy, brand new the first time I met him in his little turquoise one-piece jump suit."*

From "The Things Kids Don't Tell You" Department: After reading this chapter when we were together for Thanksgiving 2014, James (my number one son) remarked: *"Oh, the cool thing was that we kids found all this live ordnance stashed behind that big rock on the hillside above the house! We also found tons of spent and unspent ordnance that was lying about."* Well, two conclusions can be drawn from this testimony: firstly, the obvious fact that this patrol was rather messy and careless during their war games. Secondly, and more important to the author's credibility, we now have an eyewitness who has come forward with solid evidence that I was not dreaming up this whole nightmare!

Upon hearing James' recollections, Suzy (my number one daughter) recalled: *"The weirdest thing was this huge helicopter flying over the house and hovering noisily just above the hillside behind the pool. There was this huge net hanging from underneath the helicopter; it looked like a huge net full of fish. The only thing was: it was full of soldiers who spilled out onto the hillside for the next war exercise!"*

* * * * * * *

And finally, an **Echo from Eden**: *"Mike, This story is priceless! We had a small war-games at one stage too - but at night! I took out my megaphone - which I usually used to bring in the children for meals...and blasted the airways telling them to GO AWAY!!! The most precious part of the episode I remember was this very, very young Chinese guy I spotted suddenly outside of my bedroom window peering in. I brought the house down!!! He scared me to death. He made the children, who were little, cry. And so then I bellowed on my loud speaker... Needless to say, they never came back again! – Jenny"*

9. Buffalo Phil and Other Spills!

The star of this story is my second son, Philip Michael. Our family spent many happy, sweaty hours hiking the many winding trails of Lantau Island, back in the days when I was very young and very fit. Phil had incredibly amazing blue-green eyes and was a very handsome little chap, quite popular with all the local ladies. Often when we were out, if we turned our backs on him for a mere moment, we would discover he was surrounded by a crowd of admirers.

There are countless Lantau trails leading in every direction, yet I was ever in search of new detours. In the hot summers of Hong Kong, each additional step resulted in a few more drops of sweat. My detours were thus all about conserving water. My wife Erica felt duty-bound to try to save me from my follies as much as humanly possible, yet there were still the occasional run-ins with baboons, wild boars, and firecracker throwers, as I have confessed to elsewhere in this book. Yet I remained undaunted. On this particular outing, we had wound down from our lofty hillside home, past the "bus stop" out of the Tung Hang Mei valley and back close to sea level. We were headed for Butterfly Hill, a beautiful shady spot en-route to the waterfalls which featured—you guessed it—gorgeous butterflies enjoying the relatively cool moist air.

The beaten, concrete path wound way down to the village and then joined the path we were seeking at an acute angle V-junction. Down and back the two legs of the V was probably close to a mile; the distance across the relatively dry marshland traversing the back of another property was only a couple hundred meters or so. This was a no-brainer decision for such an inveterate detour-taker as myself. I also had some embarrassing, unpleasant memories about my faulty parenting skills on that long stretch of pathway resulting in an accident, which I was trying to avoid and which I will explain later.

Over Erica's worried protests, we set out across the grass with the five kids, baby Andy in a backpack. I think I still have grooves in my shoulders from all those years of backpacking with the kids, but that is a consequence of my own doing, obviously. The first part of my new shortcut was easy going and before long we were about halfway, right behind the yard of a nice big three-story building set right in the middle of nowhere. Here the space between the back wall of that house on the left and the thick woodsy hill to the right narrowed considerably. And here a huge, muddy, old, black and formidable-looking water buffalo chose to take up the entire path.

So we had come face-to-face with a dilemma: try to find some way to proceed, or take the dreaded long way around. After a while, wives can tell what their husbands are thinking, I believe. I stood there pondering which was the lesser of two evils: (a.) to go around the front of the beast; but what about those big horns or (b.) to go around the back of him instead; but does a water buffalo kick backwards, like the horse did to James when he was little? The mother of these five children psychically declared: "No!" She did have an inordinate tendency to worry, I felt.

You need to know about that horse incident, I can sense. This was back in our even younger days in Australia. My parents came for a visit one Christmas and we took them around to see the various grandparent-friendly venues in Sydney like the Taronga Park Zoo. I spotted a nature reserve/petting zoo marked on the map out in the western suburbs and felt we could give that a try. It was a mistake.

The owners had apparently long since given up trying to maintain a respectable establishment, but they were still collecting admission. My dad paid up and in we went, searching for fun and adventure. The animals did not look like they had had any fun for quite some time, and not that much food either. James, my number one son, was all of about two years old at this point and full of energy and mishaps. He easily broke away from our grip and went charging after an old sway-back horse in the distance. Our calls to him to wait up for us went unheeded. So we charged after him, trying to get to him before he could get to the back of that horse. Somehow his little legs outran us all and we resorted to frantically yelling after him to stop.

Then it happened. The old cantankerous horse was in no mood to entertain strangers, let alone an energetic little ankle-biter. So he did what horses do in such situations: he reared back and kicked for all he was worth, and unfortunately, right on target. A quick prayer went up from the gathering of horrified adults. The horse's hind foot connected squarely with James who came hurtling back towards us, flying through the air, landing with a thud in a heap on the ground.

Erica claimed it was entirely my fault for picking this miserable park and, for punishment, ordered me to go collect the corpse. Meanwhile, everyone else held their breath. With heavy heart I set out with shaky legs to collect my firstborn, who promptly broke out into giggles when he saw me. Exhale! I examined him to find what must be the huge imprint in his little torso, but there was none! I asked the little rodeo clown where the horse had kicked him, and he pointed to his left knee. I could find no mark or swelling and he ran off to his mother. To this day my left knee still aches in weather changes.

Let's return to our tale about the buffalo. While I hesitantly pondered alternative shortcuts and mother hen kept clucking "no," young Phil decided he had had enough of this standing around doing nothing and decided to take matters into his own hands by charging directly at the afore-mentioned huge water buffalo. What was it with my young sons and charging after large beasts? As with James and the horse, we could not catch up with Phil before he came upon that mountain of flesh. He gave it a firm swat on its hind side with his determined little fist. When I dared open my eyes again, I gratefully saw that, like an elephant with a mouse, the buffalo had been spooked out of its wits by little Phil and took off, yielding the path to our family. Phil proudly led the way across the rest of the shortcut, understandably quite pleased with himself.

I mentioned earlier about a previous mishaps on these paths. That episode took place on a cold winter day when I was out biking along these narrow pathways with James and Suzy. James was old enough to ride his own "China-Store-special" bike, the heavy kind made of indestructible Chinese steel. Suzy rode on the back of my bicycle, the family vehicle, as it were. There were no railings alongside the path for safety. But there was a steep drop to the frigid waters below.

James (pictured below) over-corrected on a turn and went off the edge, much to my horror. He had on one of those ubiquitous Chinese-made quilted jackets which were very warm, but also very absorbent. James became the forerunner of Sponge Bob when he landed in the stream, his jacket instantly gobbling up gallons of cold water. Hypothermia was my feared enemy!

I squeezed the hand brakes and skidded to a stop. Throwing down the kick stand, I hopped off the bike and leapt down to the stream and extracted James, who was suddenly fifty pounds heavier. Also suddenly, the bicycle on the back of which I had left Suzy balancing precariously in my haste to rescue James now fell over so I ran back up the slope to check her for broken parts. The two kids were both crying and I didn't have enough arms to go around.

Suzy, my daughter-editor and confessor, refreshed my memory with further details leading up to this debacle: training wheels. Ironically, it was the parental emphasis on safety which apparently led to young James' demise. Suzy clearly recalls that James was quite competent pedaling with just two wheels beneath him, but his over-protective parents had insisted, OSHA-like, that the training wheels be reinstated. It was one of these said training wheels which had lodged in the pathway's edge that sent the bike with James atop it tumbling into the frigid waters of the local stream.

James, ever the strong one, attempted to lift himself and bicycle out of the quagmire and would probably have succeeded, but for those same training wheels becoming entangled in the long grasses. This was a classic example of unintended consequences: too much concern for safety led to his accident.

Suzy also vividly recalled that I had repeatedly instructed her to always put her foot out to catch herself whenever a bike would start to fall over. However, under these circumstances, no matter which foot she extended, gravity was not to be denied its harvest.

Apparently it was all a very humorous scene to the outside observer. Two such passers-by, more sure-footed older villager ladies, burst out into amused cackling at the sight of this skinny young gweilo and his two hapless children. So I miserably dragged the two cold, sore, crying children and our two bikes back up the long, steep path home. I tried to coach the battered and frozen children to squelch their tears so as to down-play the nature of their accidents.

As I approached our gate I began to imagine the reception I was about to get when the wife saw what I had done to her two defenseless young children. Then I did what any man would do in my shoes: I burst into tears myself.

10. The Four Seasons – by Hong Kong

Like Vivaldi, Hong Kong has its own four seasons, viz: Too Dry and Windy; Too Cold and Foggy; Too Hot & Humid; and finally, Three Days of Perfect Weather in October. The big typhoon I wrote about in "Ellen's Nasty Visit" took place just between those third and fourth seasons—towards the end of hot-and-humid and just before perfect-weather. I will now elaborate on these four seasons:

Too Dry and Windy: Around Christmas and beyond, the very strong monsoon winds originating north in the near-arctic Mongolian plateau begin to blow very strong and cold blasts across Hong Kong. It's a high pressure / low pressure phenomenon where the cold air in Siberia gives rise to a high pressure while the relatively warm waters of the South China Sea create a tempting low pressure just begging to be filled. Thus the north-south wind pattern.

It never freezes or snows in Hong Kong, so of course "cold" is a very relative term, much as humidity is. Anything below 50 F° (or 10 C°) is considered cold. This is much like Texan meteorology. When you have survived 100 F° (40 C°) for months on end, then the blood tends to thin out, making the possessor of said thinned blood easily susceptible to chills. Housing in Hong Kong is much the same as the human body in the subtropics: while designed mainly to keep cool and safe during the hot summer typhoon months, the reinforced concrete structures are very chilly in winter.

Hong Kong is at latitude 22.267 N—similar to that of Hawaii or Havana—such that when the winter winds do not blow, it can be very pleasant. We have had nice sunny February days in the 80's F (28 C°) where we swam at the nearby beach. If only we could put a wall up along the border of south China to keep out the cold north wind! Anyways, unfortunately it is exactly during this dry blustery time that at festivals such as the Chung Yeung (Double Ninth), folks will visit their ancestors' graves on the hillsides and burn incense in their show of respect.

The winds themselves show no such respect, and fan the little embers into giant hill fires, which Jenny and I describe elsewhere in "The Lady Who Planted Trees." This season comes on the heels of the Too Hot and Humid period whose abundant rains engender lush thick hillside growth, which turns into vulnerable tinder in the too dry months.

Too Hot and Humid: This is the season where Hong Kong is at its most characteristic state. I've already documented the joys of this season with its typhoons [in "Ellen's Nasty Visit"], its incredible humidity [in "Little Green Pacifier"] and its incredible thunderstorms and torrential downpours, below. There is little left to be said, other than this season lasts for about half the year.

Too Cold and Foggy: In between Too Dry and Windy and Too Hot and Humid comes this season. I relate about the dense Hong Kong fogs of late winter in "The Gray Wall of China" episode where the ferry boat I was on nearly went down at sea, narrowly missing a mammoth container ship and its malevolently churning propeller blades. This constant fog happens as the warm moist air of the South China Sea battles to regain its supremacy over the cold air that has usurped it during the winter months. Basically, for six weeks there is no sunshine and vision is limited to just a few feet. When you fly through a cloud and look out the airplane window at the gray goo: that's what Hong Kong is like during this time.

The peaks of mountains and the top floors of the sky scrapers vanish in the clouds. Pilots curse their luck. Ship captains wear out their fog horns. The shoes in your closet all turn moldy green. This was when asthma would visit me, like a hated in-law, and would seek to snuff out my life each year. I always managed to outlast it, thanks to the re-emergence of the healing sun at the advent of Too Hot and Humid. When I first arrived in Hong Kong, several of the British ex-pats advised that it was best to go back to the home country for these six weeks, or else commit suicide. Instead I toughed it out, for eleven years non-stop; but it wasn't easy!

Three Days of Perfect Weather: This season is self-explanatory. Everyone in Hong Kong waits for these few precious days, like a young child awaits Christmas or birthday presents. Sometimes Perfect Weather arrives in October, sometimes in November, and occasionally in early December. If you are lucky enough to be there then, on some years you get a couple nice days in each of these last three months of the year. Now that we have covered the basics, it is time for some of my own personal weird weather stories.

I realize that some of these stories, although true, are hard to believe. I know for this next tale, Nikola Tesla would believe me. That is because he could make his own. His own what? You will soon learn this. Never heard of Mr. Tesla? (There he is above, borrowing my hat during my recent visit to MIT.) Do a quick google search and you will be amazed by this genius' accomplishments. I don't lay any claim to the same level of genius as Mr. All-Things Electricity himself, but—while we did not stay in the Holiday Inn Express that is reputed to make you smarter—we did live on Lantau Island in the South China Sea where my family and I were startled observers of the eerie phenomenon: Ball lightning!

Never heard of it? Spooky stuff! What is spookier yet is that scientists can't yet fully explain it: there are dozens of plausible theories, but no clear winner as of yet. We had some tremendous thunderstorms in the Tung Hang Mei valley on Lantau Island. The distant steep hillsides across the valley from our little mountain haven were instantly transformed into roaring majestic waterfalls after just a few minutes of torrential downpour. It was during one of these particularly vigorous storms, when lightning was striking loudly, often and nearby—that it happened! Bang! Boom!

The smell of freshly created ozone pervaded the room while our ears were still ringing from the tremendous crash of thunder that accompanied the blinding flash of lightning that cut through the dark. Then there was a hum, like the sound of an old vacuum-tube radio. [Ask your great-grandpa what that is.] Like an other-worldly apparition which the natural senses struggle to deny, a compact blue orb of pale light hovered near the northwest corner of the living room, close to where the electric wires all entered the building.

About a meter (three feet) above the concrete and tile floor, this uninvited visitor meandered across the length of the room, rising and falling ever so slightly and constantly humming as it traversed some invisible pathway towards the back door. Then it was gone as mystically and suddenly as it had appeared! What must have only taken seconds seemed like hours!

After exhaling, all voices questioned in unison: "Did you see that!?" There have been many reported sightings of ball lightning over the centuries. The ball varies in size, noise, and destructive nature; but all accounts have two things in common: first, the ball happens during a strong thunderstorm and second, it is spooky!

Since it's my book and my story, I'll offer my theory. Our building was entirely made of reinforced concrete. Most lasting structures in Hong Kong are made thusly in order to withstand the tremendous winds of the typhoons and the degenerating forces of the prevailing subtropical climate. So our two-story house was basically two giant concrete shoeboxes, one atop the other; with half-foot thick concrete walls, floors and ceilings into which were imbedded on all six surfaces a mesh of reinforcing bars of steel.

Have you ever been to one of those interactive science museums where they do the cool demonstration with artificial lightning? They zap millions of volts of electricity at a metal cage, but the person inside is unharmed. It's called a Faraday cage—instead of a Tesla cage—probably because there are more English than Serbs in the scientific community. But it was the pioneering Serbian inventor and electrical engineer who set up his ground-breaking laboratory in Colorado Springs. If you were to click your ruby slippers and wish all the concrete to disappear from my house, you would be left basically with just such a wire cage. Voila! This cage—hidden in the otherwise non-conducting concrete—is what temporarily trapped that blue ball of lighting in our downstairs living room. Ah, I can see Nikola smiling and nodding to me from on high.

When it Rains, it Pours!

Although that expression is registered by the Morton Salt Company and they have been using that slogan in their advertising for a century or two, I think it will still safely work out OK to use for this story. [James informs me that Morton is still his favorite salt brand.] Later on I tell the story about the mystery water tap in "Fragrant Harbor." That was the relief valve for the septic tanks that protruded from a massive stone retaining wall which lined the concrete pathway snaking up from our gate. Now about that wall: each of those huge stones weighed hundreds of pounds. How they all got placed there without the aid of modern machinery on a remote hillside seems to be a noteworthy engineering miracle, not unlike the pyramids. There are times when I long for the "way-back" machine: I would love to be able to travel back in time and see just how they did it. There were other massive stones on the property similar in size and composition which made up our mysterious swimming pool, but that will be another story.

One day it started to rain. So also, probably innocently, began a chapter from old Noah's log. So also began a late spring day after a particularly long dry spell in Hong Kong that had left the hillsides parched (and as you know, thereby less absorbent to sudden large quantities of rain water in that condition.) Many folks, I'm sure, had been wishing and praying for rain.

It appears that when making such wishes and prayers, it is important to be very specific. For example, don't say "we want a real lot of rain!" unless you are prepared for the torrential consequences. A trough of low pressure arrived and parked itself along the coastline bordering the sea for a couple days. It rained. It poured. It rained so hard and thus so loudly at one point that we had to shout to each other inside the house in order to be heard.

Fortunately it did not rain cats and dogs. That happened in the olden days of thatched roofs when a real gully-washer of a storm deposited so much rain that roof collapsed, sending the slumbering animals tumbling to the ground. But you already knew that trivial factoid, right? Back now to our storm where we fortunately, as you've read above, had a half-foot thick reinforced concrete flat roof over our

55

heads. During that cloudburst, in just 60 minutes, twelve inches of rain fell. All told, in that 24 hour period, a total of four feet—yes, 48 inches—or 1.22 meters of rain fell on our property! And then it stopped. I planned to head to Central via the ferry that morning and got ready to head down our path. Not so fast! That big tall imposing wall built of those huge granite stone blocks was gone! What was left in the wake of the storm was a huge mountain of rubble in front of our gate, blocking our pathway out of the property.

I'm not a particularly big person, and certainly I never had serious aspirations of being a weight lifter. But I am a determined individual, and that day I was determined to get to Central HK for work. I also had gravity on my side. The hillside sloped steeply away from the path on the side opposite from where the stone wall once stood. Far below was our banana plantation, surrounded by lush vegetation.

With enough effort and proper leverage I was able to send those huge slippery stones, one by one, off the path and tumbling, crashing to the awaiting valley below. I would imagine they are still there. There was no easy way to get them back up that steep slope, which would be like trying to put the proverbial toothpaste back into the proverbial tube. If Jenny Quinton ever wondered how all those big stones got down there, now she knows!

We wrote to my mother-in-law, Beth, all about that exciting big storm. She lives at her property called "Kengol", near the town called The Rock, in New South Wales, Down Under. Her place was named eponymously after the nearby sacred Aboriginal site. She has a modest sheep farm there. Well, it is no reflection on the sheep. They are not particularly modest, but the property is. In the near-arid Outback, grass being so sparse, thousands of acres—or half as many hectares if you prefer—of land are needed to supply sufficient grazing material.

Beth raised black sheep, and I am not referring to her children. She was somewhat famous for the black wool that was produced there on her property. Anyways, suffice it to say that it rains seldom and only slightly there. When we wrote of our four feet (') of rain, she wistfully replied that she wished that she could have gotten some of those four inches (") of rain that we were blessed with. There was no way on earth to convince her that we could have actually gotten four feet of rain in one day, or as much as they would have received at The Rock in an entire decade.

*****

When it was not being drenched by storms or buffeted by typhoons or burning from wild fires whipped up by fierce winds or being zapped by violent lightning strikes, our little corner of the earth was indeed paradise! Jenny captured the beauty of Lantau Island and its Tung Hang Mei valley in a poem she wrote called "A Poem for Lantau" which you can find at the end of the chapter "The Lady Who Planted Trees."

11. The Gray Wall of (the south) China (sea)

Alternatively: "I haven't the foggiest"

Elsewhere I refer to an era of my life as the "young, penniless and silly" stage. This story takes place later in my life, during the "older, better-off, yet still impatient" era. I have already made reference to the vagaries of Hong Kong's four seasons. When the too-cold-and-windy season is ready to yield to the too-hot-and-humid season, an unwelcome intruder stays for several weeks: Foggy Gloom is her name.

As I mentioned in the last chapter, when I first arrived in Hong Kong from the sunny land Down Under, I was informed that sane expats leave for the home country during this time; if they can't afford to do so, they commit suicide. Well, it really is quite gloomy to go six weeks without seeing the sun, while being swaddled in thick misty chilling clouds that touch the ground. Meteorologically, the cold air from Mongolia is fighting to retain its grip on the South China Sea while the warmer southerly winds arriving from the Philippines prevail. The result is a marine variety of Pea Soup.

On one such late February day, when it was so foggy that it was difficult to see your own outstretched hand, I decided that it was imperative that I leave the peace and comfort and safety of my cloud-enshrouded mountain home on Lantau Island and head for the ferry plying the above-mentioned waters en route to Hong Kong Island's Central district. About this time you can probably hear the refrain from The Choir of Sane and Reasonable Persons chanting "Why?!"

Hong Kong ferry operators and their crew are no less impatient than I, it seemed, and thus I was able to get a ticket and board the doomed vessel in spite of the dangerous sailing conditions. Back then for about US $1, you could sit in air-conditioned comfort upstairs, and work at a table. [I see on the "New World" ferry website that three decades later the price is up to US$3 now.] I've done some of my most inspired writing in just such a setting. But this was not to be one of those days, however. I could not even see the bow of the ferry through the front window from where I sat, so stubborn was the day's fog. Soon I heard yelling and, being the ever-curious sort, I went forward to investigate. A smear of black appeared at the ship's bow and when the light (what little there was of it) was just right, I could make out that it was a crew member—either holding on, or lashed thereon, to the flagpole at the ferry's leading point.

Imagine the setting: a three story, 60-meter long vessel—perhaps the "Xin Fa"—filled with about 1000 noisy impatient passengers scheduled to travel at about 14 knots into zero visibility across one of the world's busiest shipping lanes. I soon surmised that the crewman was the human equivalent of sonar, and his yells were the "pings" advising the captain which way to steer through this formless gray patch. To give credit where due, the ferry was indeed travelling a tad slower than usual.

The water suddenly becoming choppier was the nautical clue that we were now out of Silvermine Bay and into the open sea lanes of the West Lamma Channel. Huge container ships going to and from all points on earth traversed this waterway. Our intrepid little ferry would thus be heading perpendicular to these passing behemoths. I found it difficult to concentrate on my bowl of noodle soup; such was my sense of pending doom. Aided by my now-heightened senses, I realized that my business in town really could have waited for another, clearer day; alas I was not at the helm and there was no turning back.

Suddenly our sonar chap began yelling for all he was worth—which in Cantonese is very loud and very strident. Bells began ringing and the ship shuddered like a whale trapped in a fit of coughing, as the diesel engines below protested being thrown into full reverse. Still all ahead appeared to be just formless gray, until suddenly a massive darker gray wall bizarrely materialized in the midst of the South China Sea, directly in front of our ferry! No matter how far I stretched my neck upwards, I could not see to the top of this great gray wall. A moment later a huge blast from a huge ship's huge warning horn cleared the air enough to reveal that this wall was indeed nothing less than the side of a huge container ship, and one that was directly in our path.

An important nautical principal took over and that is: huge ships don't stop, turn or do anything rapidly, for that matter. They especially do not yield for smaller seafaring vessels. Actually, they can't swerve to avoid an obstacle, even if they wished to do so. They just pass serenely by, anticipating that smaller vessels will exercise discretion and/or a healthy sense of self-preservation and thus correctly yield right of way and do all the necessary stopping and turning. Our brave little boat was trying its best to do just that, but there was still that pesky forward momentum to deal with. Thus the yelling and bell-clanging and horn-tooting and engine shuddering continued for what seemed like an eternity, until suddenly I was afforded the view of the largest propeller I have ever seen, and at much closer proximity than I would ever care for. It looked like the blades of a giant's delicatessen meat slicer, waiting to devour the next loaf of cold cuts. In this analogy, our ship was the unfortunate salami.

Give our fearless crew due respect, as they somehow managed to miss those churning blades of the container ship's propeller, albeit by mere inches. The noise from those huge hunks of metal sloshing in the sea was awe inspiring. Out of the frying pan, now into the fire: we were not yet out of danger.

Such a three-story ferry is relatively flat-bottomed for its dimensions and thus it rocks sideways quite easily. When the thousand noisy, impatient and excited passengers all rushed to one side of the vessel in order to get a good view of the monster propeller, then the next danger struck—a precipitously-listing ferry. That many Hong Kong residents—with even the slightest of builds—still adds up to a minimum of 50 tons, or the equivalent of a locomotive, and one that is precariously perched on the far edge of the ferry at that.

The floor became a mountainous slope. Cups of noodles went sliding downhill across the tilting tables. I grabbed the edge of my table to avoid taking flight. Soon a new round of yelling and screaming and cursing ensued as the crew attempted to herd the crowd away from the edge. Mass hysteria yielded to mass common-sense and our center of mass was soon righted. The remainder of the journey was relatively uneventful. Terra Firma never felt so sweet! For the life of me, I still haven't the foggiest memory of what business was so urgent in Central Hong Kong that day! But I have since learned to wait for better sailing weather.

12. 香港 -- The Fragrant Harbor

For those of you wondering how the city got its name: "Hong Kong" is an anglicized approximation of the spoken Cantonese name 香港, meaning "Fragrant Harbor". It has been apocryphally suggested that the reference to "fragrance" may refer to the harbor waters being sweetened by the fresh water influx of the Pearl River, [mind you, this river runs dark brown in color] or to the incense from factories lining the coast to the north of Kowloon [where, I might point out, the canals were black from pollution]. Don't fall for that bit of tourism mythology, as there is nothing sweet about the smell of the harbor, except, that is, for the sweet smell of success, provided you like the scent of money. In 1842, the Treaty of Nanking was signed, and it was then that the name "Hong Kong" was first recorded on official documents.

I feel that this treaty requires some further mention here because it shows the entire foundation upon which the complex British-Sino relations were established: unflinching commerce. Indelicately put, British traders wanted to sell opium to the Cantonese. The local leaders objected to their subjects being turned into airheads by these foreign drug peddlers. The colonial traders were incensed (as it were) with this objection: after all, what else was colonialism for, but to foist upon one set of subjects the over-priced merchandise swindled from another set of subjects. Since the British navy had its guns trained upon the city of Nanking, this pragmatic point of view prevailed and thus the "unequal treaty" was signed. Jardine Matheson was one of the original Hong Kong trading houses and to this day, two centuries later, its corporate logo aptly bears the stylized image of the opium poppy.

So as you can see, Hong Kong was not as sweet smelling as some folks would have you believe. In fact, someone once dubbed Hong Kong the "land of a thousand distinct stinks and ten thousand indistinct stinks." If you know the author of that phrase, please let me know so I can give proper credit. Until then, take my word that Hong Kong has more smells per cubic meter of atmosphere than any place you have ever known! The steep mountainsides surrounding the reclaimed land upon which the city floats form a gravy tureen-shaped harbor which is as crowded with maritime activity as is its adjoining land-based counterpart. Add to these volatile ingredients the prevailing humidity that often borders on maximum, throw in the diesel fumes of the city's 20,000 taxis and 5,000 Public Light buses (minibuses) and 6,000-some double-decker buses and compress all that into just a few square miles of space and you have a very concentrated fragrance indeed! These myriad smells swirl together into a type of olfactory tapestry but the trained nose can pick out many of the individual distinct ingredients. I'll cover but a few of them in this chapter.

Stinky Tofu

No, this has nothing to do with wearing unwashed socks. Those of you who know about this delicacy are already grinning; but the following explanation is for the as-yet uninitiated. We will trace its origin in reverse, step by stinky step. Stinky Tofu is a fermented tofu with a distinctive strong odor. Tofu is bean curd, made by coagulating soy milk. Soy milk comes from those soy bean plants you've seen growing everywhere by the sides of the highways. Soy milk, and thus tofu, and ultimately, Stinky Tofu have been around for a couple thousand years. Some blame it on the Han dynasty, but they could not be reached for comment as of my publication deadline. Tofu is sold everywhere by street vendors in Asia, and seems particularly popular on cold evenings. Not unlike the chicken transporters I refer to in "Things My Mother Never Could Have Warned Me About!" the vendor often has two square metal tubs filled with hot grease / oil which he can carry suspended via a pole worn over his shoulder as he walks the crowded streets plying his trade.

It appears to me that the murkier the frying oil, the better the stinky tofu sells. There is no need for a sign, or for shouting advertisements to the crowd. The stinky smell wafts effortlessly through a crowd like that of a hundred rabid skunks in heat. There is no escaping it! There was no escaping it for me on my first close encounter with the delicacy one winter evening in Happy Valley. It was a cold night, by Hong Kong standards, and I was bundled up with my black leather jacket while awaiting the green double-decker tram to go to Causeway Bay. [Trams come in other colors, but green was most common, like the little green pacifier I wrote of.]

Along came the Stinky Tofu vendor. Up until that moment, I was unaware that it was possible to have such a violent allergic reaction to said stink. After just one whiff I was suddenly overcome with extreme itchiness and the unnerving sensation of burning up with fever. I abandoned my planned trip and raced across the road back to my eighth floor apartment [which had a great view of the horse race track]. As I raced for the elevator, I began tearing off my coat. I was on fire! Dashing into my home, I shed clothes helter-skelter as I made a beeline for the bathtub, which I filled with cold water, all the while painfully moaning incomprehensibly. My body was entirely covered with stinging red welts, and cold winter night or not, I dove into that frigid water and its anticipated relief. After a while hypothermia began to trump the hives and out I emerged somewhat relieved of my misery so that I could begin my explanation to my dumbfounded family.

From that time forth, whenever I saw, heard, or began to smell or even vaguely suspect the approach of the Stinky Tofu vendor, I would immediately cross the street and put as much distance as I could between me and that smell, much the same way as if I were being chased by a serial killer. No, I have not tried Stinky Tofu. But they say it is quite tasty…

Mid-Levels in Mid-Summer

"How Stuff Works" explains that there are two major factors which affect odors: temperature and humidity. Both factors will increase the volatility of the smell molecules. Both critical factors are also very high in Hong Kong during mid-summer. Trash removal is a big deal in Hong Kong. When I lived on Mount Davis Road, I was awakened early each morning to the cacophony of the mountain of rubbish being wrestled away, eleven floors below. It was like the Cantonese sanitation engineer's version of Verdi's "Anvil Chorus!" Visualize it: buildings of twenty or thirty stories with three or four flats (apartments) on each floor add up to a hundred or so households daily producing tons of garbage in a very small space. Multiply this scenario by many hundreds and thousands of other skyscrapers crammed closely together and the said smelly mountain grows exponentially. By one account it weighs in at 6.4 million tons each year, and growing.

Before heading off to a "strategic landfill" the trash first goes to a "refuse transfer station." That sounds sinister, doesn't it? On days when we walked from the Mid-Levels to Western, we passed such a station. You can see what the area looks like if you watch Peter Sellers as *Inspector Clouseau* in *"The Revenge of the Pink Panther."* At the movie's conclusion there's a fun car chase and gun fight in a fireworks godown (= warehouse) on the docks there in Western. The movie was released the very same year I first arrived in Hong Kong and I consider it a significant contribution to the body of comic-historic literature on colonial Hong Kong, almost on a par with this book.

Anyways, back to rubbish: like mortally-wounded beasts, the huge noisy rubbish collection trucks leaked a constant smelly trail of percolated compost all the way back to the awaiting transfer center. To step in their wake meant needing to find replacement footwear. We'd walk in the shade of the big stone wall on the east side of the street and when we neared that dump we'd take a big breath, hold it and jog past as quickly as possible. Sometimes a diesel truck or taxi or minibus would roar by, discharging its own distinctive fumes which helpfully cut like a knife through the prevailing stink. It was the lesser of two evils, I suppose you could say. It is quite amazing how many different ways "relief" can be spelled, depending on the circumstances. Actually I came to rather appreciate such pure diesel fumes – it was one reliable constant in an otherwise ever-changing vat of aromas.

King of Stink!

Things get controversial now, as I will be referring to durian. If you don't know what durian is, here is a clue: it is large, smelly and covered with thorns. Those who have been initiated are grinning. Hotels in Thailand have signs: "no durians allowed in the rooms". And durians cannot travel on the subways of Singapore. Before your imagination runs wild, here is a disclaimer: durian is known as the "king of fruits". Partake of it in privacy, but tell-tale evidence of your act will follow you publicly for a long time to come.

Still uncertain where all this is going? Durian is an edible fruit of the Durio tree, and can grow to be as long as twelve inches and up to seven pounds each. Those with durian experience are divided into two camps: aficionados and those who are disgusted. Back in the 1800's, Mr. Wallace, a creative British naturalist, tried helpfully to put a positive spin on the fruit by describing it as almond-flavored custard. But then again, he probably was one of those sorts that liked Stinky Tofu as well.

Durian grows in many places throughout Southeast Asia, but temperatures drop a bit too low in winter for the tree to grow productively in Hong Kong; however, that doesn't stop durians from arriving by the boatload. Three million tons of these smelly things circle the globe each year. Animals have been known to detect the durian's scent up to one kilometer (a half-mile) away! Besides the humans who are so inclined, the fruit is a favorite among squirrels, monkeys, elephants and the occasional desperate tiger.

Over the centuries, folks have struggled to describe the durian's smell in many ways: rotten onions, moldy gym socks, old vomit, skunk, sewage, turpentine and the kiss from a dead grandmother. For those who prefer more scientific descriptors, there is a volatile but indeterminate mix of ketones, esters and sulfur compounds responsible for the unique fragrance. Given the above, it stands to reason that there are also an infinite variety of opinions as to how to discern when the durian is truly "ripe."

Only about a quarter of its weight is edible, and it is consumed in a variety of manners—raw, as flavoring in just about anything considered to be a dessert, and—adding insult to injury—fermented, like the poor tofu. Durians have been subjected to eponymous use to describe buildings, hookers, cyclones and even cities. Well, New Yorkers have the "Big Apple" don't they? Durian is great if you like fatty, sweet things—like an avocado butterscotch pudding. But do NOT drink alcohol and eat durian! Because at the very best you will have an extended stomach, and wake up with a terrible hangover. In the worst case scenario, you won't [wake up at all, that is.] The potentially fatal reaction has something to do with being too much sugar and fat for the human body to process all at once. My guarded personal opinion: Durian tastes slightly better than it smells.

Like Heaven

As I will describe in "Ellen's Nasty Visit," there is truth to the old aphorism "It is an ill wind that blows nobody any good". Therefore it follows that among the myriad fragrances of Hong Kong, there are also some very pleasant ones to be found: for example, the mandarin orange blossoms during Chinese New Year are wonderfully welcomed harbingers of springtime. But my favorite has to be the white ginger, or Butterfly Ginger Lily (Hedychium coronarium to the botanists among you). We grew them quite by accident on our little heavenly acre up the Tung Hang Mei Valley of Lantau Island.

Our rural house had been constructed such that all of the outflow from the sinks ran to a Our Our rural house had been constructed such that all of the outflow from the sinks ran to a concrete channel that circled the building and sent everything hurdling downhill toward Mr. Stretch's [from "The Dangers of Discounted Chicks] little shack and surrounding vegetable plots.

The constant flow of domestically-enriched water gave rise to quite a proliferation of volunteer greenery on the hillside, but nothing as wonderful as the ginger lily whose tall, dark green stalks lifted their clusters of delicate white fragrant blooms to the awaiting breezes. If they have air freshener in Heaven, I imagine it will smell just like that. We would harvest a stalk or two and place it strategically wherever a situation needed improvement, smell-wise. I hoped Jenny still has some of those growing in her Ark Eden garden. You will find out in my last chapter...

Plumbing in August

Talk about baptism of fire, or rite of passage: however you describe it, Ron got it! You will learn more about Ron as the chainsaw-wielding hero from Typhoon Ellen's aftermath. [See: "Ellen's Nasty Visit!"] When Ron first arrived for an extended stay at our place a month prior, he came with the reputation of being a decent handyman. Poor unsuspecting fellow, the first thing I should have asked him to look into was that strange, big, water-tap-looking device sticking out of the big rock wall that lined the pathway coming up from our gate.

That bit of proactive plumbing would have prevented the following story; so perhaps this is a mixed blessing or another case of the wind blowing some good as well as evil. Well, we could have used a nice breeze that day, but instead it was a baking-hot, humid, stifling one – just perfect for the emergency project at hand.

We had not yet fully discovered and understood all the nuances of our new little property. There were two square concrete lids imbedded into the patio area to the south of the house proper. These had remained a mystery until one hot midsummer afternoon when they began levitating! As they rose, their mystery was solved: this was where everything went from our hole-in-the-tile-floor "commode" – the euphemistic synonym used colloquially for a flush toilet in some parts of the US South.

Apparently the underground tanks were only so commodious, as it were. All we really had to do to solve the situation was simply open that afore-mentioned tap down below, which was positioned to send all that valuable liquid compost down the slope to the banana plantation we had below. But we didn't make that connection at the time.

At this point, the more cautious or timid or wise would suggest: "just call a plumber." At this point, I remind the reader that the only way (other than helicopter) to our place was via the long, narrow, winding mountain pathway which could only accommodate pedestrians, or small push carts. No nice sanitation service trucks could roll up with their equipment. We were on our own. Here is where a bit of fly trivia comes in handy: a housefly in its prime can travel about six miles in a day, more with a good tail wind. Bearing that fact in mind, within an hour every fly within a quarter-mile radius had arrived to supervise our project, adding greatly to our discomfort.

I didn't know much about underground plumbing, but I did understand the principle of the bucket and rope. We had two of each, so Ron and I set out emptying our smelly ocean with a teacup, it would seem. We had big black China-store rubber boots, but not much else in the way of hazmat suits. You get the picture: two miserable gweilos, hot, sweaty, hotter and sweatier still from lugging away sloshing full buckets, swatting at flies with the free hand.

After a couple hours, an (outdoor!) shower, hosing down the area, a refreshing swim and the addition of the above-lauded ginger lilies nearby, all was good as new. The epiphany arrived a few days later, but of course too late, when Ron wondered, "I wonder what this tap does?" Our future plumbing careers just got much easier.

13. Ellen's Nasty Visit!

Ellen paid me a nasty visit right on my birthday, during the first week of September 1983. No, Ellen is not my mother-in-law nor a homicidal ex-lover. Let me set the background. It had been another hot and humid summer. This story takes place towards the end of the hot-and-humid period and just before the few days when Hong Kong has perfect weather. This year had been a particularly rough time for us folks in HK already.

Negotiations with China over the future of Hong Kong showed the Iron Lady there was an even stronger metallic substance, namely Chinese resolve. They had waited 99 years to get this part of the motherland back and that was long enough. Prime Minister Margaret Thatcher assured local residents that Hong Kong would never change. Now as I am writing this book, China has had control of Hong Kong for seventeen years. So much for political promises... While collaborating with Jenny Quinton of Ark Eden on this book, the "Occupy Hong Kong" movement held the world's attention for several weeks in the autumn of 2014 with their "unreasonable" demand of being able to choose their own leaders in their own elections. The more things change, the more things remain the same...

As I said, it had already been a rough year in Hong Kong. The markets were jittery over the stalled and jerky negotiations concerning the territory's future, culminating in a crash of the Hong Kong currency in October when the exchange rates wildly fell from HK$ 5.00 to HK$10.00 vs. the US$ before being "rescued" and pegged at 7.8 over the weekend. I learned the hard way that it was bad to be "long" on a currency as such times.

And Hong Kong was just getting over a long, nasty and controversial scandal, with a long, expensive and convoluted Royal Inquiry. From what I remember of the daily deluge in the press, it all was caused by The Law of Unintended Consequences. A nice young Scottish Inspector named John was involved in the special investigations to ferret out homosexuals in the police department, which may or may not have been a window-dressing exercise to appease the landlords in Beijing. Lo and behold, however, he allegedly found out that some of his higher-ups themselves favored young Chinese boys. This was certainly NOT the way this little investigation was supposed to go. But they had been warned: people who live in glass houses shouldn't throw stones.

Sometime thereafter, Inspector John was found in his apartment shot to death with five bullet wounds in his chest. It was declared a "suicide." [Perhaps you are like me and wonder how on earth do you manage to shoot yourself in the chest <u>five</u> times?] At the commission of inquiry—and Hong Kong's most expensive one ever at that—an "expert" witness for the Crown was flown out from the UK who brazenly testified that it was not strange at all, and in fact he knew of a similar case where someone had even shot himself <u>seven</u> times in the chest. And while this tale is not my own doing, my reporting of this assertion is indeed as true as it is weird. They even made a movie about it! Ms. E., the maverick Urban Councilor (a former Scottish Missionary to China) fought hard to exonerate John's name. She is alive to this day as I write this chapter, at the ripe old age of 101. Something is to be said for the sturdiness of the Scots!

Anyways, I wanted something to happen in Hong Kong to distract from all the depressing political events of late. You know what they warn, "Be careful what you wish for." I wanted something to shake things up. I got it. It was Ellen, a Super Typhoon. Ellen became one of the worst typhoons to hit the China coast for about a decade. Wreaking havoc in four countries, this storm cut off power to 50,000 folks in Hong Kong. Seven of those were my own little family, in our own little home on remote Lantau Island. Typhoon Ellen spawned the first ever tornado in Hong Kong history. All in all it was a rather messy affair, as you will read about in a moment.

For us, it was a "direct hit": the eye of the storm passed right over our house and in the midst of the stormy fury there was a moment when everything went calm and the sky directly overhead was eerily bright blue. Just for a moment... Then the fierce winds simply reversed direction while retaining their intensity. The storm stalled in its northward track and the winds howled all night, spawning all kinds of hideous sounds in the darkened countryside around us.

In Ellen's wake ships sank; large buildings were seriously damaged; hundreds of homes destroyed; thousands made homeless; hundreds were hurt; dozens were killed; and damage ran into the tens of millions of dollars. Well I got the diversionary excitement I wished for, all right! Here are some highlights:

The Flying Wallendas:

Our flat roof top had a big sturdy canopy for shade, made of thick steel pipes and heavy canvas, wired together firmly. It kept off the beating sun and heavy rains, cooling the house while giving us an extra room with a nice view of the valley. This same canopy made a great target for this mighty visiting typhoon. Ellen suffered from low pressure – Barometric pressure dropped to a scant 925 millibars (27.32 inches), if you can imagine, generating huge swirling winds. [To put this in perspective, average pressure is 1013 mb or 29.92 inches; a Category 3 Hurricane will have pressure around 950 mb or 28 inches. This was a very intense storm!] Ellen's winds gusted to 154 mph (or 248 km/h).

One such gust ripped an iron corner post right out of our concrete rooftop. The canvas stayed attached to the post, thanks to my great knot-tying skills. This corner post had a heavy three-way joint at its free end. The other end was attached to a portion of the tarp which acted as a spinnaker. Like an ethereal giant pounding our house with his huge mace, this loose stanchion was striking the house on all sides as it wildly careened in the vicious swirling winds. It was bound to come through one of our many windows at any moment. We listened in an attempt to determine some pattern to its fly-like, circuitous path and discovered in its rhythm of beating that it passed closely by the window at the back stairway of the living room. A desperate plan was hastily hatched.

The bright idea was to capture the giant's mace as it passed by and thus spare our house any further beatings. The first discovery was that any windows opened in such stormy conditions tend to take on a life of their own and sail away: it would take one person solely dedicated to grasping the window in order to successfully pull off this plan. On the mace's next pass I made a grab for and caught it, and then proceeded to be lifted out of the building before I finally let go of my quarry.

Second discovery: I was light enough to go airborne and our plan would thus require a third person, a spotter as it were, to hang on to me as I hung on for dear life to the mace. Well, the window holder needed his two hands to keep the window from smashing away. I need both my hands to hold onto the slippery wind-driven metal pipe. And the person holding onto me needed two hands to do so. So our project now required a fourth: someone to lash the pipe to the side of the window frame with a stout rope. On the fourth pass of the mace we were successful; we were sore, bruised and wet as well. But the giant's beatings were stopped.

Tree Shredder:

As mentioned in Jenny Quinton's chapter, "The Lady Who Planted Trees", there was one very special tree, a magnificent "Flame of the Forest" which towered over our front yard and spread its beautiful graceful boughs over the entire house and yard like a living, nurturing umbrella. I often sat under its welcoming shade during the hot tropical summers, editing manuscripts, all the while marveling at the spectacular huge crimson blooms which festooned the tree's massive crown. On this particularly sad September day the typhoon blew violently through our valley all night long.

The next morning we awoke to a botanical winter—all of the trees, (that had not been outright destroyed and uprooted) were totally denuded of each and every one of their leaves. Stark black branches were all that remained of what had been lush greenery just the day before. My little boy Andy [hero of "Which Way War"] looked out the window and burst into tears. The mighty ancient tree survived, but it was damaged and never quite regained its full glory. Years later it fell during a storm, almost crushing Jenny's young children, which you can read about in her chapter.

Lunar Heroes:

About 50 years before Shakespeare penned his version of the line in King Henry IV about "the ill wind that blows no man to good," John Heywood actually first penned these words in 1546. If you are not conversant with Heywood's writings you might find it worth a moment of Googling to discover just how many of our common pithy phrases originated out of this English playwright's head. Anyways, the conventional wisdom of this particular line dictates that some good is bound to come from even the direst of events, as I will now attempt to demonstrate for you.

72

In Ellen's wake, among other issues, was a huge fallen tree just downhill from the bus stop. You read about that bus stop in the chapter about Happy Ending. Our winding concrete path was only about a meter wide and at this particular juncture was bounded on one side by a steep slope and on the other with a precipitous drop-off. The tree's trunk was several feet thick and there was no getting around or over it, so all transportation and commerce came to a grinding halt in our isolated valley. There was no such thing as the Public Works Department in this neighborhood. This is where that "ill wind" karma stuff comes in. My buddy Ron and I got to be lunar heroes, albeit just for a day or so. And we did not have to leave terra firma to achieve this local celebrity status.

Machetes and sturdy long-handled garden hoes were the main tools in circulation in this particular village but neither of them were a match for the fallen deciduous giant. Ron and I sailed off to the big city and somehow managed to rent a chainsaw. After a day of uncommon noise and sweat and grunting and shoving, and—most importantly— all at our own expense, we had the path cleared! Hurray!—Just in time for the Mid-autumn (Moon) festival which fell on September 21st that year.

In the evening the villagers drink beer and eat moon cakes under a constellation of colorfully-lit paper lanterns. And while the striped red-white-and blue canvas awnings draped above the folding tables were no match for the Gemütlichkeit of an Austrian Biergarten, it was close enough to heaven on earth for us. Everyone was toasting us and buying us beer—mostly "San Miguel" and "Tsingtao" brands—and kept passing moon cakes and other food to us, all the while thanking us and congratulating us on our accomplishment. And all the while we could barely comprehend what was being said, let alone make any eloquent response worthy of heroes, so we just kept smiling and nodding and eating and drinking until it was time for us to go home. Ron and I gave gweilos a good name that evening! Prosit!

Land Ahoy!

I imagine there is no sweeter sight for those who have drifted long at sea than the approaching coastline. However, if it was never your intent to come ashore, it might be a somewhat less appreciated sight. Such was the tale of a large ocean-traversing freighter that was out in the South China Sea when Ellen blustered by. The crew was attempting to ride out the storm at sea, rather than risk being tossed about in Hong Kong's busy, crowded harbor. There are typhoon-strength moorings available, but only a limited number of them.

This particular hapless crew was 25 miles out to sea. They were dragging their heavy anchors and running their engines in full reverse, but these efforts were not enough to prevent bossy Ellen from sweeping them and their trusty ship right up onto our beach. Now, Silver Mine Bay (Mui Wo) is not known anywhere in the nautical world as a deep water port. Its shallow waters are normally sufficient only for ferries and row boats and swimmers paddling about.

When daylight broke and we ventured out, we discovered that our little beach was now entirely taken up by this beached steel whale forlornly grounded against its will and best intentions with its hull, rudder and propeller all fully exposed. It was months before the proper combination of high tides and super-sized tug boats could set the ship free once more to sail the seven seas. The kids had fun bouncing rocks off the hull and attempting to climb the anchor's slimy chain.

Every once in a while throughout these wild tales, I feel duty-bound to remind the readers of what I have stated elsewhere: the book's content is indeed true, despite its strangeness. The photo below of my two oldest sons James and Philip [appearing in the "Buffalo Phil" chapter] posing next to the beached ship serves this purpose in this story. (This was way before the days of Photo Shop, so this really, really happened.) Thanks guys! Typhoon Ellen had also taken all the sand away in her wake, as you can see by the rocks next to the boys.

Blowing in the Wind

Ellen left a huge mess in her departure. Power lines were down all over Lantau Island. With tens of thousands of people without power in the crowded, busy urban areas, the handful of village farmers without power in my neighborhood were hardly a priority for the giant utility companies. It was still summer, so we were in no danger from the cold. We had bottled gas for cooking. It was very hot without fans, though. This was before the days of the Internet, so in some ways, we did not feel any more isolated from the world than usual.

Phone lines, still somewhat of a luxury in our secluded valley, were also down. But with our phone line—a true royal luxury in those parts—down after Ellen's nasty visit, virtually no one knew about our situation and probably no one cared. I certainly couldn't call the repair center. It had caused enough of a stir when I had innocently requested a second line that I could dedicate for my fax/modem, not unlike Oliver's request: "Please, sir, I want some more!"

The tangle of broken and shredded phone lines resembled an amateur spider's first attempt at a web. Obviously, calling for help was out of the question. With thousands of skyscrapers and businesses to service, the few miserable lines looping through the trees up our valley did not rate priority service. So I did the next best thing, which I had learned well from the locals—adapt and adopt: improvise. In other words, I dubbed myself a newly-certified linesman and shimmied up the poles, clutching my phone set while tapping into the tangle of shredded wires. It took quite some time until I found a "hot" one—a line alive with electric current. I then had to splice several pieces of the storm-shredded wire together in order for the line to reach my all the way to our house.

Here I am once again duty-bound to point out my discovery that while the voltage and current levels on phone lines are considerably less than those of household electric supply lines, said levels are still sufficient to get your attention, especially on rainy days. A memorable lesson learned. This was probably a memorable sight for Stretch Jr.

[Remember him from "Danger of Discounted Chicks"?] as well when he passed by underneath upon his return from the local markets.

Now, anyone who has ever lived in the tropics understands the indescribable discomfort that comes from wearing tight under garments in hot, sweaty, humid climes, thus there is an excellent reason why you see all these pictures of tropical natives garbed in robes. A sarong also works well in a pinch when you are in the privacy of your home—which is where I was when I first started tinkering with the phone lines.

In my focused determination, I had wandered down our path and up the poles without first donning more suitable linesman attire. So, had there been cell phones in those days, the photo of me that Mr. Stretch posted on his Face Book account would have had the "NSFW" caveat stamp. I quickly slid down the pole upon becoming aware of my "wardrobe malfunction" and retreated home as nonchalantly as circumstances allowed. Silly gweilos indeed! But now at least my phone worked!

As we properly credited Mr. Heywood earlier, even an ill wind allows for some good and in this case, what blew in shortly after Ellen's rather nasty visit and unceremonious departure was an arriving jet, carrying a refugee missionary from bloody, war-torn Sri Lanka. And while our first encounter did not seem to bode anything promising at all, years later and a couple continents removed, this person later became my second wife. We have since happily raised a family of six children [my second set of six children] together during these intervening decades.

14. Primate Bullying!

"If you can't handle the monkey business, stay out of our jungle!"

S ometimes when husbands go on outings without their wives and families, they get up to all sorts of monkey business. In my defense, on this particular outing, monkey business was never my intention. When you read this tale you may wonder: "Is he making all this up?!" Trust me! You can't make up this kind of stuff! This tale will indeed be a bizarre story of survival, but I assure you it is all true, as I don't have an imagination sufficiently fertile to concoct such a tale. By way of general disclaimer, at this point I will interject that all of the stories in this book are true, for the most part. I only deviate minimally from the truth where I portray myself as stronger, smarter or more handsome than I might otherwise be attributed by the impartial observer. This is only natural, since I am the book's author. I read somewhere that you can even get an "artistic license" if you know the right folks.

I digress. Back when this bullying occurred, I really wish I hadn't digressed. Alas, it seems I am always going off the beaten path, finding detours, constantly in search of new discoveries, thus the title of this book. How else would an erstwhile and otherwise practical-minded MIT Sloan School of Management candidate end up living on a remote Chinese island far from most technology? Furthermore, how else can you experience coming face to face with a large wild boar on a remote mountain top of said Lantau Island, unless you crawl through a very tiny pathway in the shrubbery in search of the yet another shortcut. If I'm not mistaken, the compass bearing would have described my movements as a Northwest Passage of my own making.

Admittedly, I screamed like a little girl when I found my nose was just inches away from the boar's big hairy snout. He screamed too, after a fashion. On second thought, "he" might have been a "she", but I didn't have the luxury of time to ascertain the gender. Thankfully the boar retreated, while I set a new world backwards crawling record as I too retreated to safety—to be reunited with my concerned little family of hikers, and so here I am alive today to tell you this other tale. This next detour, however, almost proved deadly.

Now the Hong Kong you probably most readily recognize from all of the usual movie and travel channel shots is one that bristles with skyscrapers clinging to steep mountain slopes like the five o'clock stubble on a giant's bony great chin.

But that uber-urban image is really only the tip of this land's subtropical iceberg, as it were: the 10% most people see where the vast majority of the Hong Kong folk live and work. Meanwhile, the remaining 90% of Hong Kong is made up of islands, mountains, forests, farms, streams and waterfalls and lakes (reservoirs) virtually untouched by the developers, just beckoning the intrepid explorer. That's my cue.

As I looked out the tiny window of my tiny 13th story office, I could see the raw hillside behind this housing development. There were all these gravesites where the ancestors were treated to the best possible ocean views. I occasionally walked among those graves, enjoying the views thus afforded and getting some needed exercise and fresh air. [There are other, safer ways to get exercise in Hong Kong, albeit with less fresh air. See "No Third Turkey".] One day my eye spotted a narrow trail that led off enticingly into the woods. What I could not see was that a mile away, at the extreme other end of this dense, dark and cool, shady forest trail there was a very graphic warning sign.

As a child growing up in rural upstate New York in the picturesque Hudson River valley, I spent much of my free time hiking through the forests or riding along the country roads which surrounded our quiet little town. I could walk or pedal my bike for miles, enjoying the constantly changing landscape: rugged wooded hills whose hardwood trees erupted in a blaze of color each autumn; the pine forests which looked so serene in winter with their sugar-frosting of fresh snow; rolling fields dotted with cows, and one particular black bull that gave me a good chase one day; the stony babbling brooks with their cold water; the mysterious rock piles with all forms of geological specimens heaped together.

I imagine my love for exploring nature never really left me and yet now here I was in Hong Kong, in an extremely un-natural, noisy, crowded, concrete maze. Like the sirens of Homer's *Odyssey*, that unexplored trail on the edge of the hillside graves beckoned me irresistibly. Thus my adventure began, as I responded to my innate boyish curiosity.

Mind you, I was not totally irresponsible—not by a long shot! I was equipped with my prescription sunglasses from the Yu See Nau optometrist shop on steep Wing Wo lane above Central district. I also possessed a 375 ml wax carton of Vitasoy green tea drink. Clever Chinese discovered soymilk to be a viable alternative for the lactose-intolerant long before westerners discovered this condition even existed. Google search it for yourself if you don't believe me, since I don't think I have a Vitasoy story in my arsenal that I will be relating to you. You can see exactly what that carton looks like if you thumb ahead to the chapter "The Lady Who Planted Trees," where there is a photograph of Jenny's then-young son Angus clutching one himself.

It's hot and humid in Hong Kong in July, thus I was wearing only a thin t-shirt, shorts, sandals, and of course my glasses—not exactly proper body armor for the attack that awaited, unbeknownst to me. The trail started off peacefully and fascinatingly. The hillside I had left behind was pretty much scraped clear of most vegetation in order to build all of the concrete skyscrapers, gravesites and pathways.

The hot glare of the subtropical sun soon gave way to cool green shade as the trees grew ever taller and denser. It suddenly was quite dark and quite still. One would be forgiven for mistaking the location as something akin to a cross between the Black Forest of southwest Germany and the Rainforest of Manaus. I was enthralled! I didn't know where this enchanted narrow wooded detour led, but I was momentarily unconcerned. I had stumbled upon a beautiful treasure of nature's richest foliage, just a few steps from the edge of one of the world's densest populations, one of Hong Kong's great contradictions!

I was also about to stumble upon something entirely different. You know that feeling you get when you sense someone is watching you, but you can't see them? I suddenly had it. But no other <u>humans</u> were (stupid enough to be) in this forest watching me.

It's called a "troop". That's what a bunch of baboons is called. The premonition I had was entirely accurate. There they were, way up high in the trees, glaring down at me malevolently. I froze. I knew you weren't supposed to run from dogs, so I extrapolated that the same must be true of a troop of baboons. Suddenly a large female literally (not figuratively) dropped from the tree just a few meters away from where I stood, doing my best imitation of a statue. She was carrying a nursing little one.

The infant—I checked and that is indeed how you properly refer to a baby baboon: "infant"—was probably adorably cute but my vision was growing fuzzy right about now. I had read about how viciously mothers will protect their young in the wild. Why couldn't this baboon have been a young single? Well, maybe not, on second thought. For a few tense moments we stood staring at each other. Then my worst fear began: Mama Baboon charged at me, bully-style!

I assumed my best defensive posture, viz: I closed my eyes as tightly as the orbicularis oculi muscles would allow. For some reason, during that brief window of opportunity to reason, I had decided that the thing I wanted most to avoid was having my eyeballs scratched out. Now without vision, as my eyes were scrunched tightly closed, I had to rely on my other senses to inform me of my circumstances. I could hear and smell danger rushing at me. Then I sensed my arm had been jolted. Then all was calm. After some hesitation, I slowly opened my eyes, one at a time, not entirely certain that I really wanted to survey whatever damage I had sustained. Amazingly enough, there was none!

Did you forget that small detail I mentioned earlier? I did too, until that exact moment when I heard the baboon rendition of laughter. I dared myself to glance upwards at the sound and there I beheld Madame Baboon finishing off my Vitasoy drink, deftly sipping through the tiny white straw. It seems that she was a vegetarian, or at least fortunately for my sake, she was at that particular moment. She had skillfully scooped that drink right out of my hand while running past me at full speed without ever touching a hair on my hand.

The definition of "relief" was never as crystal clear to me as it was at that precise moment! I skedaddled out of that enchanted and dangerous forest before the baboons' next course (me) could commence. Fortunately for my shaky legs, civilization was a mere hundred meters or so away. As I emerged from the dark forest into the broad daylight I encountered a nice paved road, by the side of which was a large red government signboard with a frightening full- color picture of a toothy baboon, warning all sane individuals to beware. Needless to say, I took the long way home.

I wonder how Mama Baboon learned to pilfer a hiker's drink so expertly? Perhaps there is a support group out there somewhere I should contact. Sure enough, decades later as I wrote this story in the comfort of my office, I came across a wonderfully informative article entitled: "How to Survive a Baboon Encounter."

From reading it, in retrospect, it seems I did all the correct things without the luxury of having had this prior knowledge, except for one critical point of advice I had not heeded: "Do not walk through a troop of baboons; instead, wait for an opportunity to walk around

81

them, or wait for them to leave before you proceed." You should read the following article yourself before wandering in the woods alone. You have been warned. See:

http://survival.about.com/od/8/a/How-To-Survive-A-Baboon-Encounter.htm.

The picture greeting the reader at the article's opening says it all.

15. Close Encounters of the Scary or Stupid Kind

(Vignettes of real Hong Kong denizens)

Hong Kong is a very crowded place. There are about seven million people in 426 square miles, which is roughly a square of 20.6 miles across. For cities of that many people, only Dhaka is more densely populated. Weirdly enough, tiny Monaco is considered more crowded but only because it is a room-size country, and the rich and famous closely crowd around the roulette wheels. You could accommodate the entire Monaco crowd by putting a couple in each of Hong Kong's taxis.

Furthermore, given the fact that about 90% of Hong Kong's land area is covered by steep uninhabited mountains and large tracts of parklands, you really only have the habitable space of a square approximately 6 miles by 6 miles, or about 175,000 HK'ers/mi^2.* By comparison this is seven times more crowded than the Big Apple. [*Well, technically you could argue that Hong Kong is a cube of sorts, since on average, the Hong Kong resident lives on the 14th floor of one of its fabled skyscrapers, but let's stick with plane geometry; it's easier.] Nevertheless, this amazingly crowded city is still made up of unique individuals, and this chapter is dedicated to some of those.

Besides being filled with people, Hong Kong is filled with money. Only London and New York are considered more important in the halls of world finance. This tiny territory—probably about the space of your home town—has the 8th most traded currency in the world, rubbing shoulders with the likes of the Yen, Dollar, Euro and Pound. You probably didn't know that, right? You would have if you lived in Hong Kong. At a recent count there were 211 different banks; by comparison, how many banks does your town have?

[Mine has eight, and we think that is overkill. Of course you could fit everyone from my town into one of those HK skyscrapers. And while my town's land acreage is almost 1/10th the size of Hong Kong, it is only about 1/154th as crowded] Now, I'm not talking about individual sub branches of banks (of which there are about 1300 in Hong Kong); I'm just talking about actual individual bank brands. There are over two hundred of them! Seventy of the world's top 100 banks have set up shop in Hong Kong. So, understandably, some of these stories will deal with money or money handlers.

I had at first considered myself a savvy businessman of sorts upon arrival in Hong Kong: I had run a small import/export business and handcraft mail order business in Australia, albeit it was a business of about three employees, including myself. I imported my tan indestructible plastic attaché case with me when I came to Hong Kong and considered it a smart accessory. That was until I encountered Herman the German. Well, he never actually properly introduced himself, but he nonetheless successfully deflated my business acumen ego. This happened during one of my very first days walking down Des Voeux Road in the Central business District of Hong Kong Island, on a sunny, steamy June afternoon. [See "Street of Wishes!" for more stories and trivia about this very particular street.]

With a thick accent resembling that of "General Burkhalter" from TV's "Hogan's Heroes," "Herman" squeezed up next to me on the crowded sidewalk, helpfully confiding: "ditch the briefcase; they'll cut your wrist off to steal it from you!" Then he melted away into the passing throng. I never got to see his face to scan for a hint of a grin of playfulness or sarcasm, so in the absence of any such evidence, his spooky threat lingered, like that of a passing skunk. I kept a sharp lookout for knives, just in case.

The Hang Seng bank was a great place to exchange currency. You could make a transaction there just about as quickly as the server at McDonald's says "would you like fries with that?" There is a story about missing doors and frustrated dragons surrounding this building. According to Feng Shui experts, the dragons which inhabit the mountains must have an unobstructed pathway to the sea; otherwise disaster lurks from their displeasure. Thus buildings must have windows and doorways on opposite sides to allow clear passage.

The first bank to operate on this location failed to live up to Feng Shui standards and financial ruin ensued. Later banks altered the architecture with prosperous results. The giant Hong Kong Shanghai Bank further east on Des Voeux Road solved this issue by raising the entire building off the ground on four huge pillars. Dragons there can happily pass through and under the skyscraper effortlessly: perhaps it is thus no surprise that the Hong Kong Shanghai Bank is one of the world's largest and most successful.

In I walked (cautiously) with my afore-mentioned, sure-to-cause-hand-amputation briefcase and pulled out a handful of foreign currency to exchange. There were no questions asked, no raised eyebrows, no forms to fill out nor any bureaucratic delays, as I was used to in other countries. Next to me stood a poor local Chinese grandma, (or so I thought, judging by the tattered pajamas she was wearing and the filthy taped-together plastic grocery bag she was carrying.) Nonchalantly, she pulled out a cool half-million Hong Kong dollars from that trashy bag and bought South African Krugerrands, Swiss Francs and Japanese Yen. Upon successful completion of her transaction she gave a fleeting grin, revealing a mouthful of gold to rival Fort Knox. I had just received my first three free lessons on banking in Hong Kong: (a.) folks here loved dealing in cash, (b.) they were constantly buying gold and (c.) personal security was generated by giving off the aura of nonchalant poverty.

(This is not unlike the local custom of how the gods are appeased by speaking poorly in public about your family—even if you are actually privately very proud of them—in order to avoid the gods' mischievous and jealous wrath, by referring to family members thusly: "My worthless son," "My stupid daughter," "My ugly concubine.")

On another day, but on the same street, I had another close encounter of the scary kind. This time the message was delivered by an elderly Cantonese gentleman whose English was better than Herman's, but whose portent was even more dire. He actually grabbed my little goatee, literally shaking it and thus shaking my entire head, all the while pronouncing: "we know why you are here and we do not want you here!" I'm not entirely sure I even knew why I was there at that point; let alone how this chap knew. I had never seen him before and did not know who he was. Nor did I know who "they" were! And while I had never been to Kansas, I was beginning to agree with Dorothy's conclusion—Toto, I've a feeling we're not in Kansas anymore!" It was another very hot summer day, but the hairs on my arm remained at attention from the ghoulish chill surrounding me for quite some time.

Like at Alice's Restaurant, you can get anything you want in Hong Kong, especially electronic gadgets. There was one particular shop I frequented for such needs, situated on one of the various steep side lanes perpendicular to and above Des Voeux Road. The proprietor wins the award for Unabashed Candor. There was something wrong with my power adaptor. Sometimes the less scrupulous dealers would resolve your problem by simply taking a new replacement from the box and putting your broken item back instead. ("Sell it to the next tourist going back to Germany..." they would gloat.) This merchant had more integrity, or else more technical knowledge at least, so he proceeded to repair the adaptor on the spot. He removed the cover and pointed to the faulty part. "You see that gizmo there?" he asked. To show I understood, I reached over to touch it but he firmly intervened: "Don't touch that! I don't want you to..." and his voice trailed off as he pondered how best to finish the sentence. What he had said, however, was enough for me to notice that the adaptor was plugged in and I was about to get a dose of the 220-volt electrical supply. I helpfully finished his sentence for him: "You don't want me to... die!" He shook his head and corrected me, "I don't care if you die; I just don't want you to die in my shop!" As I noted before, this certainly wasn't Kansas. But that sure was a refreshing breath of raw honesty!

For my next encounter, this time with a luggage merchant, we cross Victoria Harbor by Star ferry to Tsim Sha Tsui [let me hear you say that, five times fast] on the lower Kowloon peninsula where I arrived early for my yearly appointed encounter with the funereal staff at Royal Hong Kong Immigrations to renew my work visa. You know the chirpy chestnut: "your day will go the way the corners of your mouth point." What you might not know is the Hong Kong merchants have their own version of that superstition here that the day's business will be predicted by their encounter with their first customer of the day. And for this particular luggage shop, that was about to be me. I really wasn't even shopping at the time, but that was inconsequential. I had learned how to bargain pretty well by this point, but today I was not looking for a bargain. I was just looking for my visa. So without really trying, I landed the bargain of a lifetime.

To kill time waiting for my appointment, I was strolling up and down the street. It was relatively early. Shops stay open quite late in the touristy areas, so they get a sleep-in the next morning till about nine or ten. All that was visible of the shop was the locked metal rolled-down shutter that guarded the glass display windows. Suddenly with a whirl the shutter zoomed skyward and the shop was open, ready for business and there I was, face to face, eyeball to eyeball with the hopeful merchant. "Come in!" he pleaded, rolling out the imaginary red carpet with his outstretched arm. What proceeded would have made great material for a burlesque routine. The simple fact was that I did not need any luggage. I wasn't planning to go anywhere. It was simply a case of being at the wrong place at the right time. "I have to go to my appointment!" I protested. "I'll make you a good deal!" the merchant promised.

I still had a few minutes to spare, so I reluctantly ventured inside the cramped luggage shop. The only item that even slightly caught my eye was an American Tourister hang-up garment bag. The hopeful merchant's eye caught my eye being caught by that bag and the sales pitch was on. The listed price was $200. The problem was I did not want it, especially if I had to carry it into my Immigration appointment; I feared that would really make me look far too transitory. I kept digging for convincing excuses not to buy it, only to have the merchant quickly make a counter offer and the ensuing exchange went something like this:

Me: I don't really want a garment bag.
Him: $175.
Me: It's a bit too bulky, I think.
Him: $150.
Me: I would rather another color, say, burgundy...
Him: $125.
Me: (Taking a step out the doorway.)
Him: OK, OK! $100! You drive hard bargain!
Me: Thinking to myself – "What is going on here? Already 50% off without trying?" Then it dawned on me: it was the first-sale-of-the-day thing! The persona of the hunter emerged. "I don't have that much money right now!"

Him: You have $75?
Me: Maybe, but I don't know if that zipper tag is reliable...
Him: $50!
Me: Let me feel it... Seems a bit heavy.
Him: $40.
Me: Now, on my way out the door: I'm late for my appointment!
Him: Ok, Ok! First sale of the day! I give it to you, $20!
Me: OK! But you have to keep it here till I get back from my appointment.

I returned later. Things went well at Immigrations. The successful garment bag deal had given me a needed boost of swagger. The officials did their obligatory best to be intimidating. "What will you do when we deny your visa? Where will you go?" Sort of a variation on the old trick question: "(where will you go when) you stop beating your wife?" I cavalierly brushed aside their challenge, telling them I had a distant relative, Abraham Lincoln, who advised me not to cross the bridge until I got there. That one wasn't in their play book, so the interrogation ended soon thereafter. I got my yearly work visa, went back to the luggage shop and got my bargain garment bag. It looked like business was going well for my friend. "You very lucky customer!" he crowed. Looking around at the now busy shop where money was coming in at a nice pace, I replied "And you lucky too, today!" I congratulated him. I still have that garment bag today. It's black, not burgundy; but it was a great buy— at 90% off!

For the next too-close encounter, where I got way too silly, we have to hop a slow ferry for the three-hour journey west to the erstwhile Portuguese colony of Macau, and then take a crowded mini-bus ride to the southern-most tip of the tiny island of Coloane. The time of year is February during Chinese (Lunar) New Year – a nearly week-long event where most all business comes to a grinding halt, except for the business of feasting and firecrackers. If you have never tried to shepherd your flock of little ones through a crowd during a Chinese holiday, there is no way for you to grasp the magnitude of the terror. Think of Disneyland crowds at Christmas and then by some giant, magic fusion process, squish everyone into $1/10^{th}$ the space. Scary indeed for the young concerned parent!

My nerves were already quite shot from the day's journey by this point, and being the A-type personality back then, I didn't really know how to relax. I'd tried it once or twice, but it seemed so much effort. Anyways, one reveler at the bus stop thought it would be fun to throw firecrackers at my little kids' feet. Watch the little white kids turn even whiter, something to that effect. You know how worry-wart and over-protective new young parents can be. And these were whole long strings of firecrackers that popped endlessly. I asked him to stop. It happened to be the Chinese Year of the Goat and this guy was definitely getting mine! He laughed and threw some more, ha ha! And then some more again. Ha ha!

By now, the kids—James, Suzy and Joanne, pictured below—were screaming, my ears were ringing, my nerves were frayed and so I snapped. I went charging after the culprit, yelling and screaming like a madman. Never mind that I was the tourist, and near the birthplace of gunpowder! I was determined to protect my three little ones. At this point I should have heard the Choir of Sane and Reasonable Persons chanting "Be careful!" But I didn't.

Thankfully I did hear a tiny voice of reason when I was within arm's length of my target, my fist already raised. It was my wife, pleading: "Honey!" The caution dripped heavy from her one-word alarm and, in a blinding moment of clarity, I surveyed the scene. I was an irate white visitor surrounded by a sea of local Chinese revelers. This must be akin to the moment when the bull says to himself "Oops!" when realizing he is no longer in his safe querencia but instead is surrounded by those in the ring about to send him to cow heaven.

I quickly backpedaled, bowing and scraping and apologizing profusely while the crowded giggled and shouted. I'm certain I gave them all some great material for a Lunar New Year story to tell for years to come: "The Gweilo Who Came Unhinged!" We also learned to time our vacations better.

Today, while reflecting after writing this chapter, I was thinking how great all these kids of mine – James, Suzy and baby Joanne pictured here – turned out! I'm very grateful that children can develop and mature to become successful, productive, happy adults in spite of all the silly and stupid parenting they received. Thanks, kids!

16. The Street of Wishes!

Adventures on Des Voeux Road

Des Voeux Road is a major Hong Kong Island street in the Central business district, festooned with many huge banks. Des Voeux is apparently a French word that loosely translates to "street of wishes." Indeed, there were many times when I wished I didn't have to walk down that dangerous street! Why on earth was there a French-named street lined with banks (not the left and right kind either, as in Paris) in a Chinese city that was a British colony? I don't know; I guess you'd have to ask the Rothschilds and the other bankers there.

The humor of it all escaped me somehow. I also have it on relatively good authority that this particular use of "Des Voeux" descends from an ancient French version which more accurately means "Cursed Street" but I will let you be the judge of that. Actually, long ago, the tenth Governor of Hong Kong by this very name presided over the gigantic reclamation project and construction of the eponymous street.

I feel that the above-mentioned construction of this street calls for a brief aside to humor the civil-engineering types. Much of what are now the most crowded and prosperous streets of Hong Kong did not even exist when the British Opium traders happened upon this delightful harbor in the mid 1800's. The steep mountainsides ran pretty much directly into the waters of what was to become known as Victoria Harbor. So new flat land was created along the coastline, and this new man-made geography now extends several city blocks into what was once the sea. The process continues to this very day. Where there was once seawater and fish there are now towering skyscrapers with a modern subway running beneath.

Humor me here for a moment: I don't know where you stand on this particular issue, but I myself have often chafed at the incorrectness of the term "reclaimed land." If you lost your briefcase on the train, you might try going to the Lost and Found department to reclaim it. If you had too much to drink one night, you might have a shower and some strong coffee the next morning to reclaim your dignity. In other words, you reclaim something that is yours but was temporarily lost.

But no one ever had this land before, correct? The sea had this space for millennia and developers suddenly decided to claim it from the sea. But they couldn't properly reclaim it because they never had it before. I felt duty-bound to point out this subtle yet important inaccuracy.

I'll start off my stories about Des Voeux Road in a lighter vein. Lerner and Loewe wrote great lyrics for *My Fair Lady*, and you probably recall these great two lines sung by "Freddy":

> *I have often walked down this street before;*
> *But the pavement always stayed beneath my feet before.*

It was a figurative expression, of course; for me, however, one day it turned quite literal. One particularly pleasant sunny day I was walking along Des Voeux Road, happily swinging my briefcase, when a singularly attractive young Hong Kong Chinese woman passing by caught my eye. Turning my head around to catch another glimpse of her, I kept walking forward, but without the aid of my eyesight. Suddenly the faithful Choir of Sane and Reasonable Persons sounded in my brain: "Watch Out!"

I have learned over the years to heed their voice, especially at times when somewhat lacking in sanity and reason myself. So I obediently stopped dead in my tracks and turned around carefully, not knowing exactly what to expect. There was nothing! Literally, and that was the danger: Like love-struck Freddy, with my next footstep the pavement would not have been beneath my feet any more. A manhole cover had been removed; and safety standards being what they were in Hong Kong back then, there was no warning barrier, just a clear view to the dark sewer far below.

Sometime later, I still had my faithful tan briefcase. I never did hear from Herman again after that spooky encounter with him. I kept my briefcase and considered his dire warning to be a hoax. But I was careful, as it was quite easy to get separated from possessions or loved ones in the constant stream of rushing pedestrians. The street was particularly crowded right then and folks going in both directions were bumping into my briefcase. I was uneasy and glanced across the side street and noticed that the sidewalk opposite me was almost empty, by Hong Kong standards. My impulse and basic logic suggested I dash across the street and navigate the remainder of the block in relative privacy.

The faithful Choir of Sane and Reasonable Persons resounded in my ear: "no, just wait!" I heeded their advice, and defying common sense and logic, I plowed on through the crowded sidewalk. A bus passed by and stopped at the corner when it reached Des Voeux Road. There was a small crowd of pedestrians on the opposite corner waiting to cross. It was exactly where I would have been had I crossed the street at my first impulse.

The buses of Hong Kong are large, double-decker affairs. Their drivers are even more aggressive than those piloting the taxis, if you can imagine that! There's a little stick shift mounted right on the steering column and the drivers can change gears with the flick of a thumb. Often they will flip into neutral and rev the engine while waiting impatiently at the traffic light.

I heard the engine revving and then I saw the most bizarre phenomenon: The huge blue-and-white double-decker bus reared up off the ground on its rear wheels, not unlike a horse in a rodeo— excepting that the tare weight of this "horse" approximated twenty tons. Next came an unforgettable sight: after the front end of the bus soared high off the ground, the bus then pivoted toward the curb before falling back to earth with a loud crash, crushing the half-dozen folks waiting at the corner: exactly on the spot where I would have been. As Daniel Defoe's character "Robinson Crusoe" wisely mused:

"How wonderfully we are delivered, when we know nothing of it. How when we are in a quandary, as we call it, a doubt or hesitation, whether to go this way, or that way, a secret hint shall direct us this way, when we intended to go that way; nay, when sense, our own inclination, and perhaps business has called to go the other way, yet a strange impression upon the mind, from we know not what springs, and by we know not what power, shall overrule us to go this way."

My good friend Melanie called me later that evening and asked matter-of-factly: "Were you there today?" She had heard about the tragic accident on the radio. "How did you know?" I questioned. She said that after hearing about my encounters with Herman the German, warning of my wrists being slit; the Chinese elder shaking me by my goatee; my almost-departure for the nether world while girl-watching and the bouncing I-beam, she simply concluded that I was a lightning rod of sorts for bad luck on Des Voeux Road. What bouncing I-beam you ask?

Once while walking on this same street of wishes, I witnessed a huge 10-meter (33-foot) long steel I-beam slip from the grasp of a building crane perched atop a newly-emerging skyscraper and plummet earthbound. [For you locals who are keeping score, this was the Landmark Building to-be, on Pedder Street, between Queen's Road Central and Des Voeux Road.] I quickly wondered what this I-beam would do when it struck the ground.

It was more than intellectual curiosity at this point, since I was just across the street, a mere fifty paces away. Would it fall to the center of the earth and emerge in Kansas? Ricochet wildly? More bizarrely than any of my musings was the actual event: the I-beam bounced with the other-worldly sound of a huge Chinese (of course) gong! It then proceeded to eerily wiggle skyward like a monstrous huge tuning fork/salmon, its tons of shaking steel defying gravity, all the while emitting a deafening vibration. But even in Hong Kong, what goes up must eventually come down. Down the I-beam came, this time tragically harpooning a bus and its load of passengers. I can still close my eyes three decades hence and see that image.

Do you have time for one more image? First I must confess I probably would not make a very good German citizen. This conclusion is based on my couple years living in the Germanic universe of Austria, Switzerland and southern Germany. Once while waiting to cross a German street, I noticed that there was absolutely no traffic coming in any direction. I took this to be akin to a K-Mart "blue light special" and headed off the curb.

First mistaking it for a gas leak, I heard a loud hissing sound. The hissing was in fact being emitted by my fellow pedestrians who were expressing their profound displeasure at my reckless disregard for their sensible laws. Give me the rough and tumble of Hong Kong any day! No peer pressure there, except for the person behind you nudging you to go faster. Jaywalking is a way of life in Hong Kong, one of the many corners to cut in order to get ahead in this frenetic caldron of capitalism.

City planners have added new overhead pedestrian walkways in the fancier areas—like around the Stock Exchange—where they don't want the better clientele getting flattened by one of the many forms of transport flying down HK streets. However, the unfortunate in this particular story was an older laborer woman who tried dashing across the street in front of one of the heavy, ancient, green, two-story trams, without the aid of such an overpass. "Ding, Ding" went the tram's warning bell. "Thump, thump" was the sound as the tram's front wheels passed over her. Someone frantically dragged what was left of her out from underneath and the tram went on.

I only caught a fleeting glance of this scene from the dirty window of the speeding mini-bus I was in at the time, so I don't know the outcome but I still see it all when I close my eyes. So, tourist shoppers coming to Des Voeux Road: Caveat Emptor. The four events I just described in this chapter all took place along just a mere four-block stretch of the street of "wishes" which, in my humble yet informed opinion, bodes more of concentrated bad karma.

As you can see, all is not smooth as silk when journeying along Des Voeux Road. But there is silk to be found. I used to buy some beautiful Chinese silk for Christmas presents each year: it was the one gift I could afford which impressed my more affluent relatives. Somehow, in my many travels, I missed the news of my maternal grandmother's passing far away on the other side of the world. So I kept sending her presents until I eventually found out about her demise, years later.

In a moment of candor, my younger sister Joni confided that when my mom had asked: "Shouldn't we tell Mike to stop sending presents to his dead grandma?!" Joni had countered, "No! I love getting the extra presents!" Back then, Chinese silk was beautiful and plentifully available in Hong Kong, and for just a fraction of the price anywhere else worldwide.

On a good day, you could even make your purchase right there on Des Voeux Road, since push-cart hawkers would often ply their goods up and down the already crowded sidewalks. Of course, this practice broke a number of traffic rules, and to deal with it, the Hawker Squad was formed. These officers prowled the streets trying to catch the vendors red-handed in a sale. [Apparently, legally you could make the argument that you were just pushing the items to a legal sale location.]

There are companion scouts for the hawkers, who shout. When the shouts are heard, the vendors quickly whip a canvas cover over their carts and flee down the street. Be sure not to stand in front of a fleeing pushcart if you want to live to shop yet another day. If you have timed it just right, [like I did with the luggage merchant in "Close Encounters'] you can sometimes get a real bargain. You get to keep whatever prospective purchase you have in your hand when the vendor flees for his life. There's no time for him to collect your payment: the resultant loss of sale is offset by greater need to escape jail time, even in this capitalistic stronghold. Chalk it up as "cost of doing business," as the accountants love to say.

This fleeting principle works both ways, so take care not to hand a large bank note to the vendor, expecting change at such a moment. Overall, I think I have pretty much come out ahead over the years, but that's because I am particularly lucky, as you have no doubt surmised by now.

17. Busted!

*Or: the Perils of Importing Powdered Substances,
Even if Purportedly Healthful*

I had a friend, a very persnickety friend, who lived in Manila. He had very particular tastes for things that weren't available in The Philippines. Since he lived on an island, or more accurately an island chain, let's dub him "Gillogan" for the sake of this story. Gillogan knew, as I've alluded before, that Hong Kong was like Alice's Restaurant, where you could get anything you wanted, but for a price of course.

Gillogan was a health nut. We first met when he lived in Sai Kung, in the northeast extremities of Hong Kong's New Territories. One salient memory was that his children's governess, Dianne, had one eye that was half blue, half brown. Other than that, his was a normal expat family with a large number of children, such as mine. Eventually, he hired a local young Chinese woman to teach his children Cantonese, and she also did some of the shopping. Gillogan was very proud of his eating habits, insisting on calf's liver being a cornerstone to his physical and mental prowess.

I thought this was a rather odd boast since there were many pigs in Hong Kong, but I never saw any cows other than the handful of the dairy variety at the Trappist Monastery on Lantau Island. [Stay tuned, because these very cows will make a special guest appearance in the last chapter!] There were plenty of water buffalo, but that, of course, was a horse of a different color.

One day at the local market his new employee went to his preferred meat stall to buy his weekly ration of the reputed super-food, calf's liver. Katrina asked for calf liver and the vendor laughed. "We don't sell that! Never have!" When pressed about Mr. Gillogan's purchases, the vendor confided conspiratorially that for years she had been slipping him pork livers, of which she had plenty. Outraged at her deceit (and probably at his blustering British naiveté) Gillogan rushed to confront the meat monger. Her reply was a broad smile and an unabashed triumphant cackle "I clicked [i.e.: 'tricked'] you!!" This, of course, was nothing more than a fine example of Hong Kong's entrepreneurial laissez-faire capitalism. The Brit had to admit that he had been bested.   I never heard him talk about calf livers from that day onwards.

His next health crusade focused on nitrates. He was convinced that we would all die hideous, cancerous deaths at the hand of this sinister food additive. His convictions were about to be put to the acid test. His family of four young children met up with our family of four young children one sunny day for an outing at what was then the newly opened "Ocean Park," Hong Kong's answer to "Sea World."

Ocean Park is truly fantastic, a multiple award-winning marine animal and animal theme / amusement park with breath-taking views of the South China Sea afforded from high atop the cable car ride. One of the awards garnered is The World's Seventh Most Popular Amusement Park; it is indeed a very crowded affair. On a later visit, my second daughter Joanne once got gobbled up in the excited melee and separated from us for an agonizing hour. We used child tethers pretty consistently after that trauma.

Lunch time came and both families pulled out their sack lunches. Contents for our family's meal came from the Chinese Emporium (Communist China's local version of Wal-Mart) and the WellCome (that is correct: with two l's) Grocery store. That's where we bought our "Klim" brand powdered milk which came from Australia. [It took a while for it to finally dawn on me that klim was simply milk spelt backwards: a fine example of Aussie tongue-in-cheek marketing.] Meanwhile, Gillogan preferred shopping in more exclusive haunts, such as Watsons.

Unsuspecting of scrutiny, I pulled out a corned beef sandwich much to Gillogan's horrified gasp: "You are not going to feed that to your children are you?!" "Sure, they like it!" was my uncomplicated reply. I put more mustard on my sandwiches than the kids preferred, but that was the only questionable feature that came to my mind. He launched into a professorial diatribe about the cancerous evils that lurked in the nitrates (or was it the nitrites?) that laced the corned beef.

I think we agreed to disagree so that lunch could proceed for the hungry children. There was a heavy silence as we munched away. Apparently his superiorly healthful meal had, alas, nonetheless left him somewhat less than satiated. After we had finished our own poisonous repast, Gillogan leaned over and guiltily whispered "Do you

97

have a sandwich you could spare?" "What! And risk giving you cancer?" I protested with mock indignity. I couldn't help myself. The set-up was too irresistible: like a ball lingering above the volleyball net, just begging to be spiked. I don't think we met for too many family excursions after that day. His sense of humor was blatantly underdeveloped, in my humble opinion.

Perhaps Gillogan wasn't a health nut after all; maybe he was just a nut. When he moved to Manila (he liked the weather better there, he claimed) he found out that not all countries are created equal in the Far East. Hong Kong was a special blend of British engineering and Chinese industriousness where petty theft of another's belongings was beneath consideration. Steal an entire territory or take over a company—now that was different, something noble.

I remember following the contentious battle between two property developers in the Mid-Levels when I lived there on Conduit Road. One firm won the bid to lease the land and build a new skyscraper. The other company—with the losing bid—owned the adjoining property. There was a surveying error of uncertain origin. The new building encroached by one inch onto the neighboring plot of land. The competition knew of this fact before construction began in earnest, but patiently waited until the building was fully completed before going to court to assert their rights to that inch of land. The legal complaint was valid and the building was ordered demolished, thus inflicting the double expense of construction and demolition on the opponent. Now, that is real class!

Where this all is leading has to do with the reliability of the mail system. Based on the logic outlined above, Hong Kong mail was relatively secure; whereas the service across the South China Sea in The Philippines was much less so. Packages arriving at Post Offices in Manila were often considered early Christmas presents for the underpaid postal employees. So I became Gillogan's offshore supplier for his much-needed specialty items.

One such item was a certain blend of Guatemalan coffee which he fancied. Hong Kong being the world market that it is allowed the buyer to shop the world without leaving the block. There was such a coffee shop in one of the lanes above Des Voeux Road in Central—the street described in "The Street of Wishes." This shop wasn't any larger than your average living room, yet it boasted hundreds of types of wonderfully aroma-laden offerings. I loved that shop; it was a welcome olfactory change to the surrounding smog and diesel fumes.

"Next time you come this way, bring me five pounds of fine-ground Guatemalan coffee," Gillogan requested. And so I obliged; only to have my delivery rejected. What could be wrong? Was it from the wrong region of Guatemala, I wondered. "You didn't have this double-ground!" That was my sin. Actually I think the original sin, as it were, was my stupidly agreeing to buy the coffee for him in the first place. I think he never really forgave me for that incident with the corned beef sandwich. Or, maybe this was still just part of his same health-nut persona in an extreme sense.

Gillogan's next health food request proved much more dangerous for me. Carob was the newest secret pathway to healthy living now, apparently. Why someone who loved his double-ground Guatemalan coffee so dearly had an issue with the caffeine found in ordinary chocolate was a question I cared not to grapple with. Of course, the carob powder I could easily find in HK was not suitable, but he had found a particular brand he wanted to try that was available in Singapore. Interestingly enough, that city-state is also thriving and relatively safe, much as is Hong Kong. I posit that this advanced quality of life is due, at least in part, to the same marriage of convenience of British and Chinese values.

That Singapore is mainly Chinese in composition is common knowledge. The English part alludes to Lee Kuan Yew, Prime Minister for thirty years and a founding father of modern Singapore. His ancestors are Hakka from Guangdong province, just upriver from Hong Kong, and settled in Singapore for four generations before this. Prime Minister Lee attended the University of Cambridge, where he read law at Fitzwilliam College and graduated with a rare Double Starred. In other words, he was a very bright chap. He also ran a very tight ship. There was a $500 fine for chewing gum in Singapore, for example. But the mail was very reliable. This is why I could mail-order the proper brand of Carob from Singapore and confidently expect it to arrive safely in Hong Kong. Well, almost. This is where the story turns very scary and very funny at the same time, depending on what seat you are occupying. I had the former.

One morning I showed up at the GPO (General Post Office) in Central to check my business' mail. There was a blue card in with the other mail, signifying a package to be collected from the counter because it was too big to fit in my mail box. "Ah, it's Gillogan's carob! He'll be happy, hopefully," I pondered to myself while approaching the postal clerk, blue card in hand. Anticipating the usual efficient service, I was already contemplating my next dozen business errands while I waited for my package to be retrieved.

[By the way, I see that the GPO is no longer where it used to be. No, the building has not been moved. Instead, the harbor waters which once lapped the northern pier of the building back when this story happened have been moved. If you look at a map of Hong Kong today, the GPO is now five blocks inland from Victoria Harbor, or at least it was as of this writing. More of that "reclamation."]

The clerk took a long time fetching my package, which was very unusual for busy Hong Kong, where every second counts. When the clerk nervously presented the package to me, asking "Is this yours?" two very serious-looking officers appeared behind me, one at either elbow. Resistance was futile. "Come with us," they ordered solemnly. Through a hidden doorway and down a narrow hallway we marched, until we arrived at a large open space. I was told to sit on the sole metal folding chair in the center of the room. A very large German Shepherd dog was led in and set menacingly at my feet. I was not going anywhere in a hurry, it seemed.

Then my innate curiosity and fertile imagination conspired to unnerve me. With nothing else to do, I glanced around the room. There mounted on the opposite wall was an impressive, eerie collection of strange, intimidating tools: crowbars, huge pliers, odd-shaped knives, various hammers and other unnerving devices—truly a treasure trove that a technician in the employ of the Inquisition would have envied. Compounding my growing paranoia, I had just seen the recent release "Midnight Express." Google it if you haven't seen the movie and you'll quickly understand my frame of mind.

A mad scientist-type quietly appeared, stared coldly at me and then proceeded to dramatically don a pair of surgical gloves. At this point, I was not sure where this examination was headed. "It's just chocolate!" I protested, "What's all this about?" The gathered officials were unmoved. "We'll determine that" was the mechanical reply. Now my mind launched into orbits of imagined misfortunes. What if this was not my package? What if something nefarious had found its

100

way to my post office box, and this was not Gillogan's chocolate? I was somewhat relieved to find that the gloves were for examining the package, not me. "Watch out, open it slowly; it's fine powder," I suggested. The reply was a silent, cold, stony glare.

With the determination of a miner certain of uncovering a rare diamond at any moment, the package surgeon pried open the package. There was the carob; I felt some relief. The official pressed on. The foil seal offered resistance and so he tugged harder. When the foil seal gave way, a cloud of fine dark brown carob powder exploded upward. When the dust settled, the inspector's face suddenly sported a dark, tanned look.

My natural response was to laugh, but the large dog at my feet did not look like the type with a sense of humor. I adopted my best poker-face, the one meant to convey "told you so!" After sampling the chocolate substitute that now covered his face and gloves and shirt, he nodded to the others. The package was carefully re-wrapped and handed to me. I was led out of the bowels of the GPO building and ejected onto the dock behind the building without a word. After that encounter, I stopped doing favors for Gillogan and eventually we lost contact with each other. And I never have used carob since then.

You will read about "M" in the "Wizard of Oops" chapter. I asked her to read this story as "Gillogan" had been a mutual acquaintance. She reacted as follows: *"Ha ha, that was great! You poor guy: having to deal with his snobbery. We did a Christmas show at a children's hospital wing with [Gillogan's] family in our early days of Hong Kong. I think your two little ones were there too—James and Suzy.*

"The show went real well and everyone was very appreciative. Afterwards, we were treated to cookies in the break room. There was a big storm in a tea cup because our two kids greedily accepted the chocolate covered cookies, much to the disgust of the two sanctimonious young Gillogans who carefully took only the soda crackers, under their nanny's eagle-eyed guidance. My husband and I still joke about this incident to this day. Don't stop the stories coming! Love, M."

18. No Third Turkey!

This is another silly but true tale from Hong Kong. I want you to know that it becomes increasingly difficult to keep coming up with clever new chapter titles. However, there seems to be no end of new material to draw from. This particular misfortune took place close to the locale of my near-fatal brush with the baboon troop, only this time I was indoors, in air-conditioned comfort. I was actually in the basement of the same skyscraper where I suffered an attack by a jealous Persian cat. [See part four: 'The Owl and the Pussycat II', of "Things My Mother Never Warned Me About!"] Regarding the title, this story has nothing to do with wildlife. In fact, I don't believe there are actually any turkeys native to Hong Kong. Those nasty baboons probably would have scared them off. This is a tale of a different turkey, this turkey being the bowling term for three successive strikes.

If you have that same affliction I suffer from, you just have to know where these terms originated! Until someone coins a better phrase, I'll call the condition of extreme curiosity, "etymologitis." To satisfy your current craving for knowledge minutiae, I offer the following: The term "turkey" became associated with the sport of bowling a century or two ago, depending on the "expert" you cite. In either era, the legend goes that a live turkey was given to the bowler who could manage to bowl three strikes in a row, usually offered around Thanksgiving time.

I hear some further clamoring for a clarification, and understandably so. Granted, there are many forms of bowling: There are several varieties of pin bowling include ten-pin, nine-pin, candlepin, duckpin and five-pin bowling, while in target bowling there are bowls, bocce, carpet bowls, pétanque and boules. Look at all the free trivia you are picking up already and the story has yet to begin! In this story, I'm referring to the plain-vanilla indoor 10-pin wooden alley variety most common in the United States, and adopted far and wide in places such as Hong Kong.

I was relaxing one evening after spending a busy day fighting crowds in Central while getting various business matters accomplished. I was delighted to find a nice, new bowling alley in the basement of the very apartment complex where I had rented a room from the French topless waitress who had the killer Siamese cat. You will have to read on further in this book to hear more about those characters.

I was by myself, my favorite way to relax, and I was alone in my thoughts as I rolled the ball down the alley. I don't have that fancy smooth impressive hook shot that the burly professional bowlers use; I throw a very boring nondescript straight ball after a three step waddle. But each man to his own, as they say. Who are "they", you ask? "Chacun pour soi meme" – each man for himself: the French lay claim to the phrase.

My shot had neither French nor English on it, but it was very effective nonetheless. The first three times I rolled the ball, all ten pins went down. I had just bowled three strikes, which as you now know, makes a turkey. I sat down and drew a long breath. I could not remember the last time I bowled three strikes in a row, let alone on the opening three frames of a game. When had I last bowled, I wondered? I was fairly certain it was when I was still in high school. You didn't bowl in college at MIT in the early 70's in liberal Cambridge, Massachusetts – that was far too "Establishment" for privileged intelligentsia. Even TV was out! Only FM radio and high-end stereos were played. There was a cultural war going on, and there were casualties! In Australia we had lawn bowls and cricket and tennis and rugby for the suicidal, but I never saw bowling alleys in my six years Down Under. So, suffice it to say that I had not bowled in over a decade. Apparently, this weirdness of my bowling three strikes was a case of the reverse of "practice makes perfect."

No one seemed to be noticing me, nor had anyone started laughing at my awkward delivery form. For all everyone knew, I might have been a professional bowler exiled from Pittsburg for putting too much chalk dust on my hands. All of that being ignored suited me just fine. I resumed bowling. Lo and behold, the fourth ball I threw was also a strike. I began looking around surreptitiously for apparitions. Finding no one to explain what was happening, I stepped up to the line and rolled the ball again. Bingo! Another strike, this one making five in a row. Now my heartbeat picked up a bit. When the sixth ball resulted in yet another strike, I now had what must be a called – what else? A double turkey!!

I sat down for a moment to collect myself. I pinched myself to make sure this wasn't some wonderful sports afterlife I had stumbled into, twilight-zone style. I was not known as a particularly good bowler, but here I was now half-way to a perfect game score of 300—I just needed six more balls like those first six. How long could this keep up? I bowled my seventh shot and there it was again, another strike—seven in a row. Two more strikes and I would have—a triple turkey? There must be a special name for that feat, I mused. I suddenly noticed that it had grown exceptionally quiet in the bowling alley. If it is ever quiet anywhere in Hong Kong, at any time, that is exceptionally significant and usually warrants further investigation. I suddenly had that same eerie feeling I mentioned in my baboon story: that feeling where you sense that someone or something was staring at you. Turning around, I saw them. Not the baboons, but everyone else in the alley who had stopped bowling in order to stand behind me and watch this exhibition I was unwittingly giving. Never having played any sport professionally, I was totally unprepared for dealing with a crowd of admirers.

I wanted to ask them to all go away and ignore me, but I knew that wasn't going to happen, curiosity being what it was in Hong Kong, especially when it came to all things gweilo. With a bit of a wobble in my step, I resumed my game. With my usual walk, and with my usual straight delivery, I launched the ball. All the pins fell down. Except for one. There was a thick silence as that lone, unyielding, recalcitrant pin stared back at me and the crowd behind me. Well, so much for perfection! I sent my second ball for that eighth frame down the alley and nailed that rebellious loner for a spare. But the damage was done and my confidence evaporated as quickly as rain in a Hong Kong summer. There would be no third turkey, let alone a perfect game. My fleeting chance at bowling fame was gone.

The ninth frame was a repeat of the eighth, with that one stubborn pin again thumbing its nose at me, and my replying with my straight-ball conversion for another spare. I was outraged at the injustice of how one stupid, inanimate object could totally alter the course of glorious sports history! At this point I lost all grasp on composure and angrily flung my ball into the awaiting tenth frame. My game went from the sublime to the ridiculous with a gutter ball. The crowd began to drift silently away to allow me privacy for my mourning.

Trying to put a positive spin on my bowling experience, I took stock of the fact that I would never have a score that high again. Leaving the alley and walking through the evening's cooling air, I tried to remind myself of why I had gone there in the first place: to relax, and to be away from the crowd. Then I shook my head as I pondered: Why would anyone want to bowl professionally?

19. Snakes and Shakes!

–And Other Things That Can Kill You

As a young boy growing up in northern Upstate New York not that far from the Canadian border, snakes never presented much of an issue. We had the occasional harmless Garter snake wander through our breezeway and my sister would always vomit reflexively when she saw the cute thing. I never saw what the big deal was with snakes, or the fear thereof. My buddies and I only had a serious issue with one greedy such garden variety reptile which slithered into the cute frog farm we had set up in the shady oak grove at Billy Mitchell's house. We had caught several handsome bull frogs at Felliton's Swamp, and made a pen with chicken wire to keep them in. We dug a nice little pond for them, and caught crickets and grasshoppers and other such small meals to nourish our pets.

One day we went out to check on how the fellows were doing, only to discover that they had all vanished! Could frogs jump that high to get over that fence? In their dreams—they probably wished they could! On closer examination, we found a snake had squeezed in through one of the narrow fence openings but could not get back out, because it was now sporting five large lumps. We angrily beat on that invader in a vain effort to free the captive frogs; but only one of them emerged alive, as the others were already suffering from various stages of indigestion, as it were.

It would be many years before I found out that snakes can indeed be serious business. When I arrived in New Zealand, I was informed that there were no snakes on the entire island chain. Some theorized that this was because the Westerners first settling there were missionaries. Maybe it was just too far for the snakes to swim, or food was bad there, who knows? Australia, also an island nation, had no such lack of snakes and sports some of the scariest and deadliest varieties.

The Kiwis across the Tasman Straight will crow that this phenomenon was due to the fact that the first western Aussies were criminals being deported from England. But I'm not so sure that immigrant occupation is the determinant factor in reptile distribution. Later, I did find many snakes, great and small, very well distributed on Lantau Island when I myself migrated from Australia to Hong Kong years later with my own family, and that is where we'll travel for the following true tales about those with tails.

"HUGE bamboo pit viper was seen less than a meter off the path on our way up to help fertilize and mulch some tree saplings!– So beautiful!" –Ark Eden posted on FaceBook on November 14, 2014. My response: "I recognize that critter! Many years ago I was cutting some bamboo to make a fence, there at what is now Ark Eden, formerly Casa Hawron. I was using a machete of sorts, down by your front gate, just to the high side of it. I leaned my left hand on another bamboo plant to steady myself, only to find that I had barely missed grabbing the excellently camouflaged pit viper that was on the same bamboo pole. It was a close call for both of us!"

There were no end of close calls with snakes and other manner of things that could kill you when my family was living in the wilds of Northeast Lantau Island in the Tung Hang Mei valley. In my "Tour de Farce" chapter, I talk about how living in this valley for six years cured me of any apprehension about spiders. Today I will dwell on fears of the more slithery variety. I never really knew how many different types of snakes there were until we accepted the offer to move into this abandoned mountainside property! I guess we didn't read the fine print. Whoever does?

In Hong Kong, you were not allowed to have any weapons of self-defense such a handgun, slingshot, bow and arrow, sword or spear. Living way up a winding dark isolated pathway with a houseful of small children, I wanted to have something I felt I could use in the odd chance I was called upon to defend my family. The best legal solution I could come up with was a length of metal pipe (about three feet long) in each room, preferably one with an elbow joint at the end for greater effect and so I equipped my castle thusly. And while for the most part these old pieces of pipe sat gathering rust, one day one of them saved my life…

"Help!" came the frightened call from our cook, who had her bedroom in the small separate building behind our main house. "There's a snake!" was all she could say. By this time, I had lived there long enough to no longer fear snakes. Instead, I had developed more of a scientific curiosity to see how many different varieties I could catalog. I bought the local Hong Kong government publication on snakes and kept it handy. "I wonder what kind of snake this will be?" I mused while fingering the length of pipe tucked in the corner beside the door.

There it was, behind the set of shelves, ready to identify itself: Suddenly it said "I'm a cobra!" by spreading wide its identifying hood. It was a healthy-sized one at that! Next came the "hiss!" Next came my involuntary reaction. Somewhere in the inner confines of my mind, a thought process was rapidly formulated with two clearly-defined parameters: "It will be you or the snake" and "You only have once chance to get this right!" Today if you visit our old home, you can probably still detect the deep indentation where my pipe-weapon imbedded itself in the concrete wall after hitting its mark.

A meal fit for a king! What is six meters (nearly 20 feet) long, takes five local villagers to carry it and shows up on Silvermine Bay beach after the torrential downpour I wrote about in the "When it Rains, it Pours!" section of the "Four Seasons by Hong Kong" chapter? A King Cobra is the answer. I suppose it is called King because it dines on all other manner of snakes as well as the usual fare of rodents and lizards and such. These critters get so enormous by avoiding contact with things more deadly, which on Lantau Island would mainly just be the humans. But the huge rains and ensuing floodwaters must have flushed this creature out of hiding.

We were down at the beach with the children when we heard a commotion. Commotions are something you hear all the time in Hong Kong, so it was not particularly noteworthy until we heard sustained, feverously excited shouting. When all the hubbub subsided, a curious serpentine procession passed by: five local fisherman, each holding a length of rope tied at various spots around the huge reptile's body, cheerfully jogged their way towards the local restaurant! They would eat well tonight! Not to mention that snake bile wine is a highly sought-after elixir. I think I just dined on noodles that night, out of respect for the king's demise.

Miracle Grow? We did our best to spruce up and beautify our little bit of paradise there in that peaceful sub-tropical valley. Those efforts included planting and caring for various flowers and shrubs. On one fine summer day, I was out with my hedge clippers snipping away at the weeds and grass that were forever trying to choke out my attempt at garnering the Garden of the Month award. Some of these less-desirable plants were quite hardy and required a good bit of muscle to snip through them.

Snip! Pop! What was that? Turns out the weed stalk I had just cut in half was in fact actually the loop of a medium-sized snake which had crawled out of one hole in the rock wall and went right back in a neighboring crevice. Obviously in this condition, it was hard to make heads or tails out of the situation. I apologize for that!

Just in case you are wondering, yes: living, crawling things that are cut in half can sometimes grow back together, all on their own, as my daughter Suzy and I once witnessed. In narrow, winding mountainous roads with blind curves in countries such as Japan and Switzerland, there are parabolic mirrors installed to warn you of what lurks around the corner. On our pathway in the Tung Hang Mei valley, there were no such devices, so we always carried a big walking stick so as to be armed for any unforeseen eventuality. On this particular journey down the path, I was carrying a solid metal-handled machete as well, as we were trimming back the bamboo branches that were blocking our way down the path. Good thing!

There are thousands of species of centipedes; the one that we encountered around the next corner was of the largest variety, as it was over a foot long, with dark ugly coloration and a healthy pair of venomous claws. By the way, perhaps you did not know that centipedes do not actually have 100 feet. The number can vary from about 22 to 298 legs, but oddly enough (pun intended) the total number of legs can never be an even 100 because the centipede always has an ODD number of pairs of legs. So you can get 98 (49x2) or 102 (51x2), but never 100 exactly, because there cannot be 50 pairs of legs, since 50 is an even number.

Feel free to use that little obscure factoid at your next trivia event. Why are there only odd-numbered pairs? I don't know. Mr. T.J. Rhoades, our local octogenarian plant nursery owner, told us we should always plant an odd number of shrubs, never an even number. It must be a karma thing! Now, after writing this chapter, I read somewhere that they have indeed finally discovered one variety of centipede that has an even number of legs. I wonder though, how they are certain that it was not just an amputee victim?

Anyways, as I will relate in a moment, Suzy was still nursing a sore toe from being attacked by a different creepy crawler. Since centipedes are carnivores, and her little toes might look like lunch from that critter's point of view, we took no chances. I chopped the big ugly thing in half, sparks flying off the concrete path where the heavy steel machete blade cut through the beast. Then we were treated to one of the most eerie sights I have ever witnessed: The centipede's separated halves were an inch or more apart. Dark liquid oozed out of each of the edges of the cut halves. Do Centipedes bleed? I'm no expert.

The ooze spread along the concrete from both directions until the two puddles met, and merged. Whatever it was—blood or voodoo juice—it soon congealed, and then the two halves drew back together as one and the centipede marched off as if nothing had ever happened. We ran the other way! If anyone else has ever had a similar experience, please let me know, as I would like to form a support group: this event has left me shaken.

Alright, I mentioned Suzy's sore toe. Suzy was just a little girl then, adventurous and always wanting to run around barefoot. I was a young parent, overprotective and always lecturing. "Wear your flip-flops [this was before the days of Crocs] or else something might bite you or you'll step on something sharp or, or, or..." But it was no use, of course: as soon as I was out of sight, the footwear came off. The cool tile floors probably felt great in the hot weather. Out of sight upstairs, but not out of earshot, I heard the pained shout. An aggressive scorpion had stung Suzy's big toe and it (the toe, that is) turned bright purple. What was the first thing I did? "I told you to keep your shoes on! Daddy was right!" Next, I prayed fervently for her complete healing, but secretly I didn't mind too much if the pain lingered for just a little while in order to validate all my lecturing. Thankfully, Suzy's toe healed up nicely and the footwear stayed on for a while at least.

Lest anyone think Lantau Island was the sole snake epicenter, I'll mention the nine-foot (three meter) long black water moccasin [highly venomous] that slithered through our back yard here in Texas. - Yes, it appears everything IS indeed bigger in Texas. This specimen was lying parallel to our garden house of the same color. [Perhaps he was myopic and in search of a mate?] My wife Annette went to move the hose, and scream! The rest is history! (At least for that snake.) My wife is from good Viking stock and does not suffer intruders lightly.

But snakes are nothing compared to shakes. And by shakes I mean Earthquakes. In the subway tunnel story coming later in this book, I allude to that mysterious and futile process by which the brain tries to hang a meaningful label on some sensory input that does not otherwise compute. I somehow seem to attract unique events. Of all the locally felt earth tremors listed by the Hong Kong Observatory, the closest one ever was on a 7th of October, just three months before Andy ["Which Way War"] was born. The epicenter was recorded to be 22.3 N, 114.0 E. That, by the way, was precisely the location of our home in Tung Hang Mei Valley. There were only twelve locally felt reports and mine was one of them. It was about 10 pm on a mild evening and I was in the front yard, under the big Flame of the Forest tree.

It is hard to distinguish whether I first felt or heard the quake. It was much like the bass surround-sound speakers in a well-equipped movie theatre. [Remember the high-tech noisemakers that theatres installed for the showing of the 1974 movie "Earthquake" to add a sense of realism? More specifically, Universal Studio's sound department came up with a process called "Sensurround" – a series of large speakers that would pump in sub-audible "infra bass" sound waves at 120 decibels (equivalent to a jet airplane at takeoff), giving the viewer the sensation of an earthquake.]

What I do remember very clearly was that Erica and I—new parents that we were—took our new little firstborn to the theatre with us to see "Earthquake" and despite all the noise and rumbling special effects, he slept like—well, a baby; James never woke up during the entire movie until it was time to go home. Now back to a real earthquake:

Whatever I sensed or heard, what first came to mind was: "Wow, there is a big truck or some heavy equipment coming up our pathway!" That, of course, was impossible, since our narrow foot path was only about three feet wide, and any heavy equipment would have tumbled into the valley far below. But that was the best explanation my mind came up with in that split-second of heightened consciousness.

As earthquakes just did not happen in Hong Kong, since the place got along just fine with typhoons as the natural disaster of choice, it was hard to grasp what was really happening. When it did finally sink in

110

and I phoned what was then called the Royal Observatory, they confirmed that an earthquake had been detected under or just off the coastline of Lantau Island. "No kidding!" I retorted. "I'm standing right on top of it!" I felt rather privileged. That was about all I felt, since it was not really a strong tremblor by world standards. Turns out, from checking the official records, there was an earthquake of identical strength in the identical location six weeks prior on August 30th that same year but that time at 4 am, so I must have slept through that one.

But those shakings were nothing to compare with the one Suzy and I lived through twelve years later on Dr. Martin Luther King Jr's birthday, 8,000 miles away in sunny southern California. This particular earthquake was also at 4 am, but it certainly was able to get my attention in spite of a deep sleep. This one was a 6.7, not the tame 1.5 cradle-rockers of Lantau Island days. Apparently this was quite the special event I happened to be right in the middle of, as the quake produced ground accelerations that were the highest ever instrumentally recorded in an urban area in North America. I guess that makes it special indeed. Or me...

We were moving out of our apartment in urban Glendale the next morning and taking up new digs at a beach house on Balboa Peninsula in Newport Beach. We had already packed up all the computers and office equipment into the van earlier that evening of January 16th. This was my first really big earthquake experience. The building rocked back and forth so violently that it was impossible to walk in a straight line. After bumping off a few walls and doorways, I managed to get under the dining room table for shelter. Then I saw the most amazing sight: the TV (big and bulky, before the days of flat screens) flew from one end of the apartment to the other, as if a softball pitcher of Paul Bunyan's dimensions had hurled it at home plate. But we were all safe and without a scratch so far.

Now the real spooky fun began! Gas mains in the area burst from the shifting of the ground and huge torch-like flames erupted in the night sky. This was not a desirable neighborhood to be in, to say the least, and soon we could hear all manner of screams, shouts and gun shots. It was time to head for the beach! We grabbed our few remaining bags and headed down the stairs to the garage, happy to discover our van was not covered in rubble.

We headed due south as fast as we could to get away from the brouhaha fomenting in the urban jungle behind us. As if a huge earthquake in one of the world's biggest cities was not enough of a challenge, a thick blanket of fog had rolled in off the Pacific Ocean which slowed our progress to a snail's pace. We kept the radio tuned for information on what was out there. We heard reports of sections of the freeways being down, and in one case, an LAPD patrol car went over into the abyss, not able to see that the section of highway ahead was out, due to the dense fog.

So we crept along carefully, while all sorts of crazy idiots zoomed past us, literally like bats out of hell, without regard for the dangers that lurked all around and ahead. I got out and kissed the sand on Newport Beach when we made it safely there, several slow hours later, as dawn broke on that shaky January 17th.

20. The Wizard of Oops!

Or: Pay No Attention to the Man (& Woman) Behind the Curtain!

Sometimes the best comedy is totally unrehearsed and unscripted and, unfortunately, there are usually no cameras to record it. (I must keep reminding the young reader that there really was a time when there were no cell phones!) There was an audience in this story, but no laughter. You'll understand that in a moment.

This particular event happened not long after my arrival in Hong Kong. It was mid-summer, very hot and very humid. In those days, the skyscrapers had the complexion of bumpy squash—the outer skins of the buildings were dotted with thousands of individual air conditioning window units. It really was something to watch the crews install one of those units 21 floors up, hanging out the window on a tenuous bamboo shelf lashed to the window frame.

This story takes place in Wan Chai district, in the Tonnochy Towers to be precise. Nineteen floors below our tiny apartment [See: Hong Kong Culture Shocks] where my wife would scream every time one of the children got too close to the window, my export business had rented a small two-room office space, the larger back room with a window AC unit and the front one without one, and boiling hot— which we just used for storage.

The still air in that small room was such that you could break out into a sweat just by crossing the three paces from the front door before reaching the cool oasis beyond. On this particular day, a series of circumstances mercilessly conspired against me to rob me of any business-like dignity I may have attempted to project in my new digs.

I had an expensive paper shredder which broke. Actually all that was broken was one tiny plastic gear; the rest of the device was perfectly whole. Rather than just throw it out, I decided on a ploy. Hong Kong was full of plastics industries, small and large. After a few calls, I managed to contact one company that seemed hungry for business and so I inquired if they might be able to turn out a prototype gear for me (i.e.: a free replacement part.) Thinking that I might be a prospective customer wanting millions of these gears, the firm agreed to send someone over to talk with me about the project. The appointment was made for some days hence and I promptly forgot all about it.

My secretary was there that afternoon, typing some reports. I was out of managerial tasks for the moment and decided to tackle the storage area, which was badly in need of reorganizing. We had mounted a big curtain rod in front of the shelving and had hung some thick drapes there so as to cover up the whole mess. After a few minutes laboring behind the curtain, I was sweating profusely. I did the sensible thing and took off my shirt to get at least a little less uncomfortable. The curtain did a very thorough job of keeping the cool air away from me and the hot air trapped in my work space.

I was breathing hard and my face was flush by this point, but I was almost done. But I needed help: I was trying to fill up the top shelf and needed someone to hand the boxes up to me. There was a short list of available staff, namely my secretary. Many years have gone by since this day and she has a lovely family and is a lovely, respectable grandmother, so let's allow her to remain anonymous. "M" left off pounding away on her IBM Selectric and came to my rescue. ["Spell Check" just now took exception to the word "Selectric", so I imagine many of you who were born after the 70's might need to ask your grandparents about that bit of office equipment history.]

We were making good progress putting away the last of the boxes when there was a knock at the door. It was the two young, well-dressed Hong Kong Chinese salesmen here for their big sale. I really felt sorry for them. They were in for a surprise! Out I popped from behind the curtain, red-faced and glistening with sweat to greet them. The two well-dressed salesmen were graciously pretending not to notice my disheveled state. Moments later, M appeared from behind the curtain with her usual fabulous smile. This is the stuff tabloids love!

The conflict racing through our visitors' minds was almost audible. This was one of those "The Emperor's New Clothes" scenarios where the enlightened thing to do was ignore that anything was amiss. They were no doubt well aware that "the customer is king" and one slip of a knowing grin would kill their sales pitch for sure. They did an admirable job of keeping poker-faced, although they did manage to telegraph each other a furtive, knowing glance.

With as much decorum as I could scrape up at short notice, I ushered the two callers into the cool of the back office. This was going to be a short meeting, we all sensed. I showed them the gear I needed and they confidently promised they were up to the task. With a flurried exchange of business cards, they were out the door as suddenly as they had arrived. I knew not to detain them for niceties, as my secretary was much less adept at keeping a straight face and was using every available ounce of her concentrated will-power to hold back her laughter.

A few days later, the prototype gear arrived in the mail. It was a perfect fit! The vendor had actually sent a duplicate gear as well. My guess is that they did not want to risk having to make another visit. This amusing anecdote had been long forgotten; perhaps it was filed in my "repressed memories" lobe. That was until just yesterday when I wrote M telling her I was at long last writing my book about Hong Kong. We have not seen each other for decades.

Suddenly I laughed out loud when the vivid image suddenly appeared in my mind of the horrified look on the faces on those two unsuspecting plastics salesmen. I'll be curious to see if M remembers this day from way back. And just for the record, I still have an old beige-colored IBM Selectric in my workshop, just gathering dust until such time as it is needed. Thanks for the memories, M!

*****

MEMORY: M. replied: *"Ha ha, yes, M remembers! Your memory is incredible. I had forgotten all about that. Hilarious! And good times! No objections here to your including this story in your book. –M."*

21. Life in the Fast Lane

Occasionally the many years I served in Hong Kong paid off with some fringe benefits. Besides getting to experience all the fun, dangerous and bizarre events I have described so far, sometimes I had the odd side assignment for some extra cash. And of course, these assignments often turned out to be just as bizarre!

Groom for the day

I had met Jackie and her live-in boyfriend on a business trip to Manila. They seemed nice enough. Apparently he was not nice enough for her family—wrong nationality or something like that—so she had never made her liaison known to her rich family back in the US. As she was pushing 40, her family feared she would become a hopeless spinster or worse yet in their minds, perhaps a lesbian. There was talk of cutting her out of the Will, and apparently the family estate was not inconsequential. Her worrying mother and meddling aunt were planning a visit to check her out before settling the matter. Seems Jackie was between a rock and a hard place. Her desperate situation led to my receiving one of the strangest phone calls ever.

Could I help out? She had hatched a plan. Could I pretend to be her fiancé for a weekend? The old ladies were coming to Hong Kong to meet her. [They were not adventurous enough to visit The Philippines, perhaps after Jackie had undoubtedly filled them with Third World horror stories to throw them off the scent of her beau's true location.] She would pay for the five star hotel accommodations, meals and all: my only obligation would be to smile and try to charm the old ladies. Since this all sounded like the script from an exotic, yet non-violent spy movie, I agreed.

Before mother and aunt arrived, Jackie and I spent a day rehearsing facts which two responsible adults should know about each other prior to exchanging vows. This exercise was both exhausting and entertaining. If only we could keep straight faces, we might pull off the charade. The next day I must have been at the peak of my charm as the two family scouts fresh off the plane from the Mid-West took an instant liking to me.

Crawling all over Hong Kong looking at interesting stuff was something I had specialized in over the years, so it was quite easy to play the role of tourist guide. I tried to keep them so busy by dragging them from one place to another at breakneck speed that they had little breath left to ask potentially embarrassing questions. Soon they were clucking about wedding plans, so obviously I had passed muster. Eventually we were relieved to be at the airport, seeing them off. Auntie turned to me: "Well! Now that we are all one big happy family, we must contact your folks when we get back to the States! What is their address?"

It seems we had been too successful in our masquerade! I hung my head in momentary resignation of impending defeat. I thought fast and furiously. There was only one thing I could do. Like the Phoenix arising from the ashes of defeat, my head arose, my face solemn, as I broke the sad news: "My parents both perished in a horrible accident." This disclosure garnered me much sympathy and most of all, relief from any further questioning. All that remained was for Jackie to suppress her grinning admiration of my creative prevarication until her mom and auntie were safely through the boarding gate. I have never heard from Jackie all these years but I assume she got her inheritance in the end. Perhaps I should ask her for some palimony...

In search of the 38E

In hindsight, I should have just said "no!" This experience did, however, lead to one of the better-received humor articles I wrote on commission for a private circulation travel newsletter. As I explained earlier in the chapter entitled "Busted," Hong Kong was a place where you could get virtually anything for a price, much to the envy of those living in other nearby countries where the options were much more limited. But I suppose that even Shopping Nirvana has its limitations.

It was just one item, tucked amidst a list of otherwise innocuous shopping requests: powdered ascorbic acid [Vitamin C]; ground coffee; vellum stationery; micro cassette recorders; gold coins and finally: one woman's brassiere, size 38E. Depending on where you are reading this, this last request might not strike you as odd. But in Hong Kong, where all those slender ladies went shopping at the one-size-fits-all underwear stalls, the bra alphabet only went about as far as the letter B. I really had not reckoned that this would turn out to be a major quest. In my wake I left a trail of red-faced sales girls who could not believe their ears; or my nerve, apparently.

Part of my problem was my approach: I'd walk into the shop and matter-of-factly state: "I need a bra." [Usually in Hong Kong you could ask for anything without raising an eyebrow. The sale was the important consideration, not ethics: that was why we were able to buy Agent Orange to defoliate our pathways at Tung Hang Mei.] But I guess when lone male gweilo walking into the panties shop was beyond the bounds of normal laissez-faire capitalism. Maybe I was one of those kinky Brits they had read about. So when met with stunned silence, I would quickly explain: "Well, it is not actually for me, it is for my friend." Further attempts to clarify only made matters worse: "Well, actually for my friend's girlfriend." I think the relevant principle here for me to observe would have been: "When deep in a hole, stop digging."

After coming away empty-handed from all the various shops I knew of, I tried a sporting goods store where a polite Indian chap was ready to be helpful, that is, until he heard my request, at which time he shook his head, threw his hands despairingly in the air and his voice climbed an octave as he exclaimed: "My good sir. Surely you must be mistaken! C or D maybe! But certainly no man could handle such a woman!" No sale sahib!

Of course, this was before the days of the internet and Amazon, as otherwise I would not have had this assignment. I persevered and indeed eventually successfully located this rare item (by Hong Kong standards.) Several years later I actually met the lady in question in Switzerland and she did indeed exist. She kindly thanked me for my trouble.

(In my original 1980's humor article, I diverged from the truth and cast myself at the mercy of random expatriate women whom I begged to tell me where they obtained their amply-sized undergarments. Until the police led me off for questioning...)

Joy Ride—or You Can't Get There from Here!

Some of the more eccentric requests came from those financially very well off, so I usually did not hesitate to accommodate them whenever feasible. One such gentleman wanted to visit Macau without travelling to Hong Kong. At that time, the challenge was that Macau did not yet have an airport. If he had waited about ten years, he could have saved me a lot of trouble. But he was impatient, as are many older men with much money, but less time. How most people of the more conventional sort got to Macau was by first entering Hong Kong, and then taking the slow ferry, the faster hydrofoil or the speedy jetfoil across the Pearl River Estuary. I had to forge an alternative route.

There was a good rail line from Hong Kong to Canton (Guangzhou), a journey of 133 kilometers, or about 80 miles. So I went there as a starting point. Let me offer you a little vignette of travel color. Hong Kong is one of the world's richest cornucopias of all things consumer. Just a few miles away, the Communist Chinese border was just beginning to slowly open to one of the poorest, most crowded, most oppressed and bleakest social situations on earth: that very land that millions of refugees had escaped from in order to build that above-mentioned city-state filled with riches. It was such a tempting lure. Smuggling was more than frowned upon. These goodies were only for the Party officials to partake of.

The young man sitting on the train bench opposite me had an interesting solution to the smuggler's dilemma. Knowing that any bag a Mainland Chinese carried back into China would be thoroughly searched; he resorted to wearing his booty. He was a scruffy young laborer type with dirt under his untrimmed fingernails but he was dressed to the nines. From head to toe, he was a fashion statement: with designer gold-rimmed sunglasses, Rolex watch, Gucci shirt, Armani suit, Ralph Lauren tie, Yves Saint Laurent belt and classy Italian leather shoes whose brand I could not determine. He also looked about as uncomfortable as a young boy dressed by his mother for his first unwelcomed fancy occasion. It would have taken me a couple years to earn enough spare change to buy what he was wearing. I wonder how he did getting through customs that day, especially since all the shop tags were still plainly visible.

Tourism was just beginning to be discovered as a revenue source in Communist China in the early 80s, and up sprang massive new hotels in what was then the middle of nowhere, such as the White Swan Hotel. "Check it out, while you are there!" my client suggested. There it was, in the middle of nowhere. It was his dime, and being one of the first guests at a new five-star hotel was too great an opportunity to pass up. I was treated like a king! For all they knew, I might have been one!

Service was excellent. Back then, prices were incredibly reasonable, as the "management" had not yet discovered how bold they could be at asking for lots of money. The manager was constantly seeking me out for ideas and input on how to cater to the tastes and proclivities of the hordes of Westerners who were soon to follow my footsteps. We struck some great long-term deals in the dining room's buffet section. After a couple days of strenuous "research," it was time for me to find the secret passage way to Macau.

You can use Google Maps to look at the expanse of land from Guangzhou China to the northern gate of Macau. Decades after my pioneer journey, you can still discover what I did back then: there is no direct route! The smart money in China would fly directly to the new Macau International Airport. I had no such luxury, even with a pocketful of money. Negotiating with various drivers in Guangzhou, my limited Cantonese did me even more limited good among all the Mandarin-speakers. It was like trying to stay warm while wearing the Emperor's New Clothes. But I soldiered on.

澳門; or "Ou Mun"—Macau to those in the West, or Macao to the Portuguese who once ran this colony—has two world-class distinctions: At a bite-sized eleven square miles, it is both the world's most densely populated region and the world's richest country by GDP per person. This situation can be explained in one word: Casinos. Chinese love to gamble, but there are no casinos in Hong Kong. [There are horse racing tracks, but that will have to be another story.]

There are lots of Rolex watches for sale in Macau – real ones, and competitively priced with the fake Rolexes you can buy in Hong Kong and elsewhere. That is because of all the gambling losses that had to be paid off with pawned goods. Word has it that Macau is also a great place to pick up a new passport—if you happen to be a Wong or a Lee—for that same reason. But you would have to ask someone else about that.

Anyways, back to my mission at hand. My poor linguistic skills, added to the lack of highway infrastructure, made securing a ride to Macau difficult. You've read about the Little Green Pacifier by now. In this situation, desperate times called for more desperate measures. I pulled out a $100 US bill and I was able to quickly make myself clearly understood. Most taxis or rental trucks were really only licensed to

120

travel around Guangzhou city proper but for that amount of money, an eager young driver would take me to the moon, if I'd supply the gas. I pointed south, and we were soon on our way to another adventurous detour.

This was not going to be a chauffeur-driven limousine ride! Anyone willing to risk breaking the law in order to take a perfect stranger someplace he has never been is not the cautious type who meticulously maintains his vehicle. But for the money spent, it was hard to beat for sheer adrenaline-spiked, heart-pumping adventure. Off my driver friend sped. I was in no hurry, but I imagine that to his way of thinking, the faster he drove, the more his wage/hour ratio improved. That is, if we survived.

As we headed away from the big city and south into the countryside unfolding before us, the roadway steadily deteriorated from wide paved street to narrow paved street then to barely paved street until becoming a dirt road and finally downgrading to the high spot in a ditch. The one thing that remained constant was the driver's speed. The vehicle's shocks had long ago ceased to offer any cushion against the vagaries of the roadway, and so I hung on for dear life, bouncing off the door and ceiling at each new turn or pothole. Just when I thought things couldn't get any more exciting or dangerous, they did!

The cracked windshield was very dusty and grimy by this point so at first I rubbed my eyes, thinking I might be hallucinating or the dupe of a mirage. No such luck! Coming our way down the narrow dirt pathway was one of those sturdy black Chinese-issue bicycles. Across the back carrier was strapped a telephone pole. Yes, you read correctly. The pole protruded a good 10 feet from either side of the bike. This chap was doing an excellent job of balancing his load, with Cirque de Soleil-level skill.

I am not sure what the official rules are as to who has right of way in such an instance, but the driver with only two wheels kept coming as if he was certain he had priority. And so the game of chicken was underway. At the last moment, my driver veered off in to a field as the horizontal telephone pole sped by. After a few swerves and leaps, our vehicle was back on the "road" to Macau. Bing Crosby and Bob Hope should have added this journey to their series of seven "Road to" movies, but alas, their 1962 "Road to Hong Kong" was as close as they got to my harrowing, comic adventure.

Walking across the border into Macau was the next adventure. It obviously was not something often done, but not technically illegal. I did not get off a tour bus, and my hired driver took off as soon as I got out of the car, so I was on my own trying to explain how I got there. After much frowning and head scratching, the border guard concluded that—odd as it was—there wasn't anything dangerously illegal about what I was attempting that might get him in trouble with his superiors. I was finally waved through.

I headed for the historic and grand Hotel Boa Vista (which is now home to the Portuguese Delegation to Macau, since they lost their colony and accompanying Governor's Mansion to the Communist Chinese in 1999, two years after Brittan lost their colony, Hong Kong). After a nap in my corner room overlooking the picturesque harbor, I ventured out and treated myself to a good, long, delightful massage to work out all the dislocations that had been inflicted upon my poor body during my southwest passage. Aaahhh!

You can read more about Macau in the last chapter. Below is my grandson Javan next to a charming, old Macanese Catholic church in Coloane village on Macau's southern extremity. Note the cobblestones

22. Unhinged!

No matter how you slice it, every once in a while we all accomplish something of which we are less than proud. In some of these other tales I have described myself as the victim / hero of circumstances which were not necessarily of my own making. However, in this chapter I disclose events that were entirely my own fault. I have long admired and enjoyed the work of British actor Peter Sellers, especially his masterful portrayal of "Inspector Clouseau." My wife, who is Scandinavian as was Sellers' wife, has sometimes been apprehensive of this affinity of mine, perhaps because she was concerned that I sometimes channeled his mishaps much too accurately for her comfort. In any event, it is my wish that you can enjoy a laugh or two as I recall these events.

When one is young and attempting desperately to assert oneself as a serious contender in a corner of the world's stage, as I was then, such mishaps have a habit of deflating the over-sized egos. Enough water has since flowed under life's bridge that I can now sit back and enjoy telling you about some of my unhinged moments. An anonymous aging philosopher once stated: "When I was young, I always worried what others thought about me. When I grew a little more mature, I stopped worrying about what people thought of me. Finally, when I reached full age, I suddenly realized that no one was even thinking about me!"

In this chapter and in the next several chapters, we will venture out beyond the borders of Hong Kong for some events that took place on some of the other continents I explored in my long, winding journey.

Flying Saucer

I enjoyed dining out in Hong Kong for lunch. Service was fast and prices were very reasonable. There was no limit to the variety of menus and venues available—revolving restaurants atop skyscrapers and floating dining rooms in the harbor. I believe this first scene occurred in "Maxim's" which bears no resemblance to the fabled Parisian restaurant by the same name. The Maxim's I frequented was one of hundreds in the chain of restaurants established by the Brothers Wu back in the 1950s. I was in the Central business district, and long ago, so I may have been in the original Maxim's in the old Lane Crawford building before it gave way to progress and the bigger, taller new Landmark Building. [That's where the falling I-beam happened, which you read about in "The Street of Wishes."]

I guess I am one of those people who has a speech impediment: I cannot for the life of me talk expressively without using my hands. Make me keep my hands at my side and I'm speechless. On this particular day, I was merrily regaling my lunch partner with some particular tale. Who knows? It may have been the story about the baboon attack or where I faced the Postal Inquisition over that can of Carob powder. It matters not; suffice it to say I was animated in my retelling of the tale. At what must have been the climax of the story, a hapless waiter passed, routinely carrying a cup of coffee for some other unsuspecting diner. Intent on punctuating my story, while totally oblivious to the passing waiter, I swung my right arm out in a grand flourish.

It was a perfect shot. The back of my hand squarely caught the bottom of the saucer on its ascent to the exclamation point I was gesticulating. There was apparently sufficient momentum to launch said saucer and its accompanying cup arching skyward across the crowded dining room. We heard no pained screams and thus assumed that, fortunately, no one had been struck by the airborne coffee. There was a temporary hush amongst the diners, but, graciously, no real fuss ensued. However, when the waiter returned from the kitchen with the replacement cup of coffee, we noticed he took pains to avoid coming near my table.

Magic Table Cloth

It was another day at another restaurant in Hong Kong at lunch time. I loved the four course "set menu" deal – ordering was quick and simple. This time I dined alone. Is it any wonder? After the meal, and while finishing my own coffee, I opened my briefcase to study a few papers pertaining to my next appointment. When I was finished, I closed the case and prepared to leave. Fortuitously, this was one occasion when I was not hurrying about and I was actually dining in a relaxed fashion. You know that premonition you get sometimes where you imagine everyone is staring at you? Sometimes this feeling is followed by the realization that everyone is indeed staring at you, and for a good reason. I guess the Choir of Sane and Reasonable Persons sounded a timely note of alarm in my inner ear which caused me pause. Curiously turning around, I saw the reason for the wide-eyed stares that were focused on me.

As I slowly turned to survey the scene behind me, all of the elements appeared to be present and in order. However, on closer examination it became shockingly obvious that everything was seriously out of place. The table and chairs were as they were. The tablecloth was still on the table. The dinner setting—plates, cutlery, napkin, water glass, salt and pepper shakers and coffee cup—were all intact, but upon closer examination it could be determined that they were no longer resting on the table surface. They were balanced on the span of tablecloth which stretched between the table's edge and the hinged side of my briefcase where the edge of the cloth had apparently been trapped when I shut my briefcase. I had almost unknowingly pulled off the old magician's trick.

Not wanting to launch yet another coffee cup to its doom, I carefully sought to reestablish the status quo. While holding the briefcase still—and thus keeping the tablecloth taut—with one hand, I cautiously and individually replaced the various items back on terra firma (or more accurately, mensa firma) with the other hand. I imagine you could have heard a pin drop during this time; but none did. When I had successfully completed resetting the table, and after having freed the tablecloth from my briefcase, I made a mock-dramatic bow to underline my accomplishment. If this had been New York, I imagine there would have been loud cheering and applause, or at least an invitation for a career move. But my audience was a room filled with the proverbially inscrutable Chinese and I was left to depart without fanfare. I would not be surprised after this stunt if posters with my likeness were pinned up inside restaurant doorways everywhere in Hong Kong: "Do not seat this man under any circumstance!"

Lumberjack Ballet

Let's leave Hong Kong and its many fine restaurants in peace for a moment and take my antics elsewhere, to another time and another place. As you will read in the chapter "Why I Now Love Goats!" I was still in my formative stage of competently coping with Texan rural living. I had that brief unsuccessful attempt at cattle rustling. Undaunted by my dangerous level of inexperience, I acquired my first chainsaw. Actually, my wife bought me a rather nice new bright green one, aptly called "Wild Thing," for my fiftieth birthday. Whether or not she was secretly hoping to assist in hastening my demise, her true intentions will undoubtedly go with her to the grave. I think I have finally lived long enough to appreciate the fact that there are some mysteries that will never be unravelled; the majority of which are: "what are women really thinking?"

More likely, before this tale is finished, you'll soon wonder "what was HE thinking?!" Our backyard is blessed with seven natural water springs and, over the years before our arrival, while the property was not properly attended to, giant unruly willow trees had taken advantage of this abundant naturally-occurring resource, some of them growing to nearly a meter thick at their base. Unlike oaks or elms that faithfully grow sturdy to a predictably ripe old age, willows peak after only a couple of decades and then randomly and unceremoniously bend and/or topple over at will.

One such precariously leaning tree was about to trespass on my wife's newly-planted peach orchard, and so I helpfully came to the rescue, extension ladder in one hand and the "Wild Thing" chainsaw in the other. I carefully reasoned that if I felled the tree at its base, it was tall enough that it would surely topple onto the new saplings, such was my luck. So, wisely, I thought to "top off" the tree first. [I've since learned that there is a reason that only a handful of lumberjacks are "toppers" and that these specialized gentlemen are well remunerated.]

About halfway along the now-nearly horizontal trunk, I set up base camp and extended my ladder sufficiently to reach the height with a foot or two extra to spare, for good measure. Here is where I failed to fully appreciate the physics of the situation. The thick, heavy bending willow had two opposing vectors. There was the obvious one: the force of gravity pulling down on the massive tree. The other also unseen, and yet unthought-of, opposing force was the innate resilience of the willow's massive inner fibers. This force would exert its will shortly, once some of the weight was removed from the furthest extremity of the bending trunk, thus lessening gravity's pull. Those clever readers of the scientific sort are already seeing where this story is leading.

After starting up the chainsaw, I climbed the ladder: chainsaw in my right hand as I climbed with my left. I was perhaps twelve feet or so off the ground. The sharp new points of the new chain cut through the thick willow wood like butter. I had planned ahead to cut in a way so that when the falling segment travelled earthward it would not hit my ladder and thus dislodge me. But what I hadn't planned on seeing was that as the cut piece fell, the remainder of the tree thus freed of its heavy top load began to rise! Perhaps this entire emergency took only seconds to unfold, but as you may have experienced for yourself, when you are in the midst of such an emergency, time seems to (mercifully) slow and seconds feel like minutes.

I watched with sheer unbelief and horror as the tree began to eerily rise like an elevator. Meanwhile, the amount of ladder that was sticking up above the tree—the part that was supporting me and keeping me safe—was rapidly shrinking. At this rate, it would only be a matter of fractions of a second before the tree had risen above the tip of the ladder and, cartoon-like, I would be temporarily suspended mid-air. What to do? "Help" I yelled for all I was worth.

But there was really nothing for my family to do other than watch—and pray. Somehow my thought process overtook the pace of events and I planned my escape. I knew I needed to put distance between myself and the spinning sharp chain of the saw. I also considered that landing on top of the metal ladder would be very painful and perhaps dangerous.

I've never attempted Tai Chi, although I often saw it practiced at dawn throughout parks in Hong Kong by young and old alike. However, I think what I did next before my fall from grace was Tai Chi-like: With one arm, I flung the chainsaw as far away as possible from my estimated impending point of contact with the earth. With the other arm, I pushed the ladder away from me as hard as I could and this had the effect of propelling me in the opposite direction.

When all was said and done, the three of us - ladder, chainsaw and lumberjack - ended up in three separate spots. Starring in the role as lumberjack, I safely landed in some soft mud, winded, but only really seriously bruising my ego. "Are you crazy?!!" I could hear my wife expressing her displeasure at my recklessness. Actually, it was not recklessness; it was just plain stupidity. In any event, the fact that I could hear my beloved yelling at me was a good sign: somehow, I had survived.

For this next ego-bruising confession, I take you to the suburbs of Sydney where a well-respected architect friend had arranged for me to meet with the all-powerful local Catholic Bishop. I was all of about 22 at the time. What was at stake was the free rent of some unused but strategically-located diocese property of which the said mighty cleric had the discretionary power to turn over the keys.

The meeting had taken some time and skillful delicacy for my older architect colleague to arrange, so I clearly felt the pressure that this opportunity was mine alone to lose. I would have to be on my best behavior, my young mind concluded. I had never been face-to-face with a bishop before, other than kissing the ring of Bishop William Aloysius Scully in far-away Rensselaer a decade before at my prepubescent Confirmation. But this time I was a married adult and I would actually have to speak and perhaps say something witty or respectful.

My daughter Suzy just called and opportunely reminded me: "you need to write about the wedding!" This reference requires a bit of explanation. I had become somewhat of an ecumenical poster-child by this point due to my recent controversial and well-publicized wedding. My first wife Erica was nominally Anglican and thus, as a "heathen," should not have been allowed inside the sacred confines of Australia's largest Catholic cathedral, St. Mary's.

But allow me to put things in perspective for those readers unfamiliar with the ways of the twenty-some million denizens of the land Down Under. Virtually no one in Australia takes religion too seriously. Actually, very few things are taken too seriously, and that is a matter of national pride. From what I experienced, beer, the beach, and time off from work are taken very seriously. Almost everyone drinks beer, and goes to the beach (it's hard not to, when you live on a big island) but only about 2% of the population confesses (as if it were a sin) to going to church regularly. In the most recent census, one in three Australian respondents listed "none" for their religion.

So in the grand scheme of things, this marriage was not of the earth-shaking variety of that of King Henry and Anne Boleyn; it was more on the order of a storm in a teacup. But in the recent wake of Vatican Council II, progressive clerics were given more leeway to experiment with new ways to express the Faith. Enter Father Ed, a Cambridge graduate and celebrated author, still alive and much respected today as one of Catholicism's finest minds. He must be getting old by now, because I am. Back then, as a young, liberal head of the prestigious Cathedral, Father Ed embraced my idea of letting us have a folk wedding in his otherwise somber church.

We had the full use of the cathedral for the ceremony and the annex for the reception, all free of charge! We had a big yellow bus full of hippy-looking guitarists pile out and serenade us down the grand center aisle. Fr. Ed himself happily officiated. The cathedral's long-serving organist later resigned in protest over the breach in protocol. He obviously lacked the good priest's ecumenical tolerance. The press was in attendance and our wedding was given full page coverage in the Catholic Weekly. My wife and I were invited to various Roman convents (for day visits only) and parochial schools. So I had a certain amount of unbridled swagger for a young adult.

Now let's get back to my story of meeting with the Bishop at his residence. We were ushered into the richly furnished formal dining room. Small talk ensued around the table, about which I was painfully unskilled. Searching for any opening, I leaned towards the gorgeous centerpiece of white lilies, inhaled and commented: "Ah, they are lovely!" The bishop, keen to seize upon the opportunity for one-upmanship replied pointedly: "Ah, but they are plastic!" I fell silent, never quite recovering my poise after that embarrassment. I let the elder architect and the bishop do all of the heavy lifting of the conversation from then on. Nevertheless, I was granted my wish for the use of the property I desired. I guess it was deemed that I had paid sufficiently for it.

The bishop invited my wife and I back for other visits. I think he was mainly interested in my pretty young bride, the old rascal! But it was he who freely introduced us to the finer points of port wine and sherry, for which I was grateful on those chilly winter days.

Is That You, Mike?

This next encounter took a long time before I felt comfortable retelling it. The venue was on a rural stretch of road on the North Island of New Zealand. There are two large islands in the nation's chain of scores of island groups: North and South. Depending on where you are standing at the time, either one is considered to be the "mainland." Both sides have fierce arguments to defend their territorial integrity. South Island is a few inches bigger and has more sheep. All the big cities are on the North. There are glaciers to the south, and rainforests to the north. Take your pick: it is all otherworldly beautiful, regardless of which island you chose to call the "mainland."

I first landed in New Zealand just prior to my 21st birthday. Leaving upstate New York mid-July for the 27-hour flight (before the days of 747's) and travelling to what I considered to be a "south sea island," I packed mainly light clothing, and threw in a thin windbreaker for good measure. I obviously had not paid sufficient attention in world geography class: July in Auckland is the dead of winter in the southern hemisphere and it is very chilly, with evening temperatures hovering just teasingly above freezing. We had a coffee-shop of sorts with a wood fire going in the living room fireplace and that was the only source of heat in the entire building. For the next couple months, I usually never strayed far from the hearth, and I happily volunteered to secure firewood.

This led to an interesting experience that I will leave to the metaphysicists to explain. Three months prior, I had been in Boston and one of those super-spiritual guru types challenged me to try an exercise: I was to be seriously curious as to what would happen 90 days hence and await some dream as a sign. I did, in fact, have a vivid dream where I was picking through the aftermath of a large destructive fire: there were burnt timbers everywhere I looked. I could not accurately gauge distances in a dream, of course, but I dramatically concluded the fire's reach must have been global or at least countrywide in its scope. Within a few days, life uneventfully proceeded as normal and I forgot all about the dream.

Now let's fast forward to a cold morning in the Auckland inner-city suburb of Ponsonby where I was out gathering some wood scraps to feed my precious life-sustaining fire. There had been a fire at an old, abandoned, wooden school house nearby and I found some wood that had survived that fire ready to be gathered up for today's new fire. As I surveyed the scene looking for more available fuel, I was suddenly déjà vu-ed into the identical scenario of my dream three months prior. I asked Simon, the Kiwi chap who was with me, what today's date was and sure enough, it was exactly three months since the dream. I wonder if Peter Jackson ever had this happen when he was filming in New Zealand?

Then I was a lowly young world traveler on my first visit to New Zealand. Several years later, I returned, but this time in a supervisory capacity, touring our various branches, and brimming with self-importance, with my impressionable protégé in tow. We had a great time travelling the length of <u>both</u> main islands. While we usually flew or took trains between cities, we decided on a lark to hitchhike on one leg of the journey just so we could perhaps meet some of interesting characters.

New Zealand was indeed a very safe haven back in those days, seeming to be about fifty years behind the world's haste to self-destruction. One evening we caught a ride north out of Rotarua—a town with a smell as unpleasant as the sound of its name. Actually Rotarua is a geothermal wonder, with steam coming out of the manhole covers in the main streets, everywhere smelling of sulfur (i.e.: "rotten eggs"). But there is plentiful free hot water in the town, so I should have felt right at home, seeing as I often seem to be in hot water myself.

The conversation drifted to past travels and the driver told this story how she had frequented this coffee shop in Ponsonby, Auckland years ago. The music was okay, and the coffee just ordinary, but she declared that the real attraction was this young guy who kept her in stitches. "He wasn't trying to be funny, mind you! He just WAS funny – the way he talked and acted. He took himself so seriously, but he was so innately goofy!" And on and on she went, extolling the comic qualities of this particular young man.

We recognized from her various descriptions and detailed account right away about whom she was extolling: it could be none other than—yours truly. Apparently I had sufficiently changed and matured enough in appearance over the intervening years that she could tell this story with a straight face while looking me directly in the eyes, not suspecting the cauldron of embarrassment bubbling behind my stony eyes.

Jeremy thought to interject some information into the conversation to enlighten her, but I quickly shot daggers out of my eyes in his direction. "This will pass painlessly enough if I can keep Jeremy quiet" was my strategy. The poor fellow was barely containing himself, not unlike M's battle with self-control which I described in "The Wizard of Oops!" Mercifully, our ride with my unwitting detractor finally soon came to an end and I bid a hasty goodbye on behalf of us both. As the car drove off, Jeremy's long-suppressed mirth exploded and he had a great laugh at my expense. "Never breathe a word of this!" I threatened. Well, now he can.

The Danger of a Wink

For this next adventure or misadventure—whichever you prefer—I am going to whisk you away to Europe to visit fabulous Portugal where I spent two lovely weeks in Porto, about 300 km north of Lisbon. Known as "O Porto" by its citizens, this is an ancient city which embraces the rugged Atlantic coastline. Familiar with Mateus Rosé? There was a big marketing push world-wide back in the late 70's which made this brand of Portuguese wine quite the household name.

I came to find out while in Portugal that Mateus was sold ubiquitously on the street corners not only in Rosé, but also in Red, White and Green varieties, all of them quite delicious, and very affordable. Thus I very much enjoyed my stay on this charming corner of the Iberian Peninsula. We had a very intense urgent project to deal with, involving lots of hurried logistics for many impatient people. After a fortnight of stress, we were ready at last to unwind and celebrate the project's satisfactory completion.

And thus we ventured out at sunset in search of a local neighborhood eatery. It was a mild summer evening and we ate outside in an enchanting courtyard where the potatoes and meat were roasting temptingly in big barrels nearby and the pitchers of sweet sangria flowed endlessly to wash down the tasty evening fare. Colored lights were strung overhead between the treetops and local folk music was playing.

There in the center of the courtyard she stood: a raven-haired young beauty twirling about provocatively, sending her colorful long skirt into a kaleidoscope of swirling hues. Exhaustion, relaxation, a full belly and the sangria; comfortable breezes, happy music and a myriad of colored lights in the night sky: they all conspired against me so that I could not stop myself from watching the maiden's carefree abandon.

Then it happened: the dancing girl caught me staring at her and before caution could advise me otherwise, I winked. I quickly turned away and pretended to be engrossed in conversation with my fellow diners. But it was too late, and soon I felt on my Adam's apple that uncomfortable tickling sensation that arrives just before the noose is tightened. The long colorful scarves that had adorned the dancer's lovely neck were now wrapped around my own stocky, bearded neck as she was playfully pulling me out of my comfortable chair and into the harsh lights of center stage.

Of two things that I am not, one is an exhibitionist; the other being a dancer. And while I was thus naked of these two essential characteristics, the happy crowd nevertheless expected me to cooperate with this traditional courting routine. I was a prisoner of my own making. But it was a very delightful jail at that! Around and around my lively, youthful, athletic partner spun and twirled me until all became one big happy blur and I fretted like young Dorothy: "Oh Toto! I've a feeling we're not in Kansas anymore!"

Meanwhile, my dinner party was in hysterics. Eventually my consort had mercy upon me and returned me, dizzy and dazed, to my table and parted with a wink of her own. I was totally undone. Good strong Portuguese coffee came to my rescue and brought me back to my more responsible senses the next morning, and thus without further incident we left Porto for the dignified safety of the Swiss Alps.

23. Your Call

Stories I recall but refuse to explain

I didn't plan it this way, but here I am on Halloween writing two spooky stories about true events that happened to me in the land Down Under. These are stories of the good-spooky variety, if there be such a thing. And crazy as they may sound, I had a witness in each instance: a sane, sober, and still-living person. I will relate the stories but will allow you, the reader, to make your own determination as to their possible explanation—based on whatever religion, philosophy, metaphysics or politics you may hold dear. For when it comes to the unexplained, some folks swear by the angels; others swear there are no such things as angels—only coincidence or explainable science; yet others still just swear in general.

Following the traditional setting for spooky stories, both of these did indeed happen in the dark of night. "Aha!" One group of theorists already has their explanation, but I will proceed, undaunted. This first event happened right around midnight. I remember because, for some reason, it was important that we got this batch of mail to the Post Office in downtown Sydney for a postmark before tomorrow. We were probably late paying the bills or something mundane. You know how it is: life's daily emergencies and deadlines tend to pale in their importance over the years. Completed mail in hand, Chris and I headed out the back gate.

This gate led to the alleyway behind Victoria Street in Potts Point. Potts Point is a euphemism for "The Neighborhood One Block away from Sodom and Gomorrah"—the famous Kings Cross—where in the evening hours, the streets' sidewalks are peopled by those of the persuasion The Kinks sang about in "*Lola*." The alleyway dead-ended just a few feet away, where there arose a very dark and very tall old brick wall. Oddly enough, this was the far side of a convent which had somehow found the neighborhood conducive to their mission. I never asked why.

We had an old brown Bedford panel van, the kind with the sliding side doors. It was a retired bread truck and we had gotten it very cheaply. Now that I think of it, this van deserves a bit of description. Firstly, there was the time while, driving along one hot summer day, when we decided to slide the door open for ventilation, like how all the UPS drivers do. However, the door slid open a bit too far, came off its rails and became airborne, with me still clutching the handle. I let go just in time not to be sucked out into the highway. If I remember correctly, the replacement door was red. The other odd feature was the engine compartment, which opened up into the cab area with the aid of two handles that looked better suited for a bread box. Once while driving to Hyde Park one Sunday afternoon with my new bride in the passenger seat and a bunch of other folks back where the loaves of bread usually hung out, this trap door exploded open, flames roaring out fiercely.

Somehow I had the presence of mind at that young age to immediately stop, turn off the engine, hop out (first opening that tricky sliding door), run around to the other side and pull my bride out before she was baked, and then ran around back and opened the rear door so everyone else got out safely. Just then, a big blue city bus pulled alongside us, and the driver hopped out, brandishing his fire extinguisher and put out the blaze. Bravo! The entire event lasted only seconds. But, as a newlywed, it is something you don't quickly forget. Perhaps this should have been an omen to us.

So this van did have quite the colorful history already. What had happened was the line from the fuel pump had come off the carburetor and was squirting fuel onto the hot engine block. The good folks at the local Napoli Garage on Albion Street helped us replace the burnt wiring and we were good as new, which allows me to continue this tale. Of course, as things go when you are in a terrible hurry, the battery would be flat and we were parked at the low end of the alley. Try as we might, we couldn't push the van fast enough to pop the clutch and start it that way; it was quite a challenge with just the two of us lightweights and a very heavy old van. But the mail had to get through! We prayed for help, helpfully suggesting an angel should drop out of the sky and help us. We were out of practical ideas, obviously, and had no AAA membership.

Just then, in the stillness of that dark night, we heard a loud crash behind us that made our hairs stand on end. Apparently, above the high brick wall was a metal roof. There were no structures or trees above it, so there was a very short list of possibilities of what could have fallen and made such a loud thud. It turned out to be Clarence; or whatever his name was, as he didn't introduce himself. While we were transfixed, gazing up into the darkness and trying to figure out what was going on, a dark figure dressed entirely in black, including

135

the Buddy Holly-style glasses, leapt from the roof and landed a few yards from where we stood. "Get in the van!" he ordered as he began running directly at us at full tilt.

We were only too happy to comply, as we slammed the doors closed. "Pop it into second (gear)!" were the next and final words he spoke. From my rearview mirror I could see he was nearly level with my door and at that moment he made contact with the van with another thud, this one much quieter than the last. The van roared to life, to our great relief and under these altered circumstances, fear immediately turned to gratitude. But there was no one around to thank. Our jump-starter vanished as quickly as he had appeared. Granted, it was dark and he was wearing black; but it was also a long alleyway with high fences on both sides. Your call...

The next mystery took place at night also, and this time it was cold and rainy—classic miserable setting. The scene was by the side of the Hume Highway, partway between Sydney and Melbourne. Back then in the early 70's, life was simpler and more innocent, and hitch-hiking was a fun and acceptable means of transportation. Except when in was raining. It was a great way to see the countryside and meet a variety of people, the likes of which you might never otherwise encounter. Over a period of a few years while traversing much of New Zealand and Australia, I got pretty adept at the practice. Except for this day, when we must have had cosmic headwinds. We had a dozen different rides, none of them very long. The last ride dropped us off at a fork in the road, and he motored on home, first assuring us that this was a great spot to get a ride. It wasn't.

It got darker and colder. Vehicles passed by us and none slowed other than just enough to take a look at us. The rain got heavier. The unique feature of this spot where we had been let out was that there was absolutely no shelter of any kind, tree or otherwise, to be found. We tried all different styles of hitchhiking poses, but none proved any more convincing. As it got darker and rainier, I guess we became less visible and we had a few close calls with nearly being run over. By this time, we were fourteen hours into our day. Did I mention that we were also very hungry, thirsty and tired? "We need a miracle!" I exclaimed.

No sooner had the words fallen from my rain-soaked lips than a car screeched to a halt just ahead of us. "Get in, before you catch pneumonia!" the driver barked (as if it were our choice to be in this predicament)! "Hungry?" he surmised. "I'll feed you, but first I have to get a little miracle," he explained. The two of us hitchhikers exchanged amazed glances. A few moments later, our rescuer stopped at a little store, ran in and soon emerged with a small tub of "Miracle" brand margarine. I swear he winked.

We drove off to his place which turned out to be a large ramshackle car repair garage, strewn everywhere with parts and tools, and sprinkled generously with oil and grease. In the midst of this dirty chaos, there stood a table and three chairs, with three places already set for dinner. The menu included steak, vegetables and toast. The "miracle" spread was for the toast. My hitchhiking buddy and I were too amazed for words; I think we were partly afraid to ask any questions, lest it all disappear just as magically. When our bellies were full we became sleepy. Looking around, we saw that there was just one well-worn cot in the room.

"Ready for sleep?" our host seemed to sense. We nodded agreement and he directed us to go outside around the corner and sleep there. It was still raining. If this was his house, we could only imagine what the guest quarters outside around the corner looked like. But as we reluctantly yet obediently trudged out into the darkness, we noticed a dim light and walked toward it. It was the night light shining in a brand new travel trailer. Yes, you guessed correctly: there were two beds already made up, with fresh towels, and a glass of water at each bedside table. We slept the sleep of the just that night.

In the morning he fed us breakfast and we asked him about his family. He was vague, only saying he had several sons all around the world. He then drove us to a spot where he assured us we could easily get a good ride. [Where had we heard that line before...] He parked around the corner, where he could keep an eye on us. Perhaps he was an undercover cop? Sure enough, in under a minute, a car pulled over to pick us up.

We turned around to wave goodbye, but whoever he was, was already gone. Our new ride took us 350 miles right to the front door of our destination. Again, I'll let the conclusion be your call. I'll include the best reader-proposed solutions to these puzzles in the next reprinting. Surely this book will sell well enough for a reprinting, you think? Feel free to spread the word! Thanks!

24. Two Strikes for the Grim Reaper

Or: Heating Errors of the Near-Fatal Sort

For this next chapter, we'll leave Hong Kong temporarily and first go backwards in time and then later forward—about a decade each way—to the continents of Australia and Texas, respectively. Both tales involve heating problems in a rent house we had just moved into. In both cases, my family and I escaped unharmed, albeit no thanks to me.

If you want to meet Greeks but don't want to travel to Greece, you can visit Australia, which boasts the world's third largest Greek population, in Melbourne. There are lots of Greek landlords; one of them was ours and he rented us a cute little frame house in a working class neighborhood. It came with a fireplace. This was a plus in the chilly southern hemisphere winter months of July and August as the houses were not centrally heated. So in we moved: my wife and our two little ones, James and Suzy, whom you have met elsewhere in these tales.

Some critical details you might not think to consider—unless you are a contractor, which I wasn't—when renting such a house might include the straightness of the chimney. As you will see, the chimney's straightness turns out to be very important. When we first moved in, I went all around the house and yard, checking it out. It was fun discovering the charms of a new home. I did look to see if there was a chimney before we began using the fireplace, and sure enough, there it was, sticking up straight out of the roof, and seemingly in great condition. This was a novice's assessment, undoubtedly.

We enjoyed our cozy little fires for quite a few winter days in that living room. On one particular evening before closing the living room door and going into the dining room for supper, I glanced up at the ceiling after I turned out the light. "Odd," I thought to myself, "Someone left the light on in the attic!" I could see light coming through the tiny cracks in the old-style wooden ceiling. Then three thoughts quickly dawned in rapid succession: firstly, that there was no attic and secondly, that there was no lighting up there. The third thought crashed and stopped my heart momentarily: if it was not an electric light up in the attic, then the "light" I saw was instead actually the bright flames from a blazing fire!

We quickly got the kids safely outside into the big back yard and after calling the fire department I ran back through the house to gather what valuables I could rescue. Yeah, dumb, I know; but well, it was my first fire, and I was twenty-something. Meanwhile, a "passerby"— who remained anonymous—spotted the smoke and flames escaping our roof, grabbed a neighbor's garden hose and somehow got up on the roof and began dousing the flames. His quick action kept the fire's damage to a minimum. The big official fire hoses that arrived next kept water damage to a maximum. The mystery fire-fighter disappeared, much as did the jump-starter I mentioned in the chapter "Your Call" which had happened several years prior. Coincidence? Your call.

We had to leave our happy home and stay with friends for a month or so while the restoration work was done. The time finally came to collect the keys and move back in again. Zorba, the surly real estate agent, was waiting for me in his lair with his huge gold ring, huge gold watch, huge gold bracelet and huge gold cuff links. It was like having a conversation with a jewelry store. "You owe me back rent!" he thundered. Not exactly being flush with cash, I did not quickly grasp the logic of paying for rent when absent from the home. One glance at his stern countenance told me that he did not grasp the logic of missing five week's rent.

As an aside, I've had some very nice Greek landlords. One lived nearby at another house we rented in Melbourne and invited us over once for drinks. Ouzo was the only choice of drinks. Some will affirm that ouzo is much like turpentine lightly flavored with licorice. In any event, it was much stronger than the local popular brews that I was more accustomed to quaffing.

Luckily, there was a nice potted plant next to my chair and when our hosts were not looking, I watered the thing—ouzo'd it, actually. Seeing my glass empty, the friendly Greeks promptly refilled it; I promptly hydrated the poor plant some more at the opportune moment. This went on for several rounds. I often wondered what that unsuspecting plant looked like the next morning. This reminds me of the Polish Sausage story which I will save for the chapter "Things My Mother Never Warned Me About!"

Anyways, back to the house fire. The postmortem on the disaster revealed that the chimney that led up from the fireplace stopped at the floor of the attic. Closer examination revealed that the chimney visible from the exterior was about twelve inches offset from the current fireplace's chimney. Either there had been some strange remodeling done over the years, or the house had suffered a weird tectonic plate shift. This meant that all those weeks that we were happily burning a cozy little fire in that little fireplace, the hot little embers were rising up the chimney and settling on top of the wooden ceiling. Eventually a critical mass accumulated sufficient to encourage the wooden planks to ignite. Thus the bright "light" I saw in the attic that fateful evening.

When I balked at paying the back rent, the landlord argued: "Well, you started the fire that burned down the attic!" I could surmise this was not a man easily intimidated and that I would only have one shot at being successful in my negotiations. In a moment of cunning, it came to me: "Certainly the fire department would be interested to know that you were renting houses that had faulty chimneys to young families ....." Say no more! Back rent was forgiven and I swaggered out with the keys. We bought a little electric room heater after that.

* * * * *

Now let's spin the globe and move your attention 8,000 miles northeast. About two decades later, and now raising my second family of six children [you are correct: yes, twelve wonderful children in all!], I had just rented a 100 year-old farm house in rural Texas. Apparently I was still clueless on the matter of home heating after all these years. The quaint old property had a huge propane tank outside, feeding its fuel to three ancient rickety heaters via an underground metal pipe. This was the typical pier-and-beam style foundation construction found most suitable at the time for the shifting prairie soils of Texas. Thus there was a small crawl space under the floorboards for access to plumbing, etc.

We were fresh from big city living, just like the "Douglas" couple [see "Why I Now Love Goats!"], and we had been recently introduced to the unforgettable aroma of wild skunk. One such large female had taken up habitation under the house while it had sat vacant prior to our arrival. Rivaling a "Wild Kingdom" story, a nasty possum [known as "Opossum" to you if you live outside southern USA; or "Didelphimorphia" if you live in a zoology classroom.] discovered said mother skunk wintering under the warmth of our bathroom water heater and thought her little baby skunks would make a tasty meal.

Mother skunk took particular exception to the possum's advances and the fight to the death was on. The two combatants wrestled and bounced around under the floorboards, making the most Halloween-ish sounds. Finally, the mother skunk, cornered and weary of it all, unleashed her musky scent-bomb. In case you wondered, yes the fumes easily penetrated the old oak floor boards and everything in my closet had matching smell after that for quite some time. "Skunk man" my co-workers dubbed me for a while.

What was less than funny was that the lingering skunk odor masked a more sinister problem. When we arrived at our new rent home we were far from wealthy and it was a considerable investment to have that big propane tank filled. It was a particularly cold winter for Texas that year and the old yet-to-be-replaced windows were very drafty so we ran those heaters non-stop. Still, it seemed like that tank ran out way too soon and the "skunk" smell seemed stronger than ever. These old heaters were the kind you light with a match.

Back on March 18th 1937, three hundred school children in New London, Texas perished when the pent-up leaking and then-odorless natural gas exploded, literally blowing the roof off the school, leveling the building and creating a blast felt by residents forty miles away. Some students and teachers miraculously survived the immense explosion, one of those being Judy Arnold, who I had the pleasure to meet. She was the mother of Penny Arnold, the businesswoman who had just hired me to run her direct mailing business, sixty years later. This is when I first learned about malodorants—the additives mixed with the naturally scentless natural gas to give it that distinctive skunky smell so there would never again be a disaster the likes of New London.

Unbeknownst to me at the time, this was what I had actually smelt under my back porch. And this would have explained why the huge propane tank emptied so quickly. But this mystery would go unsolved for quite some time. By the next winter we had managed to save enough money to pay for plumbers to install new gas lines and hook us up to the city gas supply. The old propane tank was hauled away, but the old underground vestigial iron pipes remained.

The following year the boys—Mikael, Martin and Richard—and I began digging some of that shifting sand out from under the living room floor where it had slithered in from the hillside to the south. While digging away, I came across a length of the old (now rusty) pipe that had fed the propane to the heater in the living room.

I dug down into the sandy ground until I could uncover the pipe. Upon removing it, I found I only had half a pipe, so to speak: The entire bottom half of the pipe for a foot-long section was completely corroded away! The sand in which it was buried had apparently acted as a safety wrap of sorts. It kept the gas trapped underground, but allowed the malodorant to rise, which was the "skunk" smell that had persisted. Furthermore, where this gap in the pipe occurred was directly under the floor boards of the living room where I had been cluelessly lighting matches all that first winter when starting that heater. The flame from my matches could not have been more than eighteen inches from the leaking gas pipe below.

I froze in place as the significance of this discovery slowly reached deep inside me. We had somehow been spared a similar fate to those in New London six decades prior. "Hallelujah!" was all I could say. Words fail when confronted with the fact that your family had been mercifully spared a certain death.

25. Why I Now Love Goats!

My son Richard enjoying the sunshine with a newborn goat, 1999.

Before settling in a sleepy little rural niche of Texas, I had lived in decidedly more urban settings, such as Tokyo, Hong Kong, Sydney, Los Angeles, Houston and, well, you probably get the idea: I was totally unprepared for the challenges that awaited me. Shades of TV's *"Green Acres"* perhaps. The peace and quiet would do me good, I thought convincingly. But all is not peaceful if you are not prepared.

I was facing a grass-roots problem on my newly acquired three acres: Grass. For decades prior, the property had hosted a thriving poultry business, with tens of thousands of chickens regularly fertilizing the otherwise sandy prairie soils. I had enough hearty grass to make any greenskeeper envious. What I lacked were the resources to tame it.

Speaking of tame, it is important to know that a harmless-looking calf—such as the one who resided across the rickety fence—possesses great strength, cunning and determination. When said calf meandered into the greener pastures of our yard, my wife sent me off to defend her garden. "Piece of cake" I thought, charging out across the yard, my tender city-slicker feet shod only in flip-flops. [There are good reasons cowboys wear boots, besides to look taller.] I grabbed the rope that was handily attached to the intruder and set out to convince

143

it to return whence it came. The little fellow had other ideas: I think he sensed an easy match, and proceeded to drag me through every thorn bush and fire-ant* pile available until I came to my senses and left him alone. My wife called the sheriff and reported the "emergency." I think he and his deputies are still laughing about that call.

*If you are "not from around here" then you might not truly appreciate the dreaded fire-ant. There is nothing smaller in this known universe that hurts more than the bite from that tiny ant. Land your foot in an ant hill full of them and you will soon be walking like Quasimodo.

Well, it became abundantly self-evident that cattle-ranching was not my forte. It was now late spring and the grass was growing at a vicious pace. Obviously, this is why tractors were invented; but a tractor I could not yet afford. I did find a $200, used, 12-hp rider mower and bravely set out for my back forty: being the north part of the property where the untended field had grass 40 inches high. Only my hat was visible at times as I tried valiantly to coax that mower through the surrounding savannah. What was not so visible at the time was a rattlesnake. It was indeed a snake in the grass. There's nothing like the thrill of your first close encounter with this deadly species. Hong Kong and all its snakes had not quite prepared me for the rattler. The old mower and I proved to be no match for the grass and rattlers.

I used the last $50 I had available to hire someone to "shred" the field. "Are there any obstructions to be aware of?" the owner of the brush-hog inquired. None that I was aware of, I replied. It turns out there were, however: below the overgrown greenery there were fallen willow trunks that were twelve inches thick and old concrete footings from the erstwhile chicken coops. Loud cursing erupted after that tractor was launched skyward upon encountering the afore-mentioned and previously-unknown obstacles. I would not be able to avail myself of that gentleman's services again, it seemed. It also seemed my grass-taming options were disappearing rapidly.

As fate would have it, there was an exotic game ranch nearby and somehow my wife acquired a collection of used exhibits – a llama, three miniature donkeys and a horse with a lame leg. The local paper even did a story highlighting our menagerie. [I'm not sure that a self-respecting rancher is supposed to be proud of that kind of publicity.] The various animals were indeed fun for the kids but they didn't really keep the property trimmed in a respectable manner. I was running short of good ideas. This was because, for the first 50 years of my life, I had never really taken goats seriously. To me, goats were just the thing you had on a TV comedy show when you needed a hat eaten for a few extra laughs.

This is where it becomes important to know the difference between a browser and a grazer. Sheep, for example, are grazers: they will gnaw the field right down to the bone. Meanwhile, your fence will be overgrown with vines and small bushes. This is where nature's weed eaters come in: and this is one of the reasons I now love goats. Weed-eating along fence lines can be a tedious and difficult process for a human. Buy a goat and save yourself the trouble.

Goats—God bless them—LOVE to eat weeds that grow along, under, behind and up the sides of fences. They even prefer such greenery to the grass below their hooves. How high will they graze? I will give you a clue: the varied species of trees at the western edge of our property have grown tall, yet they all share one trait in common: their bottom branches are a uniform two meters from the ground, in laser-like precision, like a well-trimmed hedge in reverse. This phenomenon is not caused by my compulsive gardening, but rather can be attributed to the fact that our La Mancha goats can reach about six feet high when standing on their hind legs as they reach for those tender leaves.

What they leave behind is also pretty neat. Well, beauty is in the eye of the beholder, they say. But if you have ever stepped in the messy, smelly by-products of horse and cattle grazing, you will love the tidy little piles of relatively odorless pellets produced by these helpful herbivores. Chicken and other forms of manure are "hot"—meaning they can burn delicate plant roots. Goat manure is more like the time-released vitamin capsules. Cool! My wife—who hates to dust or iron—will gladly spend her days instead gathering up all this stuff and happily spreading it all over her beds of roses and irises and day lilies and crape myrtles, and cacti, and asparagus or any of the million other plants she has growing resplendently around our yard. The stuff really works and is free for the taking.

Oh, by the way, what about those two acres of 40-inch high grass filled with rattlesnakes? Now in the wake of our goat herd's industriousness instead, there is a lush field of grass uniformly about six inches in height (remember, goats are browsers, not grazers.) Furthermore, there are no longer any rattlers in sight because goats love to dance on snakes' little heads, and word has gotten around to the local serpent population, apparently.

By now you should have begun to understand my newly-acquired appreciation for goats: These green lawnmowers noiselessly eat grass, trim trees, weed fence lines, produce valuable fertilizer, stomp out snakes—all without consuming gasoline or producing any polluting smoke. But to be a successful, albeit humble, goat herder you must have a good fence, and not just any old fence. More on fences later...

Goats are pretty smart, for never having gone to college. They have great social-ordering skills, and set up their own finely-tuned schedules. At any time of the day, you can approximate the hour by where they are browsing (not grazing) in the grass at that particular time. Whether they are chasing shade or sun or dew or whatever, they have a certain method to their madness, just like a circuit rider. When a new goat is introduced to the herd, the first day is spent bashing heads together until everyone comes to an understanding of the newly revised social order. Then each one knows their place—in the lunch line.

This works well for goats because they have a triple-skull and thus avoid brain damage in their squabbles. When the door is opened to the milking room to get grain, they line up by "seniority"—their status determined by the composite score of age, size, head-butting skills and chutzpah. My wife has been overheard muttering ruefully on more than one occasion, "I wish my children were this well behaved!"

On most days, there are usually one or two "Kodak moments." At certain times of the day the goats will purposely assemble for what looks like a group photo op, when all the serious work of eating, social ordering and fertilizing is completed. We have plenty of climbing items for them—tires, barrels, wood piles, fallen tree trunks—and nothing is better than being the goat that can climb the highest. Once they have arranged themselves to their optimum mutual satisfaction, they calmly pose, waiting for the imaginary paparazzi. I'm not really sure how this particular routine contributes to the preservation of their species. Darwin only knows!

However, don't bother to bring your camera on rainy days. Goats can take plenty of heat, plenty of cold, plenty of wind, and of course snakes. But they do not like to get their feet wet. The first few drops of rain send them running for shelter. Rocky hillsides are a great habitat for goats as the water drains off and the ground stays dry. That's another reason why you don't usually see goats strolling along the seashore. Too much rain resulting in standing water will result in goats with runny noses, and much worse.

Goats' eyes! I forgot to warn you about their eyes! You'll notice when you are taking pictures of them: Instead of the cute big round pupils of a kitten, goats' pupils are shaped like a long, horizontal bar. I guess they mainly take landscape views themselves. But the first time they stare at you, it's kind of spooky, sort of extra-terrestrial in nature.

What's really weird is when they size you up closely and want to get a good portrait orientation view of you; they rotate their heads 90 degrees so that bar-shaped pupil captures your image from head to toe. If they are really particular, they alternate between clockwise and counter-clockwise rotations until they have you focused in just right. Talk about being "given the eye" – this is it! Following is a picture of my youngest child, last but not least, #12: "P.J.", shown here successfully out-staring the baby goat.

If social science is not your bag, maybe market research is more to your liking. In which case, goats make a perfect test market for demonstrating the power of novelty! Our neighbors were happy to discover they no longer had to burn or haul away their yard clippings. They now just toss them over the fence to our little compost minions. (Please, no Wisteria, however—something in that plant kills goats.) Over the fence go the branches and leaves and out the back of our herd come those valuable fertilizer pellets.

Now here is the interesting part: You can throw 99 identical branches from a boxwood shrub or oak tree over the fence and they will happily munch away at that pile. That is, until you throw one more branch over the fence a few seconds later. The entire herd (except for "Peanut"; she's an outlier, it appears) will rush for that "fresher" offering. Throw the 101st branch fifty yards down the fence in the other direction and—you guessed it: they abandon the ninety and nine and rush after the latest model. Works like a charm every time! This phenomenon is one of the few examples of plain silliness amongst the otherwise practical-minded goat world.

Of course, if you have a dairy goat herd, the day's highlight is the milking. A productive doe will yield a gallon each day and the milk is good for you! Technically, goat milk has less lactose than cow's milk, more easily assimilated fats and a chemical structure similar to breast milk, and thus it is easier for the sensitive stomachs to handle. Many cultures worldwide have centered around goat milk for centuries before "Elsie" ever gave her first gallon of cow's milk on a modern western farm. We have had a veritable procession of people referred to our herd by doctors whose patients had ulcers, allergies or immune deficiencies. My favorite is the goat milk cheese my wife makes with caraway seeds and jalapeño slices.

In case the nutritional details are becoming boring, let's go back to the fencing issue. You will not have any of this delicious dairy produce if you do not first have a good fence. Houdini was probably part-goat, thus his ability to escape just about anything. You can string up any pathetic tangle of barbed wire and the average horse or cow will conclude: "Ok, I've got the general idea; you want me to stay inside here." Not so with your average goat. The goat will take the fence as a personal challenge and will carefully examine every inch to make sure it meets proper specifications. If not, you will find the goat in your rose bed, or tomato patch or wherever else it should not be. Remember, they are browsers, not grazers. Ever "browse" through a shopping mall? You've got the point now, I believe.

Maybe investments are your bag – and this is another great thing – this milk-producing, manure-manufacturing weed trimmer will multiply itself. The first time, a mama doe usually produces just one baby. After that, it is usually twins each year. You really only need one buck to service a field full of does, as bucks are usually well endowed in that department, so baby bucklings don't fetch as much. You have better chance for advancement being born a female in the goat kingdom.

Curiosity may have killed the cat, but the goat thrives on it. I'm not sure if it is intellectual curiosity as much as it is mischievousness. I've used a small red cart towed behind my little garden tractor to move things around the field and sure enough if I stop for something for just a moment, when I get back there is one goat in the cart, another fertilizing the driver's seat and two more fighting for their chance to do likewise. They especially love it when you have tools!

Our big, but fortunately friendly, buck does a great Abbot and Costello routine. If I put a tool in my back pocket and bend over to get something, he will pluck that tool out and sniff it as his way of examining things. If I take my hat off and put it on the fencepost to wipe my brow he will snare that thing lightning fast and playfully begin to make off with it. He is quite content to repeat the process endlessly. Same for the bucket full of fencing parts – that is fair game to stick a head in, sniff out the parts, dump them out, and then stand triumphantly on the upended bucket. I'm sure it all looks very comical to the casual observer, but it is less humorous if you are in a hurry to get things done.

But I still love him. He's pretty good at singing the blues as well. When the torrid, but alas brief, breeding season comes to a sudden halt each year and the ladies all cool to his advances, he wails a great Bobby Vinton impression of "I'm Mr. Lonely" for hours on end. That is really about the only time he has much to say, really.

One of our goats was a pretty good barber. One day I noticed that the mane of our neighbor's horse was several inches shorter on one side than on the other. Immediately I suspected one of the teen boys had been up to no good. Shame on me! The next day, I saw the same horse standing ever so still right up against our west fence line, this time with the longer side of his mane facing me. Our buck was right over at the fence. It appeared as though they were gossiping neighbor-like.

Upon closer examination, I noticed to my astonishment that the goat was chewing – albeit very neatly and precisely – on that horse's mane, like a well-trained cosmetologist. I can understand the arrangement, I guess. The horse got a free haircut, because maybe it felt cooler for the summer that way. The goat found the horse hair nutritious I suppose. Bartering in the animal kingdom?

To be honest, all is not fun and games when it comes to goats! There are—in my opinion—some rather unpleasant aspects of goat-raising. I mostly leave those to my wife since I was born with a squeamish stomach. Horn disbudding of the babies is understandably a logical alternative to mature goats injuring each other or the farmer later in life, but I hate to hear those babies complain about the process! I have assisted with the little rubber band placement on the soon-to-be non-essential parts of wethers but I have since discontinued doing so. One vasectomy in a lifetime is enough. For other assorted messy details such as midwifery, afterbirths, injections, putting down sick goats, goat funerals, etc. you will have to read from a tougher author than I.

Finally, at some point in their lives everyone has probably heard or uttered the expression: "...got my goat!" But do you know its etymology? Purportedly, this expression hails from horse racing traditions. An edgy thoroughbred could be calmed by having your goat by for a sleepover before the big race. Steal your competitor's goat and the horse was upset and so were the racing results. I've never raced horses and can't vouch for that claim, but I do know that my goats have had a calming effect upon me. Especially seeing that nicely tended grassy field.

Daughter "Bunny" (Annette Michelle) – long time goat herder.

I thought I had finished my treatise on goat herding when the goats themselves decided to add a postscript. They reminded me of how good they are with subtle hints. We keep two five-gallon (twenty-liter) buckets of water by the fence for them. Whenever we get behind on refilling them, or if the goats feel we should clean them out better, they tip the buckets over sideways and give us a knowing stare. Once in a while, they even manage to upend one of the buckets for emphasis. They have us well trained it seems, but who can resist these sweet things?

26. Reality 101: First Year at MIT

Alternatively: Higher Education Learned the Hard Way

What is it about college freshmen? They leave high school smart and well-educated, only to turn perfectly foolhardy three months later when they enter "higher education." I thought I was pretty smart. My parents always told me I was, so that makes it fact, right? I was Valedictorian of my class of 300 seniors, so that should count for some degree of intelligence.

In this chapter and several that follow, I will be relating stories from the very beginning of the series of detours that has been my life, starting with the time I left my sheltered little home town as a fledgling young adult and headed for the big city life of Boston and Massachusetts Institute of Technology. Alas, upon arrival at MIT in Cambridge on a sunny September morning, I soon discovered that the entire campus was crawling with high school valedictorians, or at the very worst, salutatorians. I was no longer special; I was now only average. This painful self-discovery is a necessary first step towards wisdom. I address the problems of stressed-out MIT over-achievers in the chapter "Let's Get Physical!"

To get over the shock of leaving home and suddenly becoming stupid again, college freshman engage in a variety of "extracurricular activities." This behavior is less flatteringly referred to by outside observers as "goofing off!" At MIT, the nerdy student body used "applied science" and did clever stupid things, dubbed "hacks" – like chemistry students flushing magnesium wrapped in paper from the 5th floor toilets to see how far it would get down the pipeline before exploding and ruining someone's day further downstream; or biology majors concocting a super high-pressure water gun made out of laboratory dialysis tubing. There were 22 separate departments at MIT, each occupying their own building, and thus the available science to use for high-tech high jinx was virtually limitless.

Subways Don't Always Run on Time!

But on those days saturated with extreme boredom and/or frustration, we would go native and leave campus in search of new adventures. The concept always sounded plausible in the heat of the inspiration, but implementation often proved more risky. And ignoring this caveat, three of us set out to see what it was like to walk through the Red Line subway tunnel from the MIT station (Kendall) to neighboring Harvard (Harvard Square) late one night after the last train ran. It was a short five-minute journey by subway car, or about a two mile walk and we had all night to accomplish the task at hand. The last train ran at 12:01 am. Shortly thereafter, we set off through the tunnel, heading northwest. I was in the lead. In hindsight, I now know that one must not trust train schedules to be an absolute truth.

There are some sounds which are first sensed in the bowels of the soul even before they are detected by the auditory nerves. Such sounds include the distant rumble of an approaching train in a subway tunnel. The mind, which has already accepted the fact that no trains will be in the tunnel at that hour, searches desperately for other train-like sounds which could be the source of the audio input. When the light comes on—in this case, the light at the front of an approaching train as it rounds the corner of a hidden turn—the brain abandons its previously-held position of an alternative reality and switches to simple panic mode.

Yes, that is correct: I was standing on the tracks watching a train approaching! As I observed in my vignette "Lumberjack Ballet" in the chapter "Unhinged," during such extreme emergencies normal time seems suspended so that what only actually takes a second–or even a fraction of a second—to transpire seems like hours. Somehow in this timeless gap of heightened consciousness, I found a worker's alcove— a notch in the stone wall just big enough for someone to press into without protruding into the tunnel proper.

Then I watched as my life, and the subway cars, flashed before my eyes. And then it was gone; or at least the train was gone. I lived on to tell you this tale some decades later. Now many years later, and myself a father of twelve and grandfather to fourteen, I can appreciate how horrifying it must have been for that hapless train driver late for his last run back to the terminus siding to peer out into the darkness and see some young idiot from MIT about to ruin his day. Sorry, sir!

The Evil Ronald McDonald Happy Cup

There is no substitute for quality, the marketers will tell you. Sometimes, as I found out the hard way, there are also no viable substitutes for orange juice. For example, Tang powder does not possess the same properties as orange juice when it comes to making a Screwdriver. You will need much more vodka to fill up the glass if your only other ingredient is a spoonful of Tang. You guessed correctly, this story occurred in the same epoch as the subway adventure related earlier in this chapter: Freshman year at MIT, living in East Campus dorm, fourth floor, east wing. Up until this moment, my total experience with all things alcoholic was limited to two items: the mass-produced 12-ounce aluminum cans that possessed what passed for beer and some stolen sips from my mom's bottle of Italian Swiss Colony sweet Muscat wine that she won at St. Joseph's bingo night and hid in the cellar.

"Never had a Screwdriver before?" was the taunt. Being young, fearless and with the self-perception of being invincible, I was certain I was up to the challenge. I did not have any glassware, but I did have a red and yellow plastic Ronald McDonald Happy Cup. I would soon learn to hate that cup...

The other ingredient I did not have to make my first-ever Screwdriver was orange juice. But I was undaunted. I filled the glass with the colorless, odorless distilled liquid. After all, "vodka" derives its name from the Slavic word for "water"—harmless enough. The gang that gathered in the common room of the dorm suppressed their various expressions of disbelief and watched poker-faced, much as one would while witnessing a bungee-jumper prior to a jump, using a cord that is too long. I added a spoonful of Tang and commenced to respond to the dare.

All was fine at first until I grew sleepy and went to lie down in my bottom bunk and instantly fell fast asleep. Shortly thereafter, I awoke to a violently spinning room. The real fun was about to begin. There would be two things I would never do again. *The American Top 40* hosted by none other than Casey Kasem was blaring on the AM radio. My body began helpfully rejecting the poison I had consumed. Fortunately enough, there was a sink in my dorm room within staggering distance. It would become my place of residence for the next 24 hours. After a long unpleasant spell of vomiting, I soon discovered there was something even worse: dry heaves, another new experience to add to my fast-growing list. If you have never had the pleasure, the best description I can offer is that you are being pummeled by a champion boxer, but from the inside out. I could occasionally get my mouth under the tap for a sip of water, and then the cycle would begin again in earnest. Meanwhile, America's top forty hit tunes repeated in a nauseatingly endless loop; but I was too weak from the torture my body was inflicting upon me to reach the annoying radio on top of the shelf.

My roommate moved out and took up residence in the common lounge at the first whiff of my troubles: "I'll be back after you have gotten yourself together again." So I was left all alone in my misery, albeit I had the unwelcomed Mr. Kasem to keep me company. When my angry body chose other unpleasant ways to eliminate the poisons I had inflicted upon it, I happily found a large metal trash can under the sink. I was a self-contained casualty ward for one long day and night. Finally the pint of vodka was out of my system, and after a long hot shower and disposing of the trash can contents, I had our dorm room back to normal. But the first thing I did was to turn off the radio. And the two things I would never do again? I have never listened to the Top 40 since that day. And I have never gone near vodka—or any hard liquor for that matter—from that day forth. I'm a better man for it.

Hacks! --Or Applied Science; viz: Applied with Mischief

In 2015 the MIT Alumni website wished the word "Hack" its 60th birthday, so that makes us contemporaries, although I did not meet Hack until I was 18. The concept of Hack makes more sense if you can fully appreciate the collective angst of thousands of clever, frustrated students surrendering their childhood freedom to the rigors of adult studies. At MIT, true release comes only from the cleverest form of mischief, be it on a grand or minuscule scale. On the grand scale, you get phenomenon such as the time the campus once awoke to the sight of a full sized fire truck atop the great dome. [Great hacks are best pulled off under the cover of darkness.] There are considerable challenges involved in getting contraband items to the top of the 150 foot high dome, but after all, this is Engineering Mecca.

155

As a freshman, I climbed to the top of that dome one night on the strength of a dare and greatly enjoyed the view thus afforded. The fun ended when it came time for the descent, when it also became apparent that gravity was wont to accelerate objects down the steep smooth slope and over the edge to the awaiting abyss of the Killian Courtyard, the equivalent of 15 stories below. The challenge was to provide enough friction to slow the descent without losing all of one's epidermis. Obviously I was successful, since I live to tell the tale this day.

The fact that the Hack is very much ingrained into MIT subculture can be easily confirmed by even the most casual of Google searches. [Such as the one I just performed.] These daring deeds are not chronicled in the darker regions of the ether world, but boldly institutionalized on the MIT.edu website, neatly cataloged by year, greatness or theme. There are dozens upon dozens of links to Wikipedia and elsewhere that will give you more amazing photos and details than I could ever include here. Besides, someone has, or more accurately—"a bunch of somebodies"—have, already done so quite impressively. So why should I reinvent the wheel? But just type "MIT Hacks" into your search engine if you are unfamiliar with this subject and be prepared to be amazed at the volume of material. My search request today resulted in 7,730,000 results.

While hacks are officially unsanctioned, the MIT administration nevertheless recognizes their inherent worth. For example, there was a decade when the "Hall of Hacks" graced the official MIT Museum. One hack recently installed in the avant-garde Strata artificial intelligence building has been allowed to remain because it nicely fills an otherwise ugly architectural void.   Clearly, synergy is at play. Anthropologists might charitably view the phenomenon of Hacks as the tradition of a mini-culture or self-affirming group belonging. Then there are also the individual what-the-heck hacks.

Some of my favorite big-time Hacks are: the ersatz police cruiser high atop the MIT dome, replete with donuts and dummy patrolman; the two-ton, 100-plus year-old cannon filched from arch-rival Cal Tech and transported across continent where it briefly took up residence outside the Green Earth Sciences tower, adorned with a huge MIT class ring, "The Brass Rat"; and the black balloon at Harvard Stadium. This last one is my favorite: Harvard was hosting Yale's football team. The fun began when a large black balloon emerged from beneath the

46-yard line, where it had been buried along with its attendant vacuum-cleaner motor and hydraulic pump wired into the sprinkler system's electrical supply: on the balloon "MIT" was written in large letters.

A footnote here: MIT's 2014 football team had a great season that drew nationwide attention. Until this breakout year, the football program had only won a grand total of 80 games in the previous 69 years. During this same period of time, MIT folks garnered the same number—eighty—of Nobel Prizes! Brain and brawn, it would seem. After all, MIT's motto is "Mens et Manus", Latin for "Mind and hand."

There are also many, many unrecorded hacks, conducted far beneath the radar screen of fame and much smaller in scope, but nevertheless still true to the dictates of hack-ness: technical aptitude and cleverness. As with most hacks of the more grandiose scale, these are usually (a.) perpetrated by undergraduates and (b.) under the cover of darkness. I will now record for you one of the hacks that history had hitherto fore overlooked.

I can personally vouch for the authenticity of this first hack: that it was indeed perpetrated by (a.) an undergraduate and (b.) under the cover of darkness, but whose identity will remain unknown in order to preserve the hack tradition of anonymity. There was definitely technical aptitude of a sort involved, and it certainly seemed clever at the time. In the adjoining dorm room slept Tony V. The daring aspect of this hack centers on the fact that Tony was a member of the rowing team and thus a much stronger, more aggressive and larger freshman than the hack's perpetrator. Tony had a physics exam the next day and left the curtains open so that sunlight would hit his sleepy eyes and act as a back-up alarm clock, should the primary device fail. As you can see, even early on, MIT students learn to be proficient at redundancies. The hacker had to thwart this reveille plan, somehow without entering the dorm room.

Fortuitously for the hacker of this story, Tony's room was one of just a handful that had a balcony that was shared by the adjoining room. All that remained was to summon the skill set and courage to (a.) crawl out on this narrow, ancient structure on a chilly winter's night while carrying a bucket of paint and a paintbrush and (b.) reach and stretch far enough to be able to paint all the window panes with a very opaque covering of black paint while (c.) not falling 40 feet to the pavement below and (d.) without making any noise to awaken the person being hacked while also (e.) avoiding detection by any passers-by or authorities who might interrupt the hack if it was discovered whilst still in progress. I can report that the hack was a success because Tony failed to wake up in time for his exam. Revenge was imminent...

The Cruelties of Peer Justice

To the list of endangered species, please add college freshman. Evolutionary pressures from those further up the food chain are immense! Even sophomores carry an intimidating hubris. Perhaps it was meant to encourage a positive sense of belonging, but the phrase "you will never leave here" sounded more like a sentencing. We'll get into sentencing more in a moment.

This section of the chapter will be about JudComm [MIT-speak for Judicial Committee, a kangaroo court run by the students]. It had been conspiratorially conveyed to me that [the fortunate] freshmen evolve into Sophomores, then on to Junior and Senior Undergraduates only to morph into Graduate Students, Graduate Assistants, then PhD candidates, after which they mutated into Instructors. The strongest survived to become Professors, Full Professors some even Deans, before finally expiring – all this without ever having to leave the proverbial technological jungle that is the MIT campus.

Now: on to issues of justice, or the miscarriage thereof. Four of us fellow freshman lived two-to-a-room in connecting rooms on the east side of the hallway in the southern "Walcott" section. The following year, I would score my own private room on the east corner of the northern "Goodale" section, from which I had the enchanting view of the dilapidated NECCO factory. By the way, NECCO [New England Confectionary Company] is reputed to be the oldest continuously-operating candy company in the United States.

If you are old enough, you may remember the old Necco Wafers; NECCO produced their one trillionth Necco wafer in 2010. Those of our younger readers are no doubt familiar with those NECCO Sweetheart Conversation Hearts that are left over after each Valentine's Day season. On my recent visit to East Campus [see "The Return."] I was happy to see the now-vastly improved view, thanks to the Koch brothers' donation of the ultra-modern Building 68, the Koch Biology Building.

I think these "room wars" were all part of the grand scheme of the evolutionary process – mismatched Freshmen were paired up to fight it out for a year, and the survivor got to claim his own room the next year. It was late one night and the pressures of studying for a big physics exam became overwhelming when the Law of Diminishing Returns set in. [see Chapter "Let's Get Physical!" for more details.]

We had been conducting elementary physics experiments of our own – tossing water balloons out the fourth floor bathroom windows onto the passing cars on Ames Street far below. This feat required considerable precise calculations: factoring gravity, cross-currents, drag due to the shape of the missile, speed of the car, and desired location of impact to name just a few. [Windshield was considered a "bull's eye".]

After a while, this became boring, so we escalated by switching the balloon's content from water to paint. We had a perfect shot on the first attempt! Laughing and shouting, we all ran back to our rooms for anonymity – with about the same amount of security the ostrich gains by burying its head in the sand. We four freshmen were marked men.

All hell broke loose and the omniscient and omnipotent JudComm convened and passed sentence: I was to pay a $146 fine in restitution for damages caused to the car belonging to none other than the Belgian Ambassador's son. This was a huge amount of money in those days, especially for a college freshman with no income. Hoping to keep the fires of hell at bay, I dumped out my coin jar and turned over the first $17 and begged for more time.

I was now literally penniless–which was a good thing in some ways, as I needed to find a job. A sign on the campus work bulletin board announced an opening for part-time delivery work at nearby Heritage Travel agency. [The Heritage Travel was later gobbled up in 1988 by Crimson Travel, which was later gobbled up by Cook Travel, and finally ingested by American Express.—Another evolutionary tale for you!]

I had great fun delivering airline tickets all over Cambridge and Boston, learning how to drive a stick shift on the company's VW Beetle. I soon had my debt to society paid off but I enjoyed earning money so much that I kept the job. Soon I could afford a waterbed, and my own state-of-the-art stereo with locally designed AR speakers. Earning spending money and running all over the place meeting all the cute secretaries that the Boston metropolis had to offer did, however, take some of the luster and appeal out of attending classes.

It came time for our spring dorm floor party. Robert, the Columbian student who was that year's JudComm president, presided over the party. Sleazy Pierre furnished the necessary young neighborhood females. [Male MIT undergraduates outnumbered females 18:1 back then, thus the need for imports. Nowadays the male-female ratio is a much healthier 55-45% split.] As everyone was drinking [18 year olds could drink in those days, I mean, legally they could] and having a good time, President Robert stood up to make acknowledgements and give special thanks.

I did a double-take! Did my ears deceive me? Had I enjoyed one too many glasses of cheap wine? "We have Mike Hawron to thank for his $146 which we used to pay for tonight's party." There never was a Belgian ambassador with a son driving his car in Cambridge that fateful fall night. Apparently, the joke was on me, as well as all the drinks. My extracurricular education in Reality continued...

27. Things My Mother Never Taught Me!

In this chapter, I will serve you champagne on a flight from Hong Kong to Austria; we will visit the naughty nurse's station after a car wreck in Australia; you will enjoy a long train ride Down Under featuring an overly-amorous passenger; we'll drive a big lorry (truck) through the dockyards in Sydney; we'll dine on unspeakable cuisine in Poland and finally we will serve high tea in Potts Point. There is no significant rhyme or reason to this particular grouping of stories, other than these common traits: the stories all true, they all happened to me, they were the result of my ignorance and/or stupidity, they are meant to be entertaining and each story ends happily enough. None of my mother's nurturing had adequately prepared me for my life's long journey, filled with all these detours.

Three Dog Night, however, had no such excuse: their mama told them not to come! After living the first eighteen years of my life in the very secluded rural confines of DeFreestville in upstate New York, nothing my mama had told me prepared me for the adventures that awaited me when I circumnavigated the globe as a young adult. She wanted me to become a priest; my dad thought West Point military academy would better suit my developmental needs. They somehow compromised and Boston became the first stop on my live-and-learn tour when I went to MIT to become an electrical engineer, whatever that was. These tales are in no particular order or sequence – just however they float into my memory chamber.

The Cost of Free Champagne

One time on a business flight from Hong Kong to Vienna, I decided to fly the newly-christened Lauda Air. One reason for my choice was that I thought it was cool that the three-time Formula One race champion Niki Lauda had his own airline. Perhaps unconsciously driving my reasoning was the unspoken premise that surely a race car icon could get airplanes to their destination on time. Also driving my decision were the bargain introductory fares. Off I headed from tumultuous Hong Kong to the refined culture of Vienna. I thought to dress the part and wore my new gray pin-striped three-piece tailored wool suit with complimenting pink shirt and a paisley tie to match. The suit was from *Danny's Shoppe* in Kowloon, Hong Kong [you know they always charge an extra dollar or two if the shop name adds a superfluous "p" and "e" at the end.] "Danny" was nowhere to be found. I think it was just considered fashionable enough of a name for the Mong Kok region clientele, as neither the Chinese owner nor the Indian tailor were so named.

The suit was great, with the security feature of double front pants pockets with a hidden zipper and a matching zipper pocket in the coat. Totally bespoke! After mulling Herman's warning over and over in my mind—about how "they" would cut off my wrists to get my attaché case—I decided to find a more subtle and secure way to transport valuables. I'm proud to say that I still fit into this suit today, which is also so ancient that it is now in fashion again.

Not too long ago, I wore it successfully to the Fort Worth Opera where I mixed and mingled with the cast from *Carmen*. There are some advantages to longevity, it seems. The selling point of this particular suit was when the owner took a bolt of this London cloth and twisted it mercilessly. Upon his release, the fabric returned to its wrinkle free state. This garment would prove handy for globe-trotting. The price was great as well, and it was done in a day—another joy of doing business in Hong Kong which I sorely miss.

"Enough about the suit!" you complain. The suit is the leading character in this story, so without further ado, let us begin. Halfway into the long flight, I fell into a great deep sleep. I apparently have that rare quality among air travelers. By now breakfast was being served prior to landing in Vienna but I was still snoring away contentedly, slowly being awakened from pleasant dreams by a comforting warm feeling, amidst shouts and frenzied cries. Apparently, in the process of serving fresh hot coffee to the passenger to my right, the hostess spilled the scalding brew down my back. A customer service nightmare was brewing. Fortunately, my nifty new suit had absorbed most of the liquid and its accompanying heat before it reached the skin on my back beneath. Thus all I felt was pleasant warmth.

I awoke to the lovely sight of a very attractive young lady apologizing profusely. First German was being shouted excitedly, then measured English followed. The passenger next to me was arguing as to the seriousness of my injury and insisting on proper compensation, which I was to learn, was a free bottle of champagne. The sparkling drink and a glass soon appeared on my tray. Not to be outdone, my representative demanded his own bottle for helping to settle the

162

issue. The service staff complied, although less enthusiastically. He raised his glass and saluted "prosit!" I think you could say he was my first-ever agent. New Year's 1990 had just passed; Eastern Europe was still deliriously celebrating the fall of the Iron Curtain and my (fifth) son Martin had just been born, so all in all it felt quite appropriate to be drinking champagne early on a winter's morning at 35,000 feet.

After drinks, the friendly and ravishingly pretty staff invited me to their aft galley where they stripped off my coat and shirt and spot washed and dried my ensemble using hair dryers. [I once had a Swiss associate named Mr. Drier: After this event I used to delight in calling him Herr Drier in memory of the event. He never saw the humor of it all, but understandably so, for he was Swiss after all.] When they felt I had milked my misfortune for all the free coddling attention to which I was entitled, they sent me efficiently back to my assigned seat. The cost of free champagne: Priceless!

Broken Holden, Wounded Knee and Naughty Nurses

We had a sturdy old Holden when we lived in Allawah, New South Wales. Two points of explanation here: First: a Holden is a General Motors vehicle Down Under-style. Second: Allawah is a great word for dialect training in speaking the Australian "a"! I'm not sure however, that many realize this south Sydney suburb sports an Arabic name, meaning "God Lives Here." And why not?—so does everyone else! This is a real Aussie town, where a whopping 36% of the people claim to be born in Australia. Things have changed much since I lived there: now more than 30% of the residents speak a form of Chinese. Enough about Allawah; it is only significant in this story because that is where I parked our family car after the accident.

We were returning late one night along the ring road from Parramatta (another great suburb for practicing your "a", mate!) No, this is not another Arabic name; this one is fair-dinkum aboriginal Darug for "the place where the eels lie down." Bet you didn't know that either. A carload of drunken revelers totally ignored the stop sign and plowed into the front left side of our Holden, T-bone style. This was Australia, and so I was not there; the driver's seat is safely on the right-hand side. James and Suzy had been squabbling in the back seat and I offered to put one of them up front with me—you know, the "divide and conquer" parenting technique. Fortunately, my wife, who was terrified at all things driving and thus was also in the back seat,

163

hesitated and suggested that we give it a bit more time. A moment later that front passenger door was pushed half way into the front bench seat. James would have been history!

The punks got out of their car laughing, seemingly without a care in the world and proceeded, as it later turned out, to give a false address to the police, and thus were saved from prosecution, and liability. Repairs would be on me. The police wanted to ticket someone, and asked me for my license which I did not have on me at the time. "Aha! At least we will get someone ticketed for our troubles tonight!" Not so fast however, as my license was from Queensland, and you could not get a ticket for not having your out-of-state license on you. I guess that is sort of like proving a double negative, but it worked. Next I had to find my glasses before I could do much else and, after stumbling around in the dark awhile, I found them some twenty feet from the car, such had been the impact. (My window was open.) Old Holdens were made out of lots of solid metal, which probably saved us from much serious injury. Except my left knee, which rammed into the heater control knob (being in the days of total analog) bending the 1/8" thick metal bar 90°. My knee bent considerably also, and still bothers me to this day.

We had the battered car towed home and, before we could get any insurance settlement, the neighbors were complaining (in English, back then) about the eyesore, which is really saying something in Allawah. My knee was also sore, so I scheduled a visit to the local clinic. The nurse attending me was nice enough. I understood that I had to take off my shoes and socks to get my pants off so she could check out my knee. However, this was apparently going to be a more complete physical, as she ordered: "you will have to take off your underwear also!" I complied, albeit somewhat hesitantly. I've noticed that one tends to do things without question when in pain and/or in the presence of medical professionals. The exam of my knee concluded swiftly enough and I was promised a full recovery after a spell of pills and therapy. I was sent on my way.

Curiosity got the better of my shyness, so as I was walking out the examination room doorway I turned around to inquire why it was necessary to remove my underwear for an examination of my knee. "Oh that? I was just curious to see what you looked like!" was the casual reply. Well Toto, this certainly was not Kansas! And this was obviously way before the days of malpractice or sexual harassment, aka "The Good Old Days!"

The Owl and the Pussycat or:
Country Roads, Please Take me Home!

This is a train story of a journey from Sydney, NSW to Townsville, Queensland, a distance of 2279 km or 1367 miles—either way you slice it, the ride takes two sunsets to complete. This was still during my young and stupid stage, or as Bob Seger lamented *"Wish I Didn't Know Now What I Didn't Know Then!"* My travelling partner was Steve who was a very talented guitarist and vocalist. He had an amazing vocal range and variety of styles, and could play all manner of chords and tricky stuff on his twelve-string acoustic guitar, which he brought along to help the long hours pass more pleasantly. (We had only paid for upright seating.) John Denver, Cat Stevens and Don Mclean songs were all the rage back then, so we began with "Country Roads" and "Where Do the Children Play" and "American Pie" and then ran through the whole repertoire that night. I say "we," but my vocal and guitar talents were severely restricted; nonetheless, I could usually clap in time through the choruses. That was all the back-up Steve had. And all he needed, as he was quite the showman.

Like the troubadours of old, he wandered up and down the aisles along the snaking line of carriages, taking requests and passing out his business cards. He had a captive audience and they had free entertainment. It was a perfect arrangement. Come nightfall next day on the long stretch from Brisbane northward when the conductors vanished, musical chairs commenced. The scramble began in earnest for those in the uncomfortable upright cheap seats to find an empty sofa compartment, and I skillfully scored one right away and settled down for a good, desperately-needed sleep after having been up all the previous night. Not so fast! I was about to be introduced to my first "groupie." The big door slid open and in breezed this older woman—golly, she must have been way into her 30's! (I was just a young lad; age is so relative!) She began chatting me up about how much she had enjoyed the singing and how lonely she was. I just sat still as a stone and exercised all my concentrated mental will power to remove her from my newly acquired bedroom. Suddenly, to my great relief, she left as unceremoniously as she had arrived. I was a happy young newlywed and I had every intention of remaining so. I fell asleep.

The relief was short-lived! The door slid dramatically open and when I opened my eyes, I was greeted by the appearance of the groupie now clad in a sheer leopard-skin pattern negligee. Hokey Smoke, Bullwinkle! Then she uttered the threat: "When I want something... I get it!" And although Stevie Nicks would not record this lyric line for another 15 years, I instantly knew I was already eponymously in a *"Whole Lotta Trouble!"* I was a skinny young thing and she easily outweighed me by a stone or two (speaking here of the English unit of weight measurement, of course) so she proceeded to jump on top of me and pin me down, smothering me with kisses. "Lucky devil!" you snort?

I was terrified! Although this was still a decade before AIDS became news, I was aware of several other serious risks: the run-of-the-mill STDs; my wife killing me when she found out; or worse, maybe my wife would not get the chance to kill me because maybe this was one of those kiss-and-kill serial crazies! And I had never heard of a "cougar", as I don't think that phrase had even been coined yet. We still had free-love hippies left over in those days.

Well, what to do? My devout mom's earlier Catholic indoctrinations must have taken subliminal effect as I suddenly began desperately praying to St. Jude, the Patron Saint of Hopeless Cases. At this particular moment in my young adult life, that was me to a "T" – hopeless and clueless. I prayed that my attacker would calm down, or disappear; any scenario where I got to keep my pants on. [Remembering the nurse from the "Wounded Knee" episode?] Well, as they say: "miracles never cease!"

But what did cease was that suddenly the wild lady stopped all the kissing and thrashing about; she looked me in the eye and said wistfully "I wish I had peace like you do" and then instantly fell soundly asleep. She slept peacefully like a (very large) baby alongside me. Not wanting to press my luck, I tried not to make a sound or move; when I awoke the next morning she was gone.

I never saw that nameless lady again, but Steve later told me that she called him some days later, apologetically explaining that she had been diagnosed with just a short time to live, and that she had wanted to go out with a bang, as it were. Steve—talented and wonderful though he was—battled long and hard with alcoholism and depression until, like Mclean's "Vincent," one *"Starry Starry Night"* he took his own life and his beautiful music ceased. I alone remain to tell this tale.

* * * * *

M RETURNS: Remember M from "The Wizard of Oops?" She has become a regular reviewer of my tales, and added this insightful reaction and words of wisdom: *"Mike, I loved and enjoyed the stories.* [Regarding] *Steve --I remember something about an awesome Australian guitarist who committed suicide, so sad. That's hilarious that the nurse made you take off your pants! Older women are just attracted to innocent looking boys and I guess you looked the part. So funny! Especially the gal on the train! I think certain people attract adventure and hilarity. You most certainly are this type of person. I like to think I am too. Is it because we're looking for the fun in every situation? Because it's almost always there! Or is it because for sure we're going to tell the story? You and I are the kind of person who even if we break down at a truck stop, it's going to be an adventure and there will be tales to tell. Love ya, M."*

How to Get Things Done Down Under

This episode could also be called, "How to succeed: by not trying so hard!" In Australia, successful Labour (There is a U in "labor" there) Relations require the expenditure of as little labor as possible. Most Australians have perfected this art form. The NSW railroad union brought the trains in that state to a screeching halt once upon a time in order to press their demands for softer toilet tissue.

My life in Australia could be compared to the filling of a "chill" sandwich - the laid-back, easy-going, "she's right", "no worries" segment of my life crammed between two slices of stress bread: my earlier time in the uptight northeast of the USA, and my following years in frenetic Hong Kong. Neither era prepared me adequately for the next. I was young and out to change the world and demonstrate my brilliance. I ran smack into the prevailing Aussie attitude that personal ambition was a repugnant social ill, to be avoided and/or downplayed as much as possible.

167

Occasionally there are deadlines to be met, even in the Luckiest Continent. I was clearing a shipment of books from Hong Kong through customs. At this point in my life, I had no inkling that I would one day be at the other end of this supply chain, so I guess this was karma in the making. Due to a number of snafus, the paperwork only got to me the day before the final "or else" deadline—meaning my shipment was going to the landfill if I didn't clear it before close of business. The loss would be both tens of thousands of dollars, and irreplaceable. So I was feeling the strain.

Bright and early the next morning—before dawn actually, I showed up at the dock with my rented truck and my pushy Yankee attitude. I found myself at the back of a huge line (or "queue" there) of trucks, some of them quite massive. Given the ambient pace of work, it appeared I would be there until it was time to shave again. In desperation I walked to the front of line and found a customs agent; and pleaded with him that it was really important that I get my lot cleared today. He eloquently shrugged and pointed to the line of trucks ahead of me and walked off.

While I was steaming and brooding in my rented truck, I had an epiphany: when in Rome, do as the Romans. In this instance it was also a case of the Greeks having conquered the Romans. I sauntered back up to the customs office and found a different agent upon whom I would pitch my revised appeal for special preference. In as uncaring, nonchalant and uninterested a mien as I could fabricate, I conspiratorially confided that I was paid for the whole day to clear my shipment through customs and if I got done early I could spend the rest of the day at the beach, at the company's expense. "Good on ya, mate!" was the hearty response, as the sympathetic official promptly directed me to bypass the long line of waiting trucks and come up front for priority clearing. In at the office filing my papers, I noticed a holy picture pinned to the bulletin board. The official must have been one of the rare fervent Catholics in Australia. It was a likeness of Saint Jude, that "patron saint of hopeless causes!" Works for me, apparently!

The Significance of Beer

"Nuts don't fall far from the tree", "Chip off the old block", "Snot out of the same nose" (Danish) — these are all common pithy phrases referring to inherited traits and preferences. For my wife Erica, drinking beer was not one of these inherited tastes. Her mom virtually lived on beer in the dry environs of her outback sheep station at The Rock. That hardy lady—still going strong in her late 80's as I write this—could knock back a six-pack before breakfast and still function just fine. Her daughter hated the taste of beer. As for me, the jury was still out. I did not grow up with beer in our house, so it would have to be an acquired, not inherited, trait. Events on a hot dusty roadside would change things forever one day...

Erica and I were hitchhiking to visit her mom, about 300 miles down the Hume Highway from Sydney. The last ride left us off where the driver turned into his distant, isolated property. Traffic hurtled by, but no one was stopping or slowing down and the hours dragged on as the sun rose high overhead. The temperature soared and our throats became parched. No, we did not think to bring something to drink. This was the young and foolish period of our lives. This was also the 70's, and you could still get away with doing stupid things like this. In the distance I saw a pond, and much like a mirage, it beckoned me. The pond turned out to be for watering cattle, but it was still water—after a fashion—and my throat was screaming for relief. I stood at the edge of the water and pondered which was worse: to die of thirst or from whatever disease might be in that water. Just then one of the wading cows "eliminated" with a loud "plop" and "splash," which settled the matter in my mind. Reluctantly and still thirsty, I turned and walked back to the roadside.

Mercifully, shortly thereafter, a huge truck screeched to a halt and offered us a lift. "You look thirsty!" he surmised. "Grab yourself a cold one out of that esky [aka: ice chest]!" It was at this point when first I realized that not all angels have wings and halos. This one had cold beer. And this is when I learned the significance of beer. Beer can get colder than cold! Water can only get so cold, then it turns to ice which, as you well know, is hard to swallow. Beer can keep getting colder, and, depending on the alcohol content, can be a nice 12% colder than the coldest water—which on a very hot day wonderfully quenches the thirst. It was about 40°C (100°F) and we were desperately in need of some cooling down.

My young bride glared at me. "Do you have any water?" she asked our host. "Water—what's that?" was the trucker's bewildered response. So she glared some more at me, and then sat there thinking in thirsty silence. After one of those "lesser of two evil" inner debates—much as I had hosted during my time at the edge of the cattle pond—Erica was wrestling with her own demons: to die of thirst or drink that dread stuff. Suppressing disgust, she reached into the cooler, and after closing her eyes and scrunching up her face, she took a sip as if it were poison. When she didn't die, she slowly choked down some more. Meanwhile, I was happy as a clam, enjoying my cold beer while secretly relishing Erica's dilemma.

Too Hungary to Eat - no Polish Sausage

By contrast to the ubiquitous-ness of food in capitalist Hong Kong, Poland, in 1990 after the recent fall of the communist Iron Curtain, was a great case in point as to the feebleness of the "planned economy". A group of us travelled by car early one morning from Hungary where food was plentiful and cheap, and headed to Poland. We ignored the advice to bring a snack with us. We travelled all day through the countryside without seeing one solitary place to eat. We did find a place for coffee, which was served with coffee grounds in the bottom of the glass, to which was added hot water and a spoon for stirring. Not your average latte. Nightfall came and we stumbled across a humble little pensione for sleep, but still there was no sign of food anywhere. The proprietor was ecstatic! Here was an Australian, a Norwegian, a Brit and an American all showing up together at his humble abode. He said he felt like he was receiving a UN delegation, and he wanted to feed us! Yeah! This was the first hint of the existence of food we had heard all day.

We sat eagerly around the table and relaxed after our long tiring drive. There was water to drink and some crackers. The main course— which would be just one dish—was being prepared by the proprietor's wife. It was a real delicacy, we were proudly informed. And when it arrived it was a real dilemma. We were very hungry, but apparently not hungry enough. There on the platter was a pound or two of boiled pig's blood, stuffed inside some washed-out intestines: the meal is more commonly known as blutwurst. Known also as "black pudding" or "blood sausage," it is a welcomed delicacy in many places. Just not right there, at that time; perhaps because our stomachs were so empty. We just stared at our plates and each other.

Fortunately, our host left us to dine alone, so we could sort out this quandary without an embarrassing incident. I had a plastic bag in my possession. We all took our knives, cut a piece from our plate's portion and fed it into the bag we passed around under the table. We repeated the process at regular intervals. From time to time, the host would return to see that it appeared we were making good progress with our meal. Actually the plastic bag was getting filled, not our stomachs. Finally our plates were clean. Our host was ecstatic and wanted to know if we needed more. We all vigorously shook our heads in the negative, as our bag was full and could hold no more. We finished our water and crackers and I took our bag of uneaten dinner to our room. It was a broken sleep, punctuated by hunger. Too bad I didn't have my dog Zoey back then; she would have been delighted.

Not High Enough Tea

Now the tables are turned. Hunger was also a problem for some guests we hosted years earlier when I was a new Australian in Sydney's Potts Point suburb. We had rented an old three-story terrace house on Victoria Street. [The locale of one of the ghost stories in the chapter: "Your Call"]. Recently arrived from America, and trying to learn and adapt to all things Australian, I'd quickly surmised that tea was the drink of choice here, not coffee. Things have changed in the past forty years since this event, and happily, great coffee is now everywhere to be found Down Under. But back then, tea was king. Or queen? Being friendly, we invited some new acquaintances around for tea. "What time?" "How about five in the afternoon?" What we immigrants did not grasp was that the combination of tea + five in the afternoon = a meal, not just a "cuppa."

Our guests arrived and we promptly served them our best rendition of tea. We sat and chatted and we all nibbled on the cookies ["biscuits"] we'd set out. When the cookies ran out, we replenished the tray. After about the third round of tea and cookies, the conversation stalled and our guests seemed uncomfortable. Maybe we made the tea too strong? Finally, timidly, one of them spoke up: "Is there anything else?" I imagine it took the same steely resolve as when Oliver Twist demanded. "Please, sir, I want some more!" It was then patiently explained to us that when you invite someone over for tea at five in the afternoon, you intend to feed them properly. So we went out to the sandwich shop around the corner for some meat pies, and all was forgiven.

28. Things My Mother Never COULD Have Warned Me About!

My dear mother never went to Hong Kong, so there was no way that she could have warned me about the following events that happened to me there! So for this chapter, we'll make a stopover back in the now-familiar territory of Hong Kong.

Hong Kong Salute – or: Air Kleenex

Even though afflicted with poor eyesight, Roy Orbison could still spot something good when it came along and so he famously penned: "Pretty woman, walking down the street; Pretty woman, the kind I like to meet." And you will have to excuse me for being old-fashioned enough to agree with Roy that nothing quite brightens up a gray city street like the sight of a beautiful, graceful woman. And few things compliment such a graceful woman better than the long, form-flattering, Oriental dress called a cheongsam. Just such an apparition brightened my commute one morning as I jostled my way across the crowded pedestrian overpass above Connaught Road on my way to the General Post Office. There, amidst the diesel exhaust of passing traffic and the deafening cacophony of never-ending construction and commerce was a vision of beauty coming directly towards me.

Right about halfway along that elevated stretch of sidewalk, she caught my eye, her beauty and grace so seemingly out of place. As I approached, I could not help but smile. When our eyes met, I was ready to greet her "good morning" but she was faster. I was introduced to what I have since dubbed the "Hong Kong salute." In the winter months particularly, there are all types of sounds of the sinus and respiratory nature to be heard all about. Seems everyone is suffering with, catching, or recovering from some bout of nastiness, and demonstratively so. The lady in the scarlet cheongsam was one of these, as I was about to find out. They do sell little pocket-sized packages of Kleenex tissues everywhere in HK, but the "air Kleenex" is still the most popular brand, I believe.

When I was just a pace or two away, she deftly pushed her index finger against her right nostril and then exhaled forcefully, sending the irritating sinus matter bazooka-like out the opposite nostril through the air to the waiting pavement below, narrowly missing my shoes. Fortunately for me, I had slowed to enjoy the view. This process took just a split second and she continued on without missing a step. Well that was truly a liberating moment; the spell was broken. This happened early in my stay in Hong Kong and taught me well never to take anything there for granted.

Head of Cattle - or How Some Folks Turn Vegetarian

"Head of cattle" is a term commonly used on ranches to quantify the size of their herd. A hundred head of cattle would be a modest start-up operation. A thousand head would deem you to be a more serious rancher. Ginormous King Ranch in southern Texas has 35,000 head of cattle. Sounds like a harmless census term. Until you actually see a head of cattle. I did, when stepping out the side door of a Wan Chai restaurant after lunch one summer day in Hong Kong.

Back then, western dishes were rather limited, except at the four and five star hotels. But you could order Spaghetti Bolognese almost anywhere. It made sense, after all: it's mostly noodles, and Chinese cooks do that 24/7. The rest is a meat sauce, and if you wanted it to be called beef, so be it! (Remember Gillogan's butcher from "Busted"?) And although little old Avery Island, Louisiana is 8,000 miles away, you could find Tabasco sauce on every table of every restaurant in Hong Kong. Well, to be more precise, now that I think about it in hindsight: you could find a bottle on every table with a Tabasco sauce label. Enough hot sauce could mask whatever other flavors were unwelcome.

By the way, I am fairly certain that the term "fast food" probably originated in Hong Kong, because nowhere else is food faster! There are millions of willing diners, from school kids to the octogenarians, always shoveling down rice, noodles, chicken claws or something edible at all hours and on virtually every street corner. But there is limited space to sit down, and if you aren't eating, you're leaving! I learned that early on, the hard way: put down your fork, and it's soon gone. Leave you plate unattended for a few seconds, and it's gone! Waiters are lurking about, ready to facilitate your departure so the next diner in line can be seated.

On this particular occasion, I held onto my knife and fork continuously and shoveled the meal in non-stop so as not to be mistaken for someone who was finished and ready to leave. I was on a mono-diet binge for a while and no matter where I dined, I usually got Spaghetti Bolognese, even at the Indonesian restaurant my wife made me take her for our anniversary. She had all that Gado-gado, Nasi goreng, Satay and Sambal stuff. We were both happy as clams.

Stepping out the side door of the Café de Coral after my meal onto Tonnochy Road, there I saw my first head of cattle. It was in a reed wicker basket. It was just the head. There, abandoned on the sidewalk, staring up at me were these two huge languid eyes: peering out of the skull that had been stripped of anything edible. Who knows? That may have been where my Spaghetti Bolognese first originated.

Quail Nail - More Reasons to Become a Vegetarian

Folks in Hong Kong love their food fresh. It's like that with okra in Texas: ask someone if they would like some fresh okra from your garden and they will ask you when—down to the minute—you picked it. The older the lady is, the more demanding she usually is that the okra was picked just minutes ago. Freshness adds premium to the food value, apparently. In the Hong Kong seafood restaurants, there were big tanks filled with all manner of sea creatures and you could window shop for whichever one caught your fancy. Point it out, and for a price, it was yours. Curiously, this is the same city that sells lots of "hundred year old eggs" or "thousand year old eggs" which are not really that old, but they are stockpiled in dark warehouses long enough until the yolks turn green and the whites turn brown. Yummy, eh?

Fresh meat is another story. Fresh quail is today's story. This scene took place on one of the steep, narrow lanes that run basically north-south through Central Hong Kong between the busy thoroughfares like Des Voeux Road and Queens Road. I was exiting the building where I usually went to get my favorite brand of cologne, when curiosity got the better of me. This perfume dealer had won my loyalty years prior when one time I mistakenly asked for "8711." The chap politely apologized that he only had "4711" [the correct brand name] and would that do? A great friendship was born. Outside his doorway, I paused to watch a market transaction in progress. I had a few seconds to kill, so I lingered in the shade and observed.

Both the old ladies – vendor and prospective client – were deep in animated discussion as to the virtues (I imagine that freshness was the key topic) of the various live quail on exhibit in the wicker basket.

174

Finally an agreement of sorts was reached when the buyer pointed definitively to her chosen bird. Eager to complete the sale, the vendor quickly scooped the creature out of the crowd. I should have noticed the very long thumbnail and guessed its portent.

With a quick final nod to confirm the purchase and with a lightning-fast stroke, the vendor slit the live, screeching, struggling quail open at the chest with her sharp nail and then peeled off the skin which had been thus halved a second later, delivering the shivering live pink remainder, minus its feathers, to the buyer who gleefully hustled home to prepare her meal. Another great sales pitch for the joys of vegetarianism!

To the Poultry Market

While staying with the general theme of markets and fresh meat, this story will deal more with transportation issues. I first wrote about this observation years ago when publishing an article on Hong Kong Ingenuity. Fresh out of the west, and more importantly, the highly-unionized continent of Australia where everything is organized to be as effortless as possible, I was amazed at how differently, how simply, how economically and how quickly things could be done when enterprising ingenuity was allowed free rein.

If you had two dozen chickens to transport to market in Sydney you would need: two dozen properly-proportioned baskets, then someone from the poultry handler union to load them, and then a union driver and a union assistant to man the truck for the trip to market. And so on. The same process is accomplished in Hong Kong with only one man, equipped only with a six-foot-long bamboo pole and two pieces of string. Have you got it figured out?

You divide the chickens into two equal groups of a dozen each. As you will see, this is important for balance, and economy of effort. Take one of the pieces of string and tie twelve chicken necks together with a slip knot. Use the other piece of string and tie the second dozen poultry likewise. Tie the other end of each of the strings to opposite ends of the bamboo pole, utilizing the notch cut near the end to hold the string in place. Lift the pole in the middle, thus balancing, like the scales of Justice, an equal weight of fresh chickens suspended in air. The pole goes over the shoulder and with a lilting, hopping pace the load goes bouncing off, fresh to market. At the

175

market there are waiting baskets and the chickens are suspended over them and with a tug on the slip knot, they drop nicely into them. The string is rolled up, placed in the pockets for future use, and the pole is a useful aid for fighting one's way through the crowd.

Why People Install Privacy Fences

The next lesson was learned at our home in the hills above the Tung Hang Mei valley on Lantau Island. You may recall from the "18th August" chapter that we had stumbled upon this wonderful Shangri-La quite by accident. The landlords we rented a small flat from in another area of MuiWo one day asked if we wanted to rent a house with a pool. This was certainly a rarity for Hong Kong so at first I thought they were joking. But Chinese never joke about money. We were told by our landlords that the previous owner, after building and tending to that place, decided to move back to Mainland China.

I guess we had established a good reputation for faithfully parting with the rent cash each month, so that they felt emboldened to upsell us some pricier digs. It was still a good deal by Hong Kong standards, so we quickly agreed, which enamored us in their opinion. When I offered to pay cash each month, and that I did not need a formal receipt, I was immediately conferred the title of being "very wise" indeed. Years later, on my departure from Hong Kong, the English-speaking Chinese lad who was the intermediary for me and the landlord proudly told me they had devised a Chinese sobriquet for me phonetically resembling "Michael" which honorifically meant "wise height". I was honored and flattered. On second thought, perhaps it just meant I was not too tall.

Being the city slickers that we were, it never dawned on us to ask where the water came from for this remote house on the mountainside. We had simply turned on the tap: when water came out, that was the end of our inspection. As it turned out, there was no city-supplied water to the property. And there was no well. A few days after we had settled in, I set out to investigate the mystery source of our delicious-tasting water. A one-inch thick galvanized steel pipe emerged from the back of the attached kitchen house and I followed that pipe up the hill, past some steps, through tall grass and around trees and shrubs until I came to a concrete water tank.

The civil engineering of this house is quite amazing when you think of all the cement that had to be hauled up the one-and-a-half mile pathway (which itself first had to be constructed) without the aid of cement trucks, or any trucks for that matter. It was carried or pushed by human power: hundreds of thousands of pounds of concrete and sand and rebar for the house alone. Then there were paths, and patios, and another building, and steps, and finally this water tank.

This was quite an ingenious, private, naturally organic filtration system. There were actually two adjoining concrete tanks, each about a one meter cube. Their common wall was pierced with a few holes. In the first tank were large stones, in the second sand. Water came into the higher, primary tank at the top, settled through the stones and emerged into the secondary tank, where the water filtered through the awaiting sand and finally emerged from a pipe at the bottom of the second tank and then headed to the house. The tank was fifty feet above the level of the house, so water pressure was adequate. There was a float valve on the intake primary tank to stop the flow of incoming water when the tanks were full.

The next mystery was to find out where the pipe came from before it arrived at the tank. This next investigation would first necessitate some serious path cutting. There were small shrubs dotted along the hillside, but worse were the tall, thick, razor-sharp edged, unyielding grasses that grew head high. Machetes worked, as long as you had heavy gloves for protection from cuts. But it was hard work, slow going, and punctuated by the discovery of various snake species. In the heat and humidity, it was only possible to clear a few feet of the pathway alongside the pipeline each day. To speed things up, Ron got some stout weed-killer from the local hardware shop, which later turned out to be some version of dioxin or left over "Agent Orange" from the Vietnam War era that was dumped on Third World countries. It was cheap and effective, apart from the very painful boils that ensued for several weeks thereafter. So this was another side-lesson learned the hard way, tucked into the midst of this story.

Finally, we reached the source of our water. The galvanized pipe coupled crudely into a short length of larger PVC pipe which was covered with a green vinyl screen. The apparatus sat in a shady shallow rock pool where water collected after emerging from an underground spring a few meters further up the hillside. The flow was gentle, but always constant. After the major hill fire which I write

177

about later in the "Lady Who Planted Trees" chapter, all of the plant growth had been reduced to mere ash, leaving just barren soil and rock. Yet the spring faithfully continued to produce cool delicious water without interruption, regardless of changing seasons, military maneuvers [see "Which Way War"] or earthquakes [see "Snakes and Shakes".]

At the other—delivery—end of the pipeline close to our house was another mystery: a large hole in the ground—forty-five feet long, six feet deep and fifteen feet wide. It was made of stone walls of granite rock about one foot cube in size. Where the rocks came from, and how someone had placed them there without the aid of heavy machinery: those were but two of the unanswered mysteries. The more vexing question was the purpose of the structure. It obviously was to collect water since a spur of the pipe line dumped water into it, and there was a big wooden plug fashioned out of a log at the bottom for a drain. Was it a water reservoir for all the plants and trees on the property? Or had this been a fish pond at one time? In any event, we decided to turn it into a swimming pool.

We were in the middle of nowhere, and with only distant elderly neighbors. Since this was quite a natural pool in natural surroundings, some of our guests naturally took to bathing *au naturel.* This happy routine went on for some time until the hikers arrived. Somehow [this was long before the days of social media] news spread that there were gweilos skinny-dipping on the hillside of the remote Tung Hang Mei valley and a new hiking trail was blazed that ended at the hilltop overlooking our pool.

Some hikers brought binoculars with them to enhance the experience. We didn't pay too much attention, as a few curious teenagers didn't seem to pose much of a threat. Then things escalated. The military got involved. Soon random helicopter flyovers began, and then they became more frequent. Fearing one of the airborne voyeurs would one day fall out of the open helicopter bay and land in our pool, we decided to take defensive measures.

I went to the local hardware shop and bought out their entire supply of bamboo window shades, the kind that roll up when you pull a string. We fashioned a metal framework, and then strung the bamboo vertically and wired it to the frame. This gave us the privacy we needed and it worked well until the first big storm came through and blew our fence to shreds. In our next upgrade, we resorted to hanging the shades horizontally, (as they were meant to be hung). When a storm threatened, we raised the curtains to reduce the wind resistance, much the same way but in reverse of how sails are lowered on a ship to avoid catching too much wind. Soon the hikers found other forms of natural beauty to admire, the helicopters took different routes, and we were once again at peace in our happy little private Shangri-La.

I refer to my Shangri-La often in this book; here is my explanation: There was a 1973 movie called *"Lost Horizon"* where I first encountered the term. But there is a 1933 James Hilton novel which first described the fictional harmonious valley. As in our real-life Tung Hang Mei valley, this mystical Shangri-La is a happy, peaceful, green valley, isolated by mountains from the hectic outside world. The author could well have been describing our very own little cul-de-sac. "Shangri-la" may originate from Tibetan roots for "mountain pass." Indeed, we had to push our carts through a narrow break in the hillsides as the path wound around a blind turn, only then to reveal our beautiful mountain valley homeland.

No Yield Garlic - or Too Much of a Good Thing

We had a kindly landlord for the first apartment we rented when we moved from the crowded concrete jungle of Hong Kong Island to the idyllic countryside of Lantau Island. Mr. Wong lived downstairs. He tried his best to educate us in the ways of rural life, given our communication limitations: neither of us were fluent in English or Cantonese, respectively. One such failure to communicate was when I decided to cultivate some unused wetlands outside the walls of the property. I wanted to grow garlic. We were fanatical garlic eaters at that stage, believing the plant would ward off all manner of sickness and disease—which were themselves quite plentiful.

Mr. Wong tried telling me that it was too wet for garlic to grow there. "Too wet?" I pondered. Having spent the past six years in rain-thirsty Australia, I didn't believe there was such a condition. So I planted my garlic bulbs and waited for the opportunity to prove old Wong wrong. [Ah, the smugness of foreign new arrivals!] There were indeed two Wong's, as the Sergeant's wife lived there with him as well, but I did not think that would make them right, in any case. You knew that was coming.

While we are waiting for my garlic crop to grow, I will relate some tales that happened in the intervening months. Hong Kong is well-policed and while capitalism is allowed to run unrestrained, most other aspects of life in the territory are closely monitored and controlled. There was a total gun control, and not only was it impossible to (legally) obtain a firearm, you could not buy so much as an archery set or even a slingshot. So for the criminally-inclined the weapon of choice was usually a big meat cleaver—since butcher shops were legal. I lost track of how many times the news reported that "four armed men burst into a jewelry store brandishing meat cleavers." As you can imagine, it was very persuasive!

They didn't play baseball in Hong Kong; otherwise they might have used baseball bats for weapons. But no, the lowly meat cleaver was always the weapon of choice. Sometimes, to break the monotony of the report, I would mentally picture the crime scene differently. Maybe "four-armed men" could be a band of criminals with similar birth defects—that is, each possessing 20 fingers. And what about this thing where they were always "bursting" into the gold shop? Where is the originality in journalism like that? How about *sauntering* into the victims' place of business, for a change of pace? Or *waltzing*? Or *moon-walking*? But I digress…

So Hong Kong police were everywhere. So were oversized swarthy elderly Sikh guards sporting huge double-barrel shotguns outside banks and gold shops and other such buildings bulging with wealth,

180

begging to be robbed. I don't know if those shotguns were loaded or were meant to be used as a club, since I never heard of even one occasion where the shotgun was fired. I don't know, maybe meat cleavers trump shotguns, in a perverted variation of the game "rock, paper, and scissors."

Early one morning, while my first cup of coffee was still journeying down my esophagus, I glanced out the second story bedroom window that faced the winding narrow pathway which snaked across the fields from the nearby village only to behold a whole troop of police officers excitedly charging at my building. They flung open the gate and began shouting and hollering in the courtyard below at the top of their voices. As you may have learned from the "Survivor's Guide to Cantonese" chapter, yelling and shouting is not necessarily a matter of concern when used in this dialect. Most people who can, do indeed yell and shout in Cantonese. It is just the way things are done in Cantonese, much the way that the French refuse to pronounce about half of the letters in any given word.

After a moment of anxiety, I realized this was the sound emanating from good natured banter, and not that of a raiding party. And this was when I first learned that mild-mannered landlord Wong was a retired police sergeant—the fellows had come to pay him their respects. The next visit would not be so cordial.

It was a hot, humid night in mid-summer, when I was awoken from a fitful sleep to the sound of explosions and the glare of what seemed to be the noonday sun. Glancing out the window I saw parachutes descending with miniature little suns. [I would later learn that these were magnesium flares, used to light up the darkened surroundings.] Then I heard the sound of many heavy footsteps charging up the stairwell. What else was there to do but open the door in order to see what all that commotion was about? Hordes of heavily-armed and well-equipped paramilitary types jogged by towards the flat rooftop two flights above, politely greeting me but strongly advising me that I stay put.

As was usually the case in Hong Kong back then, the Chinese criminal underworld and the police officers were usually busy chasing each other, and rarely paid much attention to the handful of foreigners in the colony, unless one of those foreigners happened to be one of the British colonial overlords. When the explosions stopped, the flares were extinguished, the troops had retreated and the shouting all died down, we learned that there had been a prison break on the island. The authorities had been tipped off that the escapees were hiding in the hillside behind our up until now peaceful little cul-de-sac.

Now months have passed and it was high time to harvest my garlic crop and prove old Wong wrong. My garlic had flowered and grown to impressive heights. I could not wait to see the gigantic blubs hiding beneath the surface. Mr. Wong sauntered over to watch me. He was retired and I think he found me to be quite a source of free amusement. Up came the first stalk of garlic, sporting an impressive web of roots, but no garlic cloves! My landlord just shook his head bemusedly.

Certain that this first stalk was just an outlier—a bad specimen—I yanked up the next plant, only to find the same lack of yield. One by one the plants were all harvested, but no garlic was to be found. All the while Sergeant Wong looked on silently. I was dumbfounded as well as seriously disappointed. Up to my shins in mud and covered with sweat from the effort in the August heat and humidity, I was undoubtedly quite the picture of defeat. After the harvest—or lack thereof—was finished, Mr. Wong had the last word: all he said was: "See? Too wet!" And he went back inside to fetch himself a cold San Miguel beer.

The Owl and the Pussycat II (or Cat Scratch Fever)

Moving right along with this theme of my being in various degrees of hot water, this next vignette takes place in a high-rise apartment in Tsuen Wan, in Hong Kong's New Territories. At this point, I'm still happily married and now with four young children. I rented an office room high in one of those tall concrete towers. The hillside behind there was where I had my baboon troubles as chronicled in "Primate Bullying!" There was a bowling alley in one of the basement levels which I wrote about in "No Third Turkey!" So this is quite a little epicenter in the literary sense.

Circumstances were such then where I was often working quite late at night and it wasn't always really safe or practical to try to get back home to Lantau Island via ferry. So I found a room for sub-let in a nice, new three bedroom apartment for a very reasonable rate with no deposit or contract. The landlady was very old by my estimation, at least in her early fifties, so I did not expect any trouble from her, not like I had with the lady on the train in Australia. I was not the slightest bit attracted to, or interested in her, and I concluded the converse to be true. Ha! I guess you never outgrow stupidity.

Anyways, "Jackie"—Jacqueline—was a redheaded, divorced, French lady who had lived in Hong Kong most of her adult life. She was very polite, gracious and accommodating. I had free use of the kitchen, living room and guest bathroom. She was gone most of the evenings when I was there, so it was very much like my own place. She had a big, fat, spoiled Siamese cat "Chat" who took a liking to me and followed me around everywhere, purring loudly. In retrospect, perhaps that should have been seen as a harbinger's clue.

It turns out that Jackie worked nights, which is why I never saw her. I also never saw her because I never frequented the topless Kowloon nightclub "Bottoms Up" made world-famous when James Bond frequented there in the 1974 offering "The Man with the Golden Gun"—as so the billboard outside proudly boasted. That is where she worked.

Our paths seldom crossed until one afternoon she invited me to have dinner at her place one evening when she would be off work and cooking some French dish she did well. My own cooking was far from gourmet, and a rather bland routine at that, so I welcomed the opportunity for a nice, free, fancy meal.

The day for our dinner arrived and a lady friend of hers showed up. The meal proceeded deliciously, including a nice white wine. Had I been a bit more observant, I would probably have noticed the knowing furtive glances the two friends were exchanging. When the meal was over, Jackie's guest began humming and then singing— albeit badly—the chorus from Labelle's "Voulez-vous Coucher avec moi ce soir?"

My contented smile faded quickly with the sudden realization that, apparently, women can also wine and dine men with ulterior motives. I only had to hear the first couple syllables to know that my answer was an unequivocal "non!" I hastily made some poor excuse and quickly and clumsily extricated myself from the trap. I think I may have taken refuge in the bowling alley below, if I remember correctly.

Nothing more was ever said between us after that night about the event and life seemingly proceeded as normal. One day my wife was in town and she came over to see the place I had rented and we spent the afternoon together. The next night I was reading in the living room recliner and the usually-friendly "Chat" hopped up on my lap, as was often her custom.

She peered deep into my eyes and then, lightning fast, swung her claw and made a neat gash down my long nose, expertly splitting the skin nicely in two halves. She then hopped off the chair and hastened back to Jackie's room. When I saw my landlady later that evening, my nose still dripping blood despite my best first-responder efforts, I confronted her about her cat's attack and demanded an explanation. With a straight face, she responded without hesitation: "But of course! She is jealous!"

My skin crawled at the thought that a jealous woman could get her cat to vicariously take out her frustration in her absence by some kind of remote mind control. I was no match for this kind of voodoo! The eerie baboon incident had recently happened in the hillside above the apartment and I had had just about all the excitement I needed. I packed up that day and said good bye to Tsuen Wan and its aggressive baboons, stubborn bowling pins, killer cat, and stalker landlady. Maybe my mother was right – maybe I should have been a priest! Ha!

29. Tour de Farce

Here are a few tall, but true, tales of my cycling exploits. You have already read about one such event in "Buffalo Phil and Other Spills" when poor young James was up the creek, literally. Unlike some famous cyclists, I did not need any additional help from banned substances in order to perform the following feats of daring. In this chapter, we will travel from Upstate New York to Boston before looping back to Hong Kong for the finale.

When I was young, (see above) before boys were old enough and wealthy enough to experiment with cars &/or girls, they fiddled around with their bikes: adding baskets or carriers; fitting a 20" wheel on 26" frame; retrofitting butterfly handlebars; clothes pegging baseball cards to the struts so as to rub the spokes and thus sound like a Harley Davidson; adding stuff like bells, lights, generators, cool handgrips and streamers; modifying or entirely removing the brakes; removing fenders and so on. When speedometers became available, a whole new challenging sport was born: extreme downhill sprinting. The analog speedometer dial went from 0 to 60 and was color coded: Green for 0-15mph; Yellow for 15-30mph; Orange for 30-45mph and finally blood-red for 45-60 mph. We dreamt of travelling in that red zone!

Let's put things into perspective: a fast runner tops out at just about 15 mph. On average a horse gallops at 25 mph. A fit racer with a good bike can sustain speeds of 30 mph on a level surface for short bursts. It soon became obvious that we would need the assistance of gravity if we were to break out of the yellow zone and dare to wish for glory in the orange and red zones. We found the perfect spot: Felliton's Hill. On Google maps, this stretch of road is now officially marked Oak Street, and runs between Grove Street (the summit) and Clearview Terrace (base camp). The hill was steep enough that cars needed to be shifted into lower gear before ascending or descending. In the winter time, Felliton's Hill was impassible to cars, but great for toboggan runs.

But this was summer. This was also the dark ages of bicycle safety and, as such, helmets, gloves, knee pads and elbow pads were unheard of–still at the pre-conceived stage. Nevertheless, this same time period nurtured children who went on to design rockets and land on the moon, all without the aid of computers or cell phones. So much for the dangers of concussions... I was equipped for the speed run with a t-shirt (white, with no logos), shorts (short and no pockets) and my Keds sneakers (back then no one called them "tennis shoes" or "running shoes" or "cross-trainers", etc.) Remember, this was <u>Oak</u> Street. The neighborhood gang gathered at the bottom of the hill. At the hilltop, I pedaled with all my might until the pedals were going around faster than my legs could move. It was a perfect launch. Oak trees have <u>branches</u>. I was quickly out of the green zone and passing through the yellow zone. Little oak branches regularly <u>fall</u> off oak trees. I was now in the orange zone and yelling out my speed to the spectators below, the wind pushing the words back down my throat as the speedometer dial tickled the edge of the forbidden red zone. Then it happened: I was airborne.

I had not technically achieved escape velocity, but thanks to a random piece of oak, I went flying over the handlebars when the pesky stick somehow managed to get itself lodged in the rear wheel between the spokes and struts. The bike stopped. There are no seatbelts (or

186

airbags) on bicycles, so momentum took over and I was dislodged from my perch. I landed spread-eagled on the tar-and-stone road surface and slid unceremoniously the rest of the way down Felliton's Hill. I hurt like the blazes, but amazingly nothing was broken. It hurt to move, as the raw skin on my arms and legs was less flexible than the layers that had been peeled away. I looked like a flaying victim or hamburger before it hits the grill.

Awed by my flight, the guys gathered round me and carried me home, hero-style. At times I would start to cry from the pain. Then we would be reminded of the awesome silliness of the event and we would burst out laughing. So I alternated between laughing and crying as I was assisted down Clearview Terrace, until we crossed Teliska Avenue and I was safely delivered to my mother's kitchen. My mom took one look at me and passed out. When she recovered, she was full of cursings and threats about no more bikes!

* * * * *

But my cycling prevailed, and by now I had upgraded to a 10-speed model, which was all the rage back then, about the same time as color TV debuted in the suburbs. We were moving on up! It was still very acceptable and highly politically correct to have bikes on the MIT campus in Cambridge, Massachusetts in the crowded urban Boston metropolis. I had a new racing beauty, an ultra-lightweight white Peugeot with silk tires. There was something else new afoot in big city life: bicycle theft gangs. So I had to get a 3/8"case-hardened steel chain that could resist the bolt-cutters which were the tool of choice of the aforementioned thieves. The irony was, when I rode some place, the chain draped over my shoulders weighed more than the ultra-light bike. But I endured the discomfort, as well as the irony, because I had put out $200 for this bike, at a time when you could buy a brand new Cadillac for about $5,000.

Soon the bike thieves upgraded from bolt cutters to acetylene torches. One hapless bike owner who had chained his prized possession with ½" thick chain to a metal lamp pole awoke the next morning to see his bike was gone: the gang had cut the pole down in order to get at the bicycle. Once news of this brazen theft spread, we all began keeping our bikes in our dorm rooms with us at night. This development further inconvenienced me as my room at MIT was on the fourth floor of East Campus dorm and there were no elevators. So

I got great exercise carrying my 19 pound bike and its companion 21 pound chain up and down all those stairs each day.

East Campus Dorm at MIT has a culture of innovative diversions; in fact there is heavy peer pressure to be creative. When I opened the dorm's website today, I was greeted with the Homepage caveat: "The Weak Shall Be Eaten". The ambient intellectual curiosity has already been well-documented in my Ronald McDonald Happy Cup story. Now that the disgruntled bike owners needed to find ways to vent their pent-up sense of injustice, a new sport was hatched. The hallway was very long, so that when both the connecting doors were propped open, the three sub-sections formed one quite respectable length of runway. We would start at the North end, which was the "Goodale" section, traverse the mid-section named eponymously after its alumni patron, "Bemis" before finally arriving at the "Walcott" third on the south end of the building. The distance was equivalent to a football field in length.

The challenge was to pedal your bike at high speed (while avoiding the walls and emerging residents) down the hallway towards the open door at the end which led to the fire escape. Any one hitting the fire escape at full speed would have hurtled over the railing to the awaiting snow piles thirty feet below. The challenge was to see how late you could wait before applying the hand brakes. Thin tires of lightweight bikes skid very nicely on carpeted flooring, so careful calculation of braking distances was a required component of the preparations.

Last Minute Flash from the Past: Well, just minutes after I finished this section a timely email arrived at my address out of the blue, from none less than the new East Campus Alumni Committee. I had never heard from anyone at East Campus in the past 40 years, until the very day I wrote this chapter! Spooky? Many amazing things have transpired since I started this book project! I still hold firm to the belief that there are no coincidences. Here is their email, and some more background info: "*East Campus Alumni: Last fall, East Campus turned 90 years old, and to celebrate we're rolling the birthday party into the triumphant return of Old East Campus Day, on Saturday, May 2. The original East Campus Day was a festival from 1957 to 1964 featuring music and mayhem; after a 51-year hiatus, we wanted to bring it back. We're still finalizing the exact plans for the day, but there's sure to be lots of food, friends, and story-telling* *galore. Be sure to mark your calendars for the date: if you're interested, please RSVP."*

[See "The Return of the Cyclist - Coming Full Circle" for the story of my visit to my old dorm after my own 43 year hiatus.]

Well, as you can see from the above email, East Campus is still standing, so obviously nothing too catastrophic happened during these late night tests of daring I'm currently relating. Somewhat anti-climatically, the worst thing that happened was the embarrassment of premature cessation suffered when the run resulted in a large adult-size margin of safety between cyclist and open doorway. After several attempts, I managed to get the leading edge of my front wheel across the dark threshold before skidding to a safe stop. Enough of this nonsense, I pondered. This was a Saturday night. I needed to get my rest before Sunday's bike ride out to Logan International Airport.

Why did I want to bike to Logan Airport? I guess simply because, like Mount Everest, it was there. On a street map, the journey from my MIT campus dorm in Cambridge did not seem that long or daunting. What wasn't readily apparent from viewing the map was that most of those nice, big, straight streets were elevated highways that had signs on their entrances reading: "no horses, no bicycles!" So I had to find alternative surface routes: ones which did not have helpful overpasses to avoid dangerous neighborhoods or bridges and tunnels for shortcuts through Boston's inner harbor.

I got as far as the New England Aquarium and could see my goal in the distance across the harbor. The Sumner Tunnel would have had me there in no time, but not on my two-wheeled Peugeot. The Ted Williams tunnel wasn't built yet, but even if it were, I'm sure it too would have said "no bicycles." Backtracking northwestwardly now, instead of taking my intended more easterly course, I pedaled past the Museum of Science, Bunker Hill and the Charleston Navy Yard. It was a veritable tourist's delight, if you were in the mood for such historical detours. Turned back also at the US Highway 1 toll bridge over the Mystic River, I was forced to backtrack through Charlestown, finally crossing the Mystic River upstream over the Alford Street Bridge. I then set a course southeast which took me through Chelsea, a working class industrial town where half the residents had born overseas—Italians and Irish and all sorts of enclaves huddled against each other. Hopefully at the end of Central Avenue there would still

189

be that little bridge that would lead me to the peninsula upon which Logan International Airport sat. But I had to get across all those diverse Chelsea neighborhoods first.

This route was now eight times as long as the one I originally intended. My morning excursion was turning into an all-day outing. By the time I reached the drumlins I was quite spent. As I'm sure you remember them from Earth Science: drumlins are those quirky vestiges from the Ice Ages, hills that pop up seemingly out of nowhere. One such steep hill confronted me and I shifted into lowest gear and strained slowly up the hill. Suddenly an agitated pack of German Shepherd dogs took note of, and exception to, my presence in their neighborhood. My forward progress was little better than a standstill, so outrunning these beasts was not an option. Blind panic came naturally.

Let us pause the action for just a moment in order to humor our history and trivia buffs who may or may not be closely following this adventure. Chelsea wasn't always so. Once upon a time the area of Chelsea was first called Winnisimmet (meaning "good spring nearby") by the Massachusetts tribe which once lived there. There are two theories circulating (in my head) as to why place names were so long back then, centuries ago. One theory holds that the spacebar had not yet been invented on the early typewriters which were in use in pre-colonial days. The second theory derives from a more scholarly study of Native American culture which suggests that the long words were necessary because the tribes had not yet adopted the practice of Talking Sticks which guaranteed the speaker in possession of same from interruption by the others until he/she had finished his/her thought. What theories will they think of next?

What came next was a noisy motorcycle tearing over the top of the hill, its driver dressed all in black leather, heading in my direction. The dogs were even more incensed with this noisy new intruder than they were with me, so they left off chasing me and attacked the motorcycle, knocking it and its rider down to the pavement. No Good Samaritan instincts tempted me: I had no leather clothing for protection against all those canine teeth, so I pedaled for all I was worth over the crest of the hill, never looking back.

Whatever energy the journey to this point had not drained from me, this near brush with death finished removing. I was now running on fumes. But I rode on, not to be denied my quest. I was probably quite dehydrated and somewhat delirious when I reached a gate, squeezed through the opening, and headed down a big wide concrete roadway. Surely this must lead to the airport. But the road seemed abandoned; there were no cars in sight. Sensing opportunity, I steered straight ahead, my wheels between the two solid yellow lines. It seemed like I was all alone in the world.

The distant roar of huge turbines broke the silence and suddenly I was not alone. A posse of police and emergency vehicles converged on me and hustled me away. "What was I doing?" They wanted to know. "Going to Logan Airport" was my weak reply. "Well, you're on the runway!" [I just now looked it up and it was Runway 15 R to be precise.] It was the longest runway, about two miles long. That was fortunate, as it bought us some time until the huge departing jet whizzed by overhead, drowning out all conversation. Once the incredibly close and loud commotion was over, my interrogation continued. Once they discovered I was a just freshman from MIT they just shook their heads and let me go with a warning, but not until they had pointed me in the right direction, away from all their runways.

Many moons passed before this next cycling episode took place in MuiWo, on Lantau Island, in the outermost reaches of rural Hong Kong. Bicycles available for purchase in the village were far from being stylish but they were indeed solid and dependable Communist Chinese factory-issue, well-designed for transporting people and goods over the rough pathways. The available colors ranged through all the shades of black. My bike was black and was a great vehicle for negotiating the narrow winding pathway down from our mountain home in the Tung Hang Mei valley to catch the ferry in a hurry.

It was a good half-hour fast walk to the pier but with the bike I could do it in ten minutes, even less if there was not a traffic jam. A traffic jam in those days was when the huge boars were being transported by pushcart in large metal cages through the narrow market place. There was no "fast lane" or HOV lane—you just had to wait. I was usually in a hurry to catch the ferry into the Central business district. Back then the ferries only ran about once every hour, so if you missed it, there was a long wait with nothing to do and lots less time available for the business once I did get to Central.

I faced various obstacles besides the clock and the boars. Arachnophobia? Not me! The Tung Hang Mei valley cured me of any innate fear of spiders. Snakes also, for that matter, but we covered those creatures in another eponymous chapter. With abundant rainfall most of the year, all things living thrived in our green valley and spiders were no exception. Some grew to have bodies as big as my thumb, and their leg span could be as big as my outstretched hand. My China Store bike was fitted with great brakes, which was a very good thing. One morning, late out the gate, I headed down the path towards the ferry at warp speed.

The sunshine caught something stretched across the pathway and I quickly reacted by applying those industrial-strength brakes. When I skidded to a full stop, my nose was just an inch or two from a most beautiful specimen of an enormous spider who had been busy web-weaving overnight. There was no point in screaming. But from then on, I usually tried to keep something held out in front of me, such as an umbrella, for an ice-breaker, as it were.

The obstacle in question for this particular story, however, was water. We had one of those subtropical downpours which had cleared off in time for my bike race to the ferry. I negotiated the first couple miles without much difficulty and my goal was only 100 meters away: the smoke pouring from the ferry's stack told me the crew was firing up and ready to get underway soon. Like Moses making his Exodus, I was trapped by a deep stretch of water that was in the wrong spot at the wrong time. At the low spot where the pathway dipped, there was about two feet of standing water, spanning about ten feet. But there was no time to wait for a miracle.

Everyone else had pretty much stopped and resigned themselves to waiting for the water to recede. I considered the matter, then backed my bicycle up some, rolled up my pant legs, took off my shoes and hung them over my neck, and made sure my briefcase was wrapped in plenty of plastic. (I always carried extra plastic bags with me to expand the capacity of what I could lug home, if need be.)

My tactic was to get up enough speed so that I could coast through the watery obstacle and emerge on the opposite side on dry ground. This required sufficient momentum, but not too much as to make a huge initial splash which might cause me to stall out. I also needed to keep the bike perfectly straight and upright during my watery passage in order to minimize drag and avoid going overboard.

Everyone gathered to watch the spectacle: imagine the lone Gweilo of the village dressed in his blue safari suit biking through a river. I pulled it off perfectly with just enough forward speed to reach the far "shore" amidst a spontaneous cacophony of myriad, indistinguishable shouts. Probably the crowd was shouting something like "crazy foreign devil!" But never mind, I think I may have gained some secret admirers that day. It sure was fun. And I made that ferry on time after all.

30. Let's Get Physical!

Or: In Theory, all of Physics is Relative.

I started to write this as an additional explanatory paragraph in the chapter "Reality 101" where I described various ploys and schemes MIT students used to relieve the pressure of their studies. Stories of this nature spill over into the chapter titled "Tour de Farce". As I got limbered up on the keyboard, this nascent paragraph gave birth to its own chapter.

There was a pervading pressure on the MIT campus: the pressure to remain successful in a highly competitive and strenuous academic pressure cooker. The Boston Globe reported in their March 17, 2015 issue that MIT is "lightening it up" a bit – the less homework and more museums tours sort of thing – in view of recent student suicides there in Cambridge, Massachusetts. Allegedly, besides being over-achievers scholastically, MIT students lead the nation in this category as well: suicide rates on campus are 10.2 per 100,000 students, compared with only 7.0 per 100,000 nationwide. The administration is encouraging stressed-out students to come out of the closet as it were and talk about their newly-minted condition: the psychological phenomenon called "impostor syndrome," which is defined as "a frequent feeling of being a failure despite a record of accomplishment."

The article begins with the story of Maggie who "never scored below a 90 on a high school exam. But her first semester at MIT, she said, she got a 27 on a physics test and finished the class with a D." I can relate: I had a 100 average in physics in Columbia High School and got a 40 on my first 8.01 (Freshmen Physics) test. I remember sitting in the stately grassy courtyard of the old main building on an otherwise-beautiful autumn day, staring at this grade. I had never seen grades lower than a 90 before, and this number just did not compute. This failure became an existential concern because freshman Physics was like the letter "a" in kindergarten: You had to master it in order to progress further in your education, regardless of which degree program you were planning to pursue.

How could I tell my parents? Whenever I got a 99% on an exam in high school—even if everyone else in my class failed—my dad's first reaction was always: "what did you get wrong?" I decided it was safe to assume that he would not appreciate the news of the 40%. Instead

I spent the rest of the afternoon throwing a Frisbee around the oak-lined lawn facing the Charles River Basin. We had been told by the lecturer to "forget everything you learned in High School Physics" since it did not apply in the "real world": apparently there were too many constants and not enough unknowns in the physics problems in high school courses. This was Student Dis-Orientation at its best!

Actually, it got even better (or worse): Totally befuddled by first-year physics, I asked a 5th-year Physics major what on earth the final exam could possibly be like! He replied simply that it was just a one-question exam: "propose a theory of the atom and defend it." "What if you got the wrong theory?" I protested fearfully. "No problem—as long as you defend it adequately!" was his glib and unconcerned response. This Physics stuff was beginning to sound like one big well-orchestrated confidence scheme to me.

My freshman class of about 1000 "tools"—as we were called—struggled away valiantly, albeit some more than others. This was the seventies, the decade when the revolutions and freedoms of the sixties became more main-stream and, as such, some of the bolder types came to the physics lectures with their hash pipes alit. The rest of us benefited from the second-hand smoke. The lecture was held in a huge auditorium, much like a movie theatre, and there were many side shows going on in the audience. Those destined for greatness sat conspicuously in the front rows and asked carefully prepared and pre-scripted challenging questions so as to highlight their vast potential. I believe you may know them as "brown-nosers." The rest of us inconspicuously napped in the back rows.

After the main lecture, we had tutors who taught smaller groups of about 80. Mine was Professor Tzisa, a Russian import who knew his stuff in Physics, but never much bothered to learn conversational English. He would utter incomprehensible things like: "Bemynooseacousindater" [Translated: B – A cosine Theta.] That tutorial might have been helpful if they provided subtitles, but alas, I had to resort to availing myself of the humiliatingly lowest level of instruction: The Graduate Assistant. My GA (or TA) was a very pimply Orthodox fellow who had a very thick Bronx accent and the very annoying habit of vigorously rubbing his pockmarked and oversized nose while deep in thought. I didn't understand him either. Things were going from bad to worse for me. Fortunately my dorm neighbor "Scooter" had the solution.

Scooter played the clarinet when he was stressed out—he was the nonviolent, unadventurous one on East Campus Fourth East dorm floor—nowadays aka "Slugfest". He loved Mathematics and Bela Bartok but hated Physics. He had found the way out of the nightmare called 8.01 (mainstream Freshman Physics): it was called 8.021, or affectionately nicknamed "Physics for Poets." It couldn't be called "Physics for Slow Learners" as there were no such animals at MIT. This was the kinder, gentler version of Physics for those of the more thoughtful, philosophical persuasion. This physics-lite course still met the core basic requirement, but without the apoplexy. But it was still difficult enough to require a real struggle with the textbook each evening in order to keep up the high grades to which we were accustomed.

After sweating out the semester we were THEN told, after-the-fact by the grinning sophomores, that all the freshman classes that year were Pass-Fail—a new experiment by the administration to relieve the pressure—at least for the first year—of maintaining a high GPA suitable for future employment. This plan could have worked well, had we known about it—a harmless oversight it seems. But it was just as well because everyone <u>failed</u> the final exam.

The exam was written by none other than the esteemed lecturer Anthony Phillip French, PhD, a Cambridge (UK) graduate who worked on the British version of the atomic bomb in his formative years, later transferring to the Manhattan Project at Los Alamos. We all had to purchase his *"Principles of Modern Physics"* textbook. He was, indeed, quite the brilliant chap and a great entertainer with famous tour-de-force performances. His energy level, focus and enthusiasm were impressive. Sometimes at the conclusion of his hour-long non-stop presentation, he would receive a standing ovation by those sober enough to pay him the tribute.

He would spend the entire lecture hour working out a single Physics problem on the front blackboard – this was before the days of white boards, etc. The chalkboard ran the full 50-foot width of the stage and he would start at the left-most edge and scribble away while talking non-stop until he reached the other side. Then he rotated a rail that ran along the bottom of the display which raised the entire blackboard, revealing another beneath it. When this second board was likewise filled with equations and notations, he would proceed without let-up, armed with an eraser in one hand which cleared the path for his chalk-wielding other hand. In a good day, Dr. French could fill six entire boards full of the various steps necessary to solve the particular vexing problem of the day. Almost...

I say "almost" because I found Dr. French had the most discourteous and annoying habit of stopping just short of actually solving the problem to the point of an actual numerical value. He would dismissively state: "The rest is just Mathematics!" Scooter, my mathematician friend took particular exception to his beloved field being referred to as something akin to child's play or, worse yet, table scraps. This habit of not quite finishing the problem came back to bite Professor French that year, and we were the collateral damage. As I mentioned above, the entire freshman class filled with brilliant valedictorians and salutatorians from all over the country and all over the globe (MIT had a student body that was 25% Asian-born, way back in those days before anyone had ever said the term "globalization!") failed the final exam.

Worried tutors and anxious graduate assistants who had all been in Dr. French's teaching coalition for the semester huddled over the exam themselves. They all failed it as well! On closer examination it appeared that since a critical portion of Dr. French's prevailing modus operandi was his finishing conclusion that "the rest is just mathematics," the good doctor had not actually worked out answers to the final exam problems. Had he done so, he would have discovered that there were actually no possible answers to the exam questions the way they were constructed. There was, however, a simple solution to the problem of the exam problem: Everyone was graciously granted an "A" on the final exam to ensure everyone passed this most required of all courses.

Here's something that might interest you longevity fans: Dr. French began teaching at MIT the year before President John Kennedy was assassinated. He has gained a long list of well-deserved top international awards in the Physics Universe and has written a shelf-full of text books. Amazingly enough, as I write this chapter today, he is still there at MIT, lecturing away at the ripe old age of 94. To be honest, any lack of learning in that class would have been my fault and it was indeed a great privilege to have such a gifted instructor. I was just too young to realize that.

In the 70's when I took Dr. French's class, someone higher up wisely decided that the MIT engineers and physicists should have a "balanced education" and thus threw into the degree plan a sprinkling of a couple such courses as "Music Appreciation" or "Introduction to Art". These Humanities courses were not meant to be overly challenging so as to threaten all the near-perfect GPA's that were being earned in the hard sciences. None of us nerds took these humanities courses very seriously but rather thought of them much as you would a tetanus shot: something to endure to prevent you from getting a full-blown case of the disease. These Greeks—the art and music instructors—their hubris in full bloom, took exception to their courses being considered "an easy A" and set about to teach the Romans a lesson in humility. At least they tried.

I can still see the horrified look on our Music professor's face the day after our final grades were posted. He was bit of a peacock, his styled red hair and beard complimenting his distinguished training at the Julliard School of Music. I actually enjoyed the class. I can still remember, after all these years, that according to our instructor, the three key components of music composition were: cadence, sequence and pedal point. But I may be wrong about that. I do remember listening repeatedly to Beethoven's Violin Concerto in D major looking for those three necessary creatures. The class was not too challenging, and it was lots of fun spending time under the headphones. "Easy A!" was probably what was going through our minds. I don't know what was going through the instructor's mind when he gave us all a "C" for the course.

I marched down straightway to his office to try to set him straight. I was not alone. There assembled in his office was our entire "Music Appreciation" class, letting him know we did not appreciate his grade policy. Bravely the prof tried to hold his ground, arguing: "I don't understand all the fuss! At Julliard, a "C" is considered a good grade!" To a man, we all retorted in chorus that a "C" at MIT was only for an idiot, or those destined to be added to the suicide statistics. "Do you realize how hard it is to get an "A" in Calculus 4 or Computer Language, only to have a "C" in a fluff course?!" we remonstrated. He had no choice but to relent and change all our grades to an "A". So much for appreciating music!

Next year, my "Introduction to Art" instructor appreciated my efforts even less. She gave us our first major assignment, which to my engineering mind was very straightforward: Take a substance, and apply a process upon it. Prior to this, we had a warm up assignment: we had to master the use of a crow quill pen by filling a page with symmetrical, but not straight lines – in other words, in the language of mathematicians, curvy parallel lines. I began and soon had something that looked like Charlie Brown's perennial letter to his pen pal. Soon enough I mastered the non-blotching technique and filled one entire corner with wavy lines; I believe I visualized fried bacon for the pattern. After an hour of painstaking effort, I was only about 15% done. Adapting Professor French's dismissal line "the rest is mathematics", I observed that "the rest is just repetition" and wrote "etcetera" in the blank space remaining. You are correct to conclude I did not get an "A" for my efforts.

In retrospect, I believe I had a blind spot—a subconscious hatred of perceived meaningless repetition which dated from my childhood. At St. Joseph's grade school, there was an unreasonable chap named Father F. In the cafeteria, we said Catholic grace before and after the meal. There were eight grades with about 50 kids to a class room [poor nuns!] making about 400 of us lively students in this confined space. Father F. unreasonably expected instant silence when he called for prayer. Most of us could not even hear him over the din; we were not necessarily being disobedient. The parish priest felt otherwise and if there was not deadly silence the moment after his wooden pointer struck the table, he would utter the dreaded words: "500 Times!" Fortunately, this did not mean the number of strokes he would administer with his yard-long stick.

But his sentence doomed all 400 of us parochial prisoners to spend the entire evening at home after school to write out on lined paper the sentence "I will not talk in the cafeteria." Five hundred times! This is when my handwriting began its turn toward the illegible. Mark was clever and tried using carbon paper. [Ask your grandparents what that is!] But he was not clever enough to fool the priest who made the punishment fit the crime: Mark had to write out 5,000 times "I will not use carbon paper to write 'I will not talk in the cafeteria.'" It was a long time before we saw Mark again. I heard that some years later, Father F. was reassigned to basket-weaving or some other duties that did not involve interaction with children.

So this is my excuse for why I could not draw 500 lines across that piece of art paper – suppressed trauma is the official excuse, I believe.

Speaking of the term "believe"—I guess it must have happened during the intervening two decades while I was out of the country: When I left the USA in the early 70's to begin my world travels, most reasonable people would say "I think so" when giving their opinion or educated best guess on a subject. When I set foot again on US soil in the early 90's, everyone was now using the phrase "I believe so" instead. It's amazing how in just twenty short years personal opinion evolved to religious conviction.

Anyways, back to my big art assignment. I thought about it long and hard until I came up with something as effortless and as much fun as possible. I took a handful of the plastic cups we used on party nights and glued them to a board. I then took a cigarette lighter and applied heat—in varying degrees—in order to create various levels of deformities.

Two things happened: first, my dorm room filled with the toxic black smoke thus given off, driving me out into the hallway gasping for fresh air; and secondly, the instructor gave me an "F" as she apparently did not appreciate my efforts. I likewise did not appreciate her grade and I promptly dropped her class and took Nutrition 101 instead. You could say that I was fed up with the Humanities experiment. I then applied to Monash University in Melbourne, Australia. I planned to follow Liz, a graduate student who had captured my heart. Monash accepted me, but an intriguing detour presented itself.

Shortly thereafter, I left MIT to begin the four decades of worldwide adventures, which I have written about in this book. As I was going out the door, a 23-year old Israeli architecture student was entering. His name was Benjamin Netanyahu...

31. The Return of the Cyclist—Coming Full Circle

Javan and I visit MIT East Campus on May 12, 2015

The chapter "Let's Get Physical" ended with my departure from MIT and the beginning of my worldwide wanderings. Forty-some years, thirty countries and two generations later, one sunny weekend in early May 2015, I visited East Campus dorm on the MIT campus with my grandson Javan for the East Campus Day event mentioned in "Tour de Farce". At the end of the "Let's Get Physical" chapter I also chronicled the arrival of the then-young architecture undergraduate Benjamin Netanyahu. Recently, Israeli President Bibi Netanyahu addressed the joint houses of Congress and in the wake of his visit, two months later, I returned to MIT for the first time in 43 years. I believe that in the craft of storytelling, this is what they refer to as "book ends." My personal story now comes full circle.

The impetus for this visit was my receiving an unexpected email from Mr. Danny Ben-David of East Campus Alumni—my old dorm, on the very same day I finished the chapter about said dorm. The "coincidence" was too outstanding to ignore, so I booked a flight for myself and Javan, my oldest grandkid, who was college shopping. As you may recall, Javan is the son of my oldest daughter, Suzy. She sadly passed away at the end of the 2014, after collaborating closely with me in the initial crafting of this book.

Many things in Cambridge, Massachusetts had changed; some remained unaltered. In my student days, the blocks directly north and east of the East Campus dorms had been run-down industrial monstrosities, such as the noisy NECCO candy factory which provided the under-inspiring view out my north corner window. As in the early days of the USA, "Go West" was the prevailing developmental direction back in the 70's; however, today to the east of campus there is a vibrant new development of business and residential areas where investment and research have interacted in a delightful synergy.

There, next to the old three-story brick building where I reported to work at Heritage Travel [see: "Things Learned the Hard Way".] across Main Street, is the beautiful Marriot Cambridge tower where we stayed, just two blocks from the East Campus dorms. From the entrance of the hotel I could see the modernized entrance to the Kendall Subway station, the scene of my tunnel horror story some forty years prior, which I related in "Reality 101". Students were getting lunch at Chipotle's alongside us, whereas back in those less affluent days when I was at MIT, we ate cafeteria leftovers. [We were the pre-Ramen Noodle generation, if you can imagine such antiquity!] For a great history of MIT's joint involvement in the City of Cambridge's development see:

http://www.technologyreview.com/article/422108/the-evolution-of-cambridge/.

Javan and I conducted ourselves along the self-guided walking tour of MIT and spending hours looking into every nook and cranny. Javan was quite awestruck to see the height of the Great Dome, especially knowing that his grandfather had once stood on top of it years before when he was his age. Meanwhile I'm muttering to myself: "How did I ever do something so stupid?!"

We walked the 1/6th mile-long "Infinite Corridor" of the main old building and up and down the five levels of stairs, peeking into labs wherever we could. Javan was fascinated by the ship replicas in the Nautical Engineering wing. We even found the beautiful engineering library that occupies the rotunda under that Great Dome I had once climbed, but had never before seen from the inside.

What was most noteworthy to me was: "What are all these kids doing here?!" How could they possibly be researching new cures for cancer and developing new artificial intelligence models at their tender years? Seeing the MIT students running around with their torn jeans, hanging from ropes in tall trees and shouting a variety of happy silliness, I was suddenly painfully self-aware of my "maturity," as it were. Javan, meanwhile, was in hog heaven. He especially appreciated all the pretty co-eds passing by, which was very different from my time at MIT when it was an almost all-male campus, with its male-to-female ratio then at the long odds of 18 - 1.

After touring around we came back to East Campus dorm for the celebration. I looked around the mass of revelers, looking for heads with tell-tale signs of gray—or no—hair for those alumni that might be more my contemporaries. "Look at that old geezer!" I was able to find two who were older than I, and a couple just a tad younger than I who gave me the "who's that old geezer?" treatment. To everyone else, I guess we were like dinosaurs on exhibit, to be respectfully studied, but not prodded. I was greeted by young Danny Ben-David, who had emailed me the auspicious invitation to attend.

Amidst all the attendees was one fellow who had been an EE (electrical engineering) major who was from my old dorm hall, fourth floor, east wing and from my class year of 1974. Dean recognized me right off and exclaimed "you went to New Zealand!" He was correct on that count, as Auckland was indeed the first stop in my worldwide wanderings after I departed MIT.

As is typical with the passage of time and accumulation of experiences, some things from our youth look smaller now than they impressed us as being back then. The MIT McDermott courtyard— where students still fling Frisbees as we had done when they were first invented—was still impressive, but not so intimidating, after having seen the Australian outback and Schönbrunn Palace gardens in Vienna.

My old dorm room seemed smaller, albeit just as eclectically decorated as it was back in the 70's, when I had it painted black, with a waterbed in the corner. The lounges now were piled with high-tech equipment that didn't exist in the days when we sat around tables playing cards for diversion. The hallways that were dull gray apart from the scuff marks of our bike tires and Frisbees were now all festooned with unique student-crafted murals of all styles and themes and media.

As some alumni in their thirties spoofed about the "old days" when they used floppy disks for their computers, I bit my tongue rather than try to explain what it was like to use stacks of punch cards back in the dark ages before such high-tech storage devices were available for mere mortals.

In 1849, the French journalist/novelist Jean-Baptiste Alphonse Karr penned "The more things change, the more they stay the same." He wrote that epigram in French a century and a half ago, but it still seems to apply, even in English. What had changed in Boston/Cambridge were the dogs—nice polite canines were in the subways and even at Symphony Hall the night we attended. What has not changed is the problem I have with dogs.

Well, it is not a problem so much, unless you consider "too much of a good thing" to be problematic. I have a certain charisma apparently: small children and dogs seem to take an instant liking to me. When we go for a walk, Annette will sometimes have to order me: "don't even LOOK in that direction!" for she knows if I make eye contact with a dog, it is sure to follow me home. An early chapter in this book featured my adopted dog "Happy Ending"; this chapter, of my visit to MIT, comes full circle with the story of Nemo.

Javan and I were having the time of our lives exploring and travelling on Boston's MBTA subway system. Javan grew up in Dallas, Texas where the closest thing to public transport is the carpool lane on the vast network of freeways, so this was quite a new experience for him. On one journey on the Red Line, we found two seats available next to a young woman who had the most adorable fellow perched on her lap.

Not knowing much about dog breeds and thus lacking the knowledge of his proper classification, I thought to myself that this particular creature somewhat resembled an Ewok. Nemo—as we would soon discover his name—was obviously quite accustomed to subway travel. No matter how abruptly the train accelerated, braked or swerved from side to side, this cute beige dog remained perfectly still atop his master's lap, his eyes dispassionately fixed directly ahead with the ennui of a seasoned commuter.

I passed the time by asking the young lady about her dog: how long she had him (since a pup); what breed he was (French Bulldog) and so on. I commented to the girl on how sweet he was. At that moment Nemo turned his head and looked up into her face through those two deep brown languid eyes, and then slid silently and effortlessly onto my lap as if we were old friends. If my wife had been sitting next to me, instead of Javan, I probably would have heard "That's so typical of you!" (Or something to that effect). I petted and scratched my new acquaintance until it was my stop, saying goodbye and making my apologies to Nemo that he would have to go back to his master now. Then I noticed the lady across the aisle had been grinning broadly as this whole scene had unfolded.

As we were checking out of our hotel for the flight back to Texas, the attentive concierge remarked that her own father had been an MIT graduate himself and now her daughter was finishing up her own studies at her grandfather's alma mater. She wished me luck with the publishing of my memoirs. As we bid goodbye, I thought of how life keeps cycling around: once I was an 18 year-old standing on the very spot where I was now with my own 18 year-old grandson in tow.

32. The Lady Who Planted Trees

No, this is not the well-known and truly inspiring 1953 French allegorical tale by Jean Giono about Elzéard Bouffier. Monsieur Bouffier never actually planted a single tree, as he was Giono's fictional character: a lone shepherd who singlehandedly conducted a successful forty-year campaign to reforest a desolate valley in the foothills of the Alps during the early 1900's. Giono's beloved tale has lived on to inspire many real-life people worldwide with the vision to plant trees.

The story I will now tell, while perhaps less well-known at present, is no less inspiring; and this story—as with all the other tales in my book—is entirely true. This is the story of Jenny Quinton: the lady who planted trees. Bouffier was said to have turned his fictitious valley into a Garden of Eden through his reforestation efforts. Jenny's valley is real; she has named its brain center "Ark Eden" and over the years this brave, determined and resourceful single mom has transformed the Tung Hang Mei valley into a paradise restored, one transplanted tree at a time.

With this chapter, we are completing the circle from where this book project first began: with my chance meeting with Jenny Quinton of Ark Eden via the internet. In these next two chapters, I will describe the friendship and collaboration which blossomed through our ensuing communications. The story culminates in the last chapter when Jenny and I actually meet one year later at Ark Eden, in that special spot which my first family and I had once called home for several happy years. After a thirty year absence, my oldest son James and I took Suzy's son Javan, my oldest grandchild, to visit that beautiful acre in the Tung Hang Mei valley. Suzy will be travelling with us in spirit and I will tell you more about that later...

I did not know this amazing story about this amazing woman when we first began exchanging emails. However, for some reason, it wasn't long before we began talking about trees. I told Jenny about how much we loved that place where she has now made her home / living permaculture classroom. Years prior, my little family, fresh from the high-rise apartment living in the concrete jungles of Hong Kong Island, thought we had landed in a heavenly Garden of Eden!

Our heavenly Eden hunch was strengthened by the "12 manner of trees that each bore fruit in their own time"—as in the Revelations chapter 22 description of heaven—as indeed there were twelve different fruits trees, each with an individual month of harvest: peach, lemon, mandarin, lime, orange, guava, lychee, longan, star fruit, kumquat, mango, and banana. All this on one acre, planted long before our arrival and by someone we never met. That will have to be another tree-planting story for another day. Jenny had no way of knowing all this when she dubbed her new home Ark Eden.

There was also one very special tree, a magnificent "Flame of the Forest" which towered over our front yard and spread its beautiful graceful boughs over the entire house and front yard like a living nurturing umbrella. I often sat under its welcoming shade during the hot tropical summers, editing manuscripts, all the while marveling at the spectacular huge crimson blooms which festooned the tree's massive crown.

One sad September day a typhoon blew violently through our valley all night long. The next morning we awoke to a botanical winter—all of the trees, (that had not been outright destroyed and uprooted) were totally denuded of their leaves. Stark black branches were all that remained of what had been lush greenery just the day before. My little boy Andy [hero of "Which Way War"] looked out the window and burst into tears. The mighty ancient tree survived, but it was damaged and never quite regained its full glory.

I found a YouTube interview that Jenny had done, explaining her Ark Eden project. As it was filmed on the old property where we had once lived, I anxiously pored over every frame to catch the occasional glimpse of our former home: the double metal front door, the steep metal stairway to the flat roof top patio, the walkways around the house and down to the front gate, the steps to the hillside pool, the view of the valley vegetable plots and the trees. What was missing was that big Flame of the Forest tree in the front yard. Now, instead, there was a metal awning for shade, and what looked like a baby version of the parent tree. So I innocently inquired: "There was a lovely big Flamboyant tree (Flame of the Forest) in the front yard, under the shade of which I sat in my hammock for many peaceful hours editing manuscripts for various publishers. Is that tree still surviving?" Jenny's reply was truly amazing:

"I have a huge story about that tree! It is no longer there as it fell down one May 31st. I am not sure exactly what year it was, but it happened when the children were less than five years old, so probably 1993 or 1994. I had a musical box that started acting up strangely. It kept playing by itself, a stuck version of 'Love Story'. It was waking up me in the night and then on that fateful day it kept playing over and over and over. The children were outside sitting on that stone table in the front yard under that big tree while I was inside making their breakfast.

"The music box kept playing the beginning notes to the Love Story tune and then annoyingly kept stopping and starting over again— "la- la-la-la la." Well I got really cross with that blasted music box and snapped it shut and threw it in the rubbish bin. While doing that I noticed it had suddenly begun raining so I pulled my two small children inside. Angus, my youngest, ran back out again and Adele, my oldest, retrieved him. Moments after they were safely inside there was the huge tearing sound of the entire giant tree coming down. It fell right where they had been sitting! I shook for 3 days non-stop after that.

"At that particular stage in my life I was actually trying desperately to stay in Hong Kong after the breakup of my relationship with my children's father. I was so poor and everyone was telling me to 'come home' to England but I refused. So when that tree incident happened, coupled with the very weird circumstances surrounding the event, it made me examine my life and my decisions with a fine-tooth comb and forced me to ask myself many tough questions. Then I picked up that discarded music box (that never played again after that day) out of the rubbish bin and I made up my mind to stay! And a new tree grew out of the root of former big tree and it is blossoming today."

What made this special, beautiful, tree-filled, mountainside garden house that Jenny and I describe even that much more special was the surrounding nearly-barren countryside. Hong Kong's many islands are volcanic in origin and their peaks descend steeply to the coastline. The story goes that, centuries ago, a Chinese emperor had the trees of Lantau Island cut down to provide fuel for his pottery furnaces. Abundant rains allowed lush small vegetation to grow on the sparse soil, but not full trees.

Late autumn each year brought strong winds from the north with the most unfortunate of timing: the grave-sweeping festivals. Sparks from the candles and incense lit at the ancestors' graves on the mountain tops invariably ignited the tinder-dry grasses and entire hillsides erupted in flames within minutes. At night you could view the dramatic bright orange rings of fires circling many of Hong Kong's mountain slopes as they burned uncontrolled all night. At the time, these destructive hill fires seemed to be a yearly, unstoppable ritual; but that was before the hill fires met Jenny.

As it turns out, Jenny and I also unknowingly shared a fire-fighting legacy in that special Tung Hang Mei valley. Following is our unscripted e-mail exchange on the subject, just a couple days after we first made contact through the internet. I wrote Jenny the following: Dear Jenny, I read in your bio on the Ark Eden website that your interest in ecological and environmental issues on Lantau Island stemmed from an incident where one of those horrible hill fires swept down in the late autumn and nearly destroyed your place.

We had a similar situation in the mid 1980's when my wife and children barely escaped in time that night to run down the hill to stay with neighbors whose house was more safely surrounded by wet fields. Like that impressive scene from the old movie "Zulu", out of nowhere this huge seemingly endless wall of flames appeared at the crest of the distant mountain range to the north. At first the danger seemed far away, but driven by fierce 50 mph winds, the flames swept down that hillside with surrealistic speed, so much faster than we had imagined possible!

* * * * * * *

After completing this chapter, my number one daughter Suzy insisted we insert some much-needed comic relief here, which I had overlooked in my haste to portray myself heroically. This hillside was indeed home to many a drama, including the bombings as described in the chapter "Which Way War?" I was reminded that I was joined in the fire fight that day by a helicopter which dipped a huge bucket into the waters of Silver Mine Bay and dropped it on hot spots. Apparently, I was considered such a hot spot, or else the sight of a gweilo frantically beating out flames proved too irresistible a target for the airborne crew, but either way, a full load of hundreds of gallons of very cold "water" hit me head-on as it were. The force knocked me flat to the ground and disoriented me for a moment.

Normally, during the warm-to-hot majority of the Hong Kong year, a surprise dousing of cold water would be welcome relief under most circumstances, but this was during one the coldest months of the year, and on one of its coldest days, with a strong 50 mph cold wind blowing from Mongolia. I chilled instantly despite my fiery surroundings! At least I was temporarily fireproof and the hyperthermia of the previous moments abated somewhat as hypothermia set in. Bear in mind that at this point in history, sewer treatment meant dumping everything directly into the nearest body of water, so the load dumped on me was not only very cold, but it was very lumpy and very smelly. I must have looked quite the sight.

[This reference to the sewer treatment arrangement of that day reminds me of an odd phenomenon we experienced in our years of high-rise living whenever a typhoon was in town. The housing towers of Mid-Levels that clung to the steep hillside had gravity on their side when it came time to dispense with all that waste water: huge pipes hurried their loads down to the sea and the awaiting floating sampans and junks.

When the hurricane-force winds whipped up big waves in the harbor, the confined shoreline—due to all that land "reclamation"—the effect was bathtub-like. The waves slapped against the shore pilings, sea water being forced back up into the sewer discharge pipes. The result was that our bathroom had the sound of a steam-piston engine and the water level in the toilet exploded up and down to the rhythm of the waves far below. Perhaps the civil engineers have found a way to dampen that effect by now.]

* * * * * *

Back to my narration of the hill fire: Like the proverbial captain on the sinking ship, I stayed behind a little longer in an effort to prepare the property as best I could. I moved the LP gas tanks away from the kitchen to the middle of the large concrete front patio. I was very glad that the kids and I had faithfully chopped away with our hoes for weeks on end to clear a fire break in the thick tall grasses surrounding the property.

Preparing for a possible emergency and experiencing an actual one are two entirely different sets of emotions, however! I went to the water source—that little mountain spring up the hill that fed our water tanks—and cleared brush as best I could away from the intake pipe. Suddenly, the flames arrived on that nearby low hill, startling me. I turned quickly (too quickly) in an effort to make my escape only to hear a disturbing "snap" of my ankle as my left foot caught between two rocks. I was stuck!

In life-threatening moments like this, everything seems to stop, or perhaps more accurately, proceed silently in slow motion. Suddenly all life's petty cares, desires, and concerns seem just that: petty. Your life is distilled to its most existential basics: that which is required of you in order to prevent this being your last moment on earth. Neither panic nor dumb resignation to fate will satisfactorily respond to this challenge.

Somehow a combination of the angels, good karma and an adrenaline-induced boost of clear thinking got me out of that predicament, and I finally hobbled to safety. The flames roared and popped all night long. The next morning, when all the flames were out, I cautiously crept back up the path between the smoking bushes on both sides: half hopeful, half sick with fear with what I imagined would be a sight of devastation. The entire hillside of the valley was blackened and all that tall grass had been reduced to just ash!

Suddenly I could make out what appeared to be an acre of green in the midst of all that black—it was our home! Our firebreaks had done the trick. Not one blade of grass on that acre had burned. The water source was not damaged, and even the hoe that I hastily threw down in my escape was left untouched by the flames. We happily moved back in later that day. Jenny replied: *"Dear Mike: Oh my goodness! We are so blessed to be sharing the same intention to care so much for this incredible treasure of a valley and a home. Your fire stories are the same as mine..."*

Here is Jenny's own incredible hill fire story and a review of the progress made to date to prevent this tragedy from recurring. As you will see, Jenny first acknowledged this real pain in her life and then successfully and proactively confronted it. This open letter was penned by her in April 2014 as way of a "thank you" to volunteer tree-planters:

"To date, with help from over 28 organised groups and around 52 schools and universities, Ark Eden has planted over 18,000 native trees of 81 different species on degraded Lantau hillsides in the last seven years. This year we plan to plant 3,500 – 5,000 more native trees, and increase our total number of species to 95. AFCD (Agriculture, Fisheries and Conservation Department) visited our sites this week and congratulated us on our success - particularly on a survival rate of over 90% of trees planted. We would like to extend our thanks to all of our great tree-planting and tree-maintenance partners for this.

"Planting trees has helped greatly to abate the extensive soil erosion that pervaded the valley before, clogging up all the streams and rivers and culminating in the destructive "stream channelization scheme" in 1996 - which I fought and lost. Our tree planting project has also brought biodiversity back to the Tung Hang Mei valley. Now we see so many species of birds, insects, deer, owls, bats and more in our valley. I have someone working in my team who is a bird specialist and he is deeply impressed by the many species of birds he finds here (mostly eating our vegetables!)

"I sometimes tell the story to groups that come here about my first encounter with the hill fires: How when I stepped out onto my veranda – around 22 years ago - and saw five fires coming from different directions - and one racing down the mountain behind my house - how I put one of my babies in a front sling and one on the back and gathered all the brooms I could, raced up the hill, placed my children on rocks, and fought the fires until the helicopters came with their water buckets. That was the first of four times that I stopped my house from burning down. While clearing my room a few days ago, I found an old photo of what the hillside looked like for the first eight or so years I lived here before I began planting

trees. I have attached another photo - still a bit old - but now you cannot even see my house for the trees.[This explains why I could not view my former home via Google Maps: the once semi-barren hillside was now wonderfully populated with Jenny's trees.]

"Actually that day was the day I became who I am today - I am not sure what that term is: An environmentalist? An educationalist? A mega-tree planter? A person who just keeps on going no matter what? I don't know. It took us eight years to get fire-beaters around all of Lantau and signs put up. We nagged Government forever about laws, prosecutions, education, volunteers, firemen and police manning sites at the Grave Festivals. We formed fire-watch teams - all over HK. We wrote letters to the papers and articles and had meeting after meeting after meeting. At the same time we planted. And we planted. We learned how we needed to get permission, how to map sites, how to gauge species, how to source native trees, how to manage groups.

"I also need to extend enormous thanks to my two children for all their child labour for Hong Kong's trees over the years: their transporting of heavy trolley-loads of trees up the valley, their expert planting from probably the age of four and the managing of groups from about the age of twelve onwards. Also I need to thank them for all their expert fire-fighting skills. When we were three working together as a team, we were awesome!

"Just this year we taught schools how to do all this so they can create and manage their own sites. We taught them the whole process so that they could have 'ownership' over their projects and community engagement with the hope that in the future, schools will be able to use their sites as a curriculum resource, thus bringing students, teachers, parents and the wider community into the special forests that they design. There is also an enormous opportunity for corporations to do the same. My wish is that in the future schools, groups, and companies have their own designated ecological restoration sites. In this way we can then, as a community, take on the responsibility of restoring the forests, with all their benefits - and truly care for them.   – With thanks, Jenny."

In this book's last chapter I will detail my return to Hong Kong with my oldest son, James, and my oldest grandson, Javan. We visit Jenny and the Ark Eden project and see the beloved home where we lived some thirty years ago. The Tung Hang Mei valley will not be on fire, but rather beautifully lush and green and thriving with thousands of lovingly planted trees, thanks to the efforts of the teams led by Jenny Quinton, the lady who planted trees. And there in that peaceful valley, we will put Suzy's remains to rest, under a special tree of her own.

* * * * * * *

As if this story wasn't amazing or wonderful enough, I received this emotive **Echo from Eden** reaction, penned by Jenny in early October 2014 at the height of the nearby month-long student-led "Occupy Hong Kong" pro-democracy demonstrations which gained worldwide attention. Here's another echo of amazingly similar, yet unique, experiences that had been shared by two former strangers, without their knowledge, until this book project began. Here's Jenny:

"WOW! It's amazing, Mike. I just cried about three times!! Actually I am crying now. And then I just went cold - remembering – when you wrote about getting your foot stuck between 2 rocks: I did that. It was one of my most despairing fire-fights where I went up alone with two fire-beaters and five dogs and did successfully stop the fire from burning several amazingly beautiful glades. I was constantly calling for helicopters but they never came. In the end I had to watch the fire ring its way up the mountain and over the top. On several occasions I dived into these little valley dips - at one point because out of one tree flew about 100 giant yellow moths (so beautiful!)

"And then it happened! I made a sudden jump as the fire was all at once very near and my foot landed and jammed between two rocks. It was totally jammed. I will never forget the complete terror that engulfed me at that moment. I went ice cold in the midst of that terrific heat. Thank goodness for bloody chanting! I chanted so, so hard. And the thought was suddenly there and I was very clear in my head: this was not my time; I have a lot <u>more</u> to do. The fire was really near me now but I was calm. I fiddled and fiddled and fiddled and at last I managed to squeeze my foot out of my boot and finally my foot came free! Then I turned the boot round and it came out from the rocks (there was no going barefoot on that burning hot ground!)

"And so I lived to fight a few more fires. Blimey – I hadn't thought about that day for a very long time... But I have now remembered

another story too. It made it into the Hong Kong paper: the day my two children "came of age" to fight a fire with me. I have found the article and will send it to you soon. Here is the final slide from a PowerPoint presentation – a supporting tool I use to talk to students about the history and beauty of Lantau and its recent rapidly increasing pace of development (that for one I /Ark Eden am constantly setting up speed bumps for against fast moving juggernaut of so-called 'progress'). Your friend –Jenny"

Poem for Lantau
—by Jenny Quinton

It is big and wild and beautiful and no one really knows it at all.

Some of its dirt trails wind round the hills and upwards to the top.
Most of the land is bare, tree-less – the many vegetation fires have
left the land exposed and vulnerable.

Here a constant wind blows grasses, bushes, hopes and dreams
along.

Drives the flocks of curling scrub over the horizons and beyond,
inspiring them to try and try again. To struggle. To push. To grow.

Other trails wind down and through, into secret dells and over-
hanging dens - pockets of endangered heaven no one ever sees.

At night, giant yellow moths fly out of the trees and a hundred
emerald green pinpoints of light breathe and blow over the streams.

Watching the fireflies is seeing magic that is real.

Watching them, I tell them that this place is a priceless treasure.
How much I love it. And how we must never give up.

And I hear my brave words bang off the clouds and echo deep
across the universe.

And I feel my island grow a little older and cling a little deeper to
the Earth.

33. The Muse and Suzy!

An Ode to Friendship & Farewell to Suzy

Dedicated to all people who are truly a friend to someone.

To create the perfect sunset, the principal elements need to conspire flawlessly. Perhaps you've never analyzed the phenomenon: maybe you just glance up and say "cool!" For those readers who like to know how things work, the following is a rudimentary primer on sunsets. Obviously, there is location: you need to be looking in the right direction. Also it helps to have good color vision, patience and concentration. Amber-tinted sunglasses can boost the effect as well. Factors beyond your control that contribute to a great evening sky include the relatively low angle of our ever-faithful sun; seasonal lower variations in humidity; the height and slant of the clouds; and to a certain degree, the background levels of air pollution as well as the physics of visible color wavelengths. I took the picture above on my last day in Hong Kong many years ago, on a bittersweet evening when I thought—mistakenly—that I was saying a last goodbye to a special loved one. That woman, Annette, later became my wife of these past 28 years.

Mix all the ingredients and there you have it: a fiery sunset in all its glory, rich with reds and oranges, pinks and gold. Sometimes there are greens and blues, as well as subtle grays. The colors party on in the swirling celestial palette for a few glorious minutes. Then subtly, silently, it is over and gone. As the colors fade away, their memories still linger. I loved watching those glorious Technicolor sunsets in Hong Kong from my apartment balcony on Mount Davis Road, overlooking the western Lamma Channel and its enchanting scattering of islands.

I was usually a bit sad to see it disappear so soon; I would rather the sunset linger. But, to paraphrase, "better to have seen the fleeting sunset than never to have seen it at all." After all, it was a free gift. A new friendship is much the same. Serendipity helpfully prods events, circumstances and people into auspicious position, producing a burst of emotions, communications and learning. The two before-friends were already whole beings, their personalities and life experiences intact. But not yet connected.

When I was a young boy, my dad took me to meet the projectionist "Kelso" at the *"Auto-Vision"* drive-in theatre where he worked. Projectors were huge frightening affairs back in those days, lit by carbon-arc. I was warned not to look when Kelso fired up the projectors for the evening's movies, but I was a curious kid, and of course in my curiosity I did not heed Kelso's warnings. What I remember vividly when looking into the heart of the projector were these two dull gray rods, about finger-thick, as they were being slowly maneuvered ever closer to each other. When the gap was just right, there was a "Pow!" That loud, explosive, popping sound was followed by a brilliant flash of light and then a low resonating hum. Later, when my eyesight returned, that image was still etched in my memory. Such was my chance meeting with Jenny Quinton, as chronicled in the chapter "August 18th."

For two months in 2014 we regularly exchanged emails, with attached photos, stories, articles and poetry. It was incredible to be able to instantly journey via internet through a new friend's mind 8,000 miles away to a place I once lived. The book project bloomed under this inspiration, with Jenny enthusiastically encouraging me after each chapter I'd submit for her scrutiny. At one point, while searching for a handle to describe how her input prodded me to keep up with the arduous and scary task of writing a first book, I thought of the word "muse."

A month into our friendship I wrote Jenny: "To a great extent, contacting you has been the needed inspiration to get me going again on this project. You have been my—and when I was searching for the word, what came to me was—'muse.' I looked up the dictionary meaning just now, and it says: 'Muse: a person who is a source of artistic inspiration'."

At this point I might as well insert a caveat: if you are hoping to read about some scandalous infidelity, you will be sorely disappointed. Ours would simply remain a pen-pal relationship: an unplanned, unexpected but spontaneous friendship engendered by our mutual, unique shared experiences of raising our own young families in the same little house in the same enchantingly beautiful peaceful valley, shown below. There are skeptics who are unconvinced that such a friendship can exist without upsetting the cosmos; perhaps this is because they have never experienced such a wonder themselves. The experience actually enhances all other aspects and relationships in one's life, rather than detracting from same.

I was not exactly sure what happened, but a month went by without any word from Jenny. And thus as quickly as it had once formed, it seemed our sunset had faded. Without Jenny's usual regular feedback I found it harder to write the next chapter. Had something happened to her? Would we need to change our plans for our much anticipated trip to Hong Kong? Would those planned walks on those beautiful hillsides I loved never happen?

I sought counsel from Suzy, ever the witty and wise number one daughter (there have been four other wonderful daughters that followed.) She advised me not to worry: that the answer was probably nothing tragic, just a simple as-yet unexplained event. No sooner had I finished reading Suzy's sound advice when "Ark Eden" popped up as a sender in my email in-box. The Muse's voice had once again returned, after a short world tour, replying with her usual innate cheeriness: *"Hey Mike, So sorry! I have been in Wales, then I went to Paris and then to Newcastle and then to Sheffield and spending time with my family and friends - as well as trying to work at the same time for Ark Eden and my other job with ESF. I have had some grand adventures and now it's back to HK tomorrow where I need to hit the ground running, so don't give up on me. I am here! I just read "Ellen's Nasty Visit" and loved it! Keep writing! – Jenny"*

Cheerily humming away to myself, I settled down and began writing again that day, as instructed. There would be further rounds of rapid email exchanges, followed by lengthy silent periods. Thus it now appears to me that friendship is not like a singular sunset, but rather a series of sunsets, each one mysterious and beautiful in its own time, and always with many more to come. Our planned journey to Hong Kong was still on, or so I thought.

Some journeys are never planned; some are never even anticipated. Yet they arrive nonetheless and demand participation. On the long journey to visit my aging parents in Florida at Christmas, a round trip drive of 2,000 miles, a much more significant and overwhelming journey swept me away. This time it would be my silence and Jenny's friendly attempts to revive me that would create the next sunset, this one with much darker and richer colors: purples and crimsons, oranges and violets. Early in the morning the day after Christmas, Suzy unexpectedly and suddenly passed away. This is the Suzy of my stories herein: my oldest daughter; the same Suzy that was editing and provoking me to keep writing; the same Suzy that was going with me to visit Jenny in the New Year. I was devastated.

Jenny herself had been quite ill. She was also up to her ears with work projects. Her daughter was arriving for a visit and her son was helping her with a major reorganization of the Ark Eden project. These concerns all seemed suddenly forgotten as Jenny responded in earnest, even before my own grieving could fully set in:

"Mike, hi: I just sent a Facebook message. I am so, so sorry about Suzanne! It is hard to believe. I just want you to know my thoughts are with you. I am so shocked and so sorry. Just this morning when thinking of the year ahead, one of the big things to look forward to was going to meet Suzanne and James and you. I always have that picture in my mind of Suzanne and James up the mountain here. It made a huge impression on me.

And the emails Suzanne sent me and that I sent on to my children. Today I will make a tribute to her and leave it underneath the big flame tree. It is a stunning day today here in the valley in Hong Kong. My daughter is staying at the moment and walking these very same hills with her boyfriend– Drawn to the hills and the beauty of such a glorious morning. So from this place - which I know was a place of great joy and freedom for Suzanne - We all send our love!"

I replied: "Dear Jenny, thank you for the kind words of tribute to Suzy. That was wonderful that you put a tribute in the front yard where my favorite tree once was. This has been a total shock. I found out just minutes before I went with my sisters to help my dad celebrate his

86th birthday, the day after Christmas. Somehow I managed to keep it together for his sake: he could not have handled the news.

"Javan, Suzy's 18 year-old son, and my oldest grandson, is holding up so well; I am so very proud of him. We are letting him choose the final arrangements and respecting his wishes. He wishes to have Suzy cremated. He has often heard her say that the times we lived at –what is now Ark Eden – were the happiest days of her life. Javan's plan was to come with me to Hong Kong next year and bring Suzy's ashes with us on our visit, and allow her to have her final resting in the place she so loved. I was thinking of the hilltop way above the pool, where you can look down one way and see the Tung Hang Mei valley, and the other side you can see Silvermine Bay.

"Would you allow us to scatter her ashes on that mountain top? It will not be the visit we had planned for, but it will certainly be profound. Just before this sadness happened, Suzy was on the phone with me a couple of days ago, exhorting and encouraging me to keep writing the book and that she loved how it was coming along. Now I will have to finish for sure, so I can dedicate the book to her. "Well, a lot has sure happened since you answered my first email four months ago! Thank you for being my friend through this trying time. – Mike."

And then I held my breath; thinking maybe my request was way over the top. After all, I had never actually met these people, and here I am, wanting to bring my daughter's ashes with me! Well, nothing ventured, nothing gained. Fortunately, and conversely, when much is ventured, sometimes much is gained, as was the case when Jenny graciously replied: *"Dear Mike, Your email made me cry. Of course! The hillside above the house would be honored to be the final resting place for Suzy. I am really so glad Javan will still come with you and that we will do this. We have started to re-clear the path up to the top of the hill from the pool and will finish it next week. How I feel for Javan at this time. My heart really goes out to you. I have been thinking about Suzy and Javan and you all the time - chanting for you and also holding my daughter very close these last few days of her visit- she has just left.*

"Love and kinship and friendship - what treasures they are. There is nothing more important. Simply, they are the meaning of life and living. And dying. Because love never dies. And there are important messages from this terribleness that I am receiving: To look after

myself. To look after others. To get my fight back for Lantau and Hong Kong and the planet. To contribute more to the book, dedicated to Suzy and to the love of loving a place. I have been trying to think how I can contribute more to the book. So that it truly resonates with the passion and dedication that comes when people and nature meet and connect. So it encourages others to allow themselves the vulnerability of falling in love with a place, with nature. Yes, a lot has happened in these 4 months. I am there for you Mike and for your family. Love, Jenny"

What a gorgeous sunset was forming! These eloquent, healing words were much more than I could have wished for, from someone I'd never even met, who was halfway around the globe. Jenny's renewed determination to forge ahead with the important, nurturing Ark Eden project was encouraging and energizing and put my recent loss into new perspective. With a little more life in my fingertips, now I thankfully replied:

"Dear Jenny, I was happy to hear from you. Sorry to make you cry. I would have understood if you felt it too morbid for me to 'bring' Suzy with me. Javan was thrilled to hear that you welcomed our plans. We hope to be able to come sooner than originally planned, in early July. I found it amazing that at the time my daughter Suzy passed, your daughter was on the very hillsides that Suzy loved. I was grateful for your warm and emphatic and encouraging response and for your commitment to the book, because Suzy's recent passing has tended to take all the wind out of my sails. Sounds like you have harnessed some good positive energy; some good always manages to come somehow from pain and death, it seems. I'll write more soon. And hopefully I will be more upbeat next time. On this very cold, rainy, gray day here, your support helps! Thanks for all you are sending our way. Smiling again soon... Mike"

Fortunately, our accelerated plans to visit Hong Kong fit in well with Jenny's yearly plan. I was not in much condition for further obstacles and setbacks, as James and I were now not only busy dealing with Suzy's memorial plans and clearing up her estate, but we had also inherited the college planning work for her son, Javan. Few grandfather / grandson journeys could be as momentous as this upcoming July trip! And just when I could not have selfishly asked for more encouragement, more came my way as Jenny emailed:

223

"It is exciting you can come earlier! - And in summer we can plant trees for Suzy too! So please start planning! And it will make you feel better. You are in the calendar! I have 'saved' Eden Rock guest house for you for that entire time. I feel happy we are making plans.

"I had to stop in my tracks yesterday as Dhan, the dog-trackers and I beat our way up the back hill re-opening part of the old trail. We all refer to that path as 'the Stairway to Heaven'. Gulp! Just stopped in my tracks again thinking about it. As I sat there in the huge ferns the realization came that I too would certainly end resting up there too. I had never really thought about this before. And then the old Buddhist in me kicked straight in as I also realized that probably well before my ashes could hit the ground I would almost certainly be back in this life continuing where I had left off. No rest for us Buddhists you know!! We are the ultimate optimists!

"I had another thought too. I will tell you although I am not sure if this will go against your religious beliefs but the next thing that came into my brain was that when Suzy's ashes hit that ground then she too would come bouncing back and at that point I felt great joy and connection with her sitting up there on the mountain. I really hope you don't mind me sharing this. Thoughts with you all, Jenny"

How could I mind? These were my own hopeful, optimistic thoughts as well! Should I let Jenny know that, amazingly enough, my little family also used to call that pathway by pretty much the same nickname? Well, she'll find out soon enough when she reads this chapter. Through this all, I have faced yet survived one of my greatest fears: the loss of a loved one. The journey has strengthened me and made my sunsets that much more wonderful.

Then finally, this **Echo from Eden – or Lament from Lantau Island**, when Jenny emailed on January 18, 2015, three weeks after Suzy's passing: *"I wrote this Mike. It just came pouring out today. Please can you give it to her son Javan?*

Suzy in Your Footsteps
– By Jenny Quinton

Suzy in my footsteps.
Mine in hers. She listening all the time.
Me drifting, blowing with the wind and moon.
Both calling to the skies that it is alright.
Both hearing the need all over the world…
Both opening gates and doors
That are not really there.
Giving love endlessly to the small important things.
You know everything when you die.

Meeting you in the middle.
In dreams, dark places and light.
Suddenly alone in the silence.
Always up the hills
And under the tree.
When love and hope to all earthlings seems to have gone away.
Then there you are.

I tell you
You are coming back soon.
You say the same to me.
There is no doubt in your mind.
And so much doubt in mine.
You push out your huge timeless love.
And I receive it.
You are always ready.
Me only in spaces.

All of us are travelers.
But you carry nothing in your realm but love.
When I look at you I see only light.
It's the same you say.
And then you pour more love all over me.
Tell them you say. So I am saying it.
She is breathing all over you.
Understanding everything.
Suzy in your footsteps.

Suzy's Final Resting Spot:

The hilltop overlooking Silvermine Bay, Lantau Island

34. Return to Eden

Familiar Footsteps and Altered Landscapes

It was another Monday. It had been nearly a calendar year since the Monday that first began this story. There had been so much more than one year's worth of life-changing events: October's Occupy Hong Kong demonstrations garnered world attention; my daughter Suzy passed away at Christmas; Jacki, Jenny's close friend and valuable co-worker of many years passed away in the spring; Javan completed high school; in May he and I had visited Boston and MIT where I had studied forty years ago; now James was taking his first vacation in twenty years.

James and Javan and I found ourselves walking along the winding mountain pathway through the Tung Hang Mei valley which led to what had been my Hong Kong country home three decades ago. It had been a long journey getting back here, fraught with many hurdles. I had driven three hours through the Texas countryside, beautifully green after weeks of historically heavy rainfalls. My destination was the concreted expanse known as the Dallas Metroplex. From there on the 4th of July we flew via Seoul to Hong Kong. This route proved eventful as the MERS virus outbreak was in full bloom in South Korea and we were concerned about what restrictive quarantine measures Hong Kong had enacted upon arrivals from there. I fretted that we might be stopped at the border after an 8,000 mile odyssey, or kept for days in quarantine, as had happened recently to other arrivals from Korea and Mainland China.

Twenty-four hours later at the ultra-modern Hong Kong International airport, we passed through the two thermal imagining sensor arrays that had been set in place to detect any feverish travelers, at a special gate that was designated for all flights from Korea, happily without triggering any alarms. I had envisioned squads of paramedics armed with thermometers; I should have known that Hong Kong would find the most efficient screening method possible, so as not to hinder the flow of money into the SAR (Special Administration Region). Immigrations, Customs and Baggage Claim all went smoothly, much easier than in America, actually. We had arrived! It was midnight and our Monday in Hong Kong was just beginning. Right until the last moment, the next six days would prove to be a kaleidoscope of gorgeous rural scenery, juxtaposed against the incredibly modern, urbanized, skyscraper forest of the crowded city.

Years before, at about the same time we had left our home on Lantau Island, actress Geraldine Page gave an Academy Award-winning performance as elderly Carrie Watts in the 1985 film *Trip to Bountiful*. Mrs. Watts had struggled for years to travel for one last glimpse of her rural childhood. In the movie, Carrie's visit home was bittersweet as the town was now derelict and deserted. Our visit generated mixed emotions as well, but for different reasons. The beauty of the countryside was as majestic as ever; however the rapid

pace of development in the urban areas had altered the landscape in disorienting fashion. From our airport hotel window on the 15th floor we could see smoggy, crowded Tung Chung town.

When James was small we visited what had then been just a tiny hamlet, clinging to a small patch of the coastline. Now with the MTR subway connecting the new airport to the mainland, there were dozens of 60-story apartment buildings in Tung Chung ("eastern stream") where only dozens of people had once lived in near total isolation.

The new airport itself is situated on an island which was not on any map twenty years ago. Boasting the world's largest passenger terminal and being the tenth busiest in the world, Hong Kong airport sits on land which was recently reclaimed from the Pearl River estuary.

Everywhere we turned, intense Chinese civil engineering and property development were rushing ahead pell-mell. Once there was a nice leisurely ferry to Macau that took several hours and cost just a handful of dollars. Now there are helicopters that make the journey in just fifteen minutes for a tidy sum of US$600, buzzing noisily overhead and shattering the idyllic quiet of the Tung Hang Mei valley. To further facilitate the flood of gamblers rushing to Macau to offer their money to Lady Luck and the waiting plethora of high-end fashion malls, the powers that be saw fit to build a 50 kilometer (30 mile)-long bridge from the Hong Kong airport.

We had the great fortune to escape the concrete jungle after our first night's sleep. Jenny met us at the hotel after breakfast and whisked us away to the Eden Rock guest house, which had been prepared for our stay. This would be base camp from which we would make our daily forays up the mountains, into uber-urban Hong Kong and over to neighboring Macau. This was the view from our patio as I sipped my morning coffee Tuesday while the sun came over the mountains to the north, brilliantly lighting up the tiny Tung Hang Mei valley.

Even near the remote Tung Hang Mei valley on Lantau Island, progress made its inexorable march: where once was a sandy stream bed with tall grasses and reeds, now a square concreted channel imposed itself; where once grassy fields and vegetable crops had lined the stream, now dozens of multi-story apartment buildings filled the landscape; folks still rode bicycles and pushed carts, albeit now while talking into a cell phone rather than shouting to passersby.

The over-riding innate challenge of the visit would be the time constraints: firstly, how to reunite with a lifetime of memories in only six days; secondly, how to impart the beauty and specialness of it all, that his mother Suzy had once enjoyed, to her son Javan, who would be visiting for the first time. To assist in this task Serendipity appeared once more as many of the personalities, places and peculiarities of Hong Kong chronicled in my tales throughout these chapters presented themselves at will, in a book-in-review fashion, to wit: the evening air in the Tung Hang Mei valley was perfumed with the intoxicating aroma of the ginger plants from "Fragrant Harbor;" we walked past the "bus stop" where we had once found our dog "Happy Ending" in his eponymous chapter; on our daily commute down the pathway from the Ark Eden and Eden Rock homes we passed the meandering stream where James and Suzy had this cycling mishaps, and there was a water buffalo, the likes of which tiny young Phil had swatted in the "Buffalo Phil and Other Spills".

Wednesday afternoon after lunch at Cheung Sha beach, we caught the bus to the end of the line at remote Tai O village. We then hired a small boat for an exciting, fast, bouncy ride across the open waters to a miniscule pier. There we had to time it just right to jump off the undulating prow and onto the narrow slab of concrete being lapped by the waves. After a short walk along the shore and into the woods, we arrived at the roaring waterway of Shui Lo Cho, a series of waterfalls and infinity pools at the lower reaches of the famous Man Cheung Po stream. From the upper pool we had an incredible view of the South China Sea, spoiled only by the silly long bridge being built to Macau. This spot is the only water supply for the entire Tai O village; the water was refreshingly cold and delicious.

Returning on foot along the two mile-long, hilly pathway from our invigorating excursion at waterfall pool to Tai O village, we happened upon gentlemanly David. He remembered Jenny from years past, when she had guided a flock of school children on an environmental field trip. He reminded me of how crowded Hong Kong was still peopled by many wonderful individuals of strong character, as alluded to in "Close Encounters." Scattered across our valley and elsewhere we encountered the magnificent Flame of the Forest trees that were extolled in "The Lady Who Planted Trees." On Thursday of that week a Typhoon would visit Hong Kong, reminding me of "Ellen's Nasty Visit."

While some of our footsteps were taken on very familiar terrain, elsewhere the landscape had been greatly altered during the intervening years since I last lived in Hong Kong. In "Close Encounters" I spoke about all the banks and how easy it was to exchange currency. So I confidently led James and Javan down Des Voeux Road Central, and marched into a bank to change our US dollars to Hong Kong dollars. "Sorry sir, we have a new policy: no currency exchange unless you have an account." I scratched my ear, thinking I had heard wrong, as if the teller had said "We don't serve noodles at this noodle shop anymore." I persisted in trying several other banks, albeit all with the same, unhelpful response. We were directed to find little money change outlets, where the exchange rates varied considerably from the rates officially published. Then it dawned on me: Communist China was now in charge, and banking was less laissez-faire. I was not really liking this new Hong Kong!

Shrugging off that disorienting experience—of not being able to get money easily, in a city filled with banks, we set off uphill to the narrow lanes to buy some inexpensive souvenirs. The lanes had always been brimming with everything needed, and at a reasonable price. Was I in the Twilight Zone? It seemed all those nice little shops and stalls had been replaced with huge, ultra-modern, fancy, upscale stores and malls. It would prove easier to get a Gucci or Prada handbag than it was to get a simple t-shirt. Unbelievably, the huge Chinese Emporium department store in Central had vanished! Now I was really <u>not</u> liking the new Hong Kong. But wait, it got even worse!

I knew Central Hong Kong like the back of my hand, from eleven years of daily working and shopping there. But my information was now grossly outdated: where there had been a ferry pier to the Outlying Islands there was now a 114-story IFC building with Cartier and Louis Vuitton shops, sitting on top of more newly reclaimed land. The landmark ancient and venerable Star Ferry pier which had been right alongside the General Post Office was now four blocks out further into the sea and there was a huge Ferris wheel where once Victoria Harbor lapped the shoreline.

If development is a good thing, then this was obviously a case of too much of a good thing! On the opposite north side of the Harbor, Kowloon was suffering the same fate: there was a 118-story ICC building where once sampans and junks plied their trade. It might be safe to conjecture that in a few years' time, there would be no harbor at all—the two sides will eventually meet and the Star Ferry will be relegated to a museum, on some 120th floor.

James had wanted to visit nearby Macau to see the tiny 200 year-old hamlet where he once lived. We both remembered the quaint old charm of Macau and looked forward to a break from all the busyness of Hong Kong. We were surprised, however, to find that we had jumped out of the frying pan, into the fire. Once upon a time, when the Portuguese ruled this tiny outpost, Stanley Ho had a lovely casino monopoly with a cute, round 12-story hotel attached to it. While I believe there is nothing in Karl Marx's writings embracing gambling, the Chinese version of Communism has nevertheless done so whole-heartedly. There are now 33 huge casinos in this tiny enclave, one with over 2,000 hotel rooms. There is one 39-story gaudy affair which runs its own fleet of deluxe luxury coaches to the new Macau International airport which has been built for the sole purpose of facilitating gambling and high-end shopping. This seemed truly now a place without a soul.

Search as we might, there was no trace of the old stone buildings from James' village; now there were high-rise apartment buildings on what had once been isolated Coloane Island. In fact, it is no longer technically an island, as the space between it and Taipa Island has largely been filled in to make room for more "progress." Where once one bridge sufficed to move the traffic around, now there are four. There is also the 30-mile long monster bridge being built from Hong Kong International airport.

The simple explanation is that gambling accounts for half of Macau's revenue. Where once there were quaint little shops and stalls, now there are luxury malls. In fact, one such luxury mall there has the distinction of having the highest income per square foot of any mall in the world. This is all taking place on a patch of earth only eleven square miles in area! Once upon a time, during the countdown to the Chinese take-over from Portugal in 1999, there was concern that the new Communist landlords would clean up the gambling aspect. You are no doubt familiar with the expression "the Greeks have conquered the Romans". More accurately, this would be a case of the Romans acting more like Greeks than the Greeks themselves. I wonder if Mao would actually approve of this type of harvesting of the golden yet decadent Capitalist goose. The Old Maxim whispers again that "the more things change, the more they remain the same." We cancelled our plans to stay overnight.

Back on Lantau Island, there were changes afoot as well. The beaches have been wonderfully cleaned and upgraded. Now there are restaurants of all sorts that I hadn't dreamed possible when I lived there. We dined at a Turkish restaurant one night at Mui Wo. There were some new four-legged tourists in the area. It seems the Trappist Monastery wound down their dairy cow operation and in typical bureaucratic wisdom, the lead pathfinder cow was one culled by the appropriate government agency. So now the herd roams Lantau Island bohemian style. Each evening they come down to Silver Mine Bay beach to chill and mingle with the beach-goers.

Where there was once a haphazard collection of open stalls along a crowded narrow walkway, there was now a gleaming three-story, ceramic-tiled affair that was totally hygienic and completely devoid of character. The smelly swampy area behind the former marketplace now sported an Olympic-sized swimming pool and a neatly trimmed soccer field. Even back in the remote Tung Hang Mei valley, Lum Pa's ("Stretch") tarpaper shed had been bricked in and turned into the air-conditioned brain center of the Ark Eden operation. I'm not certain that Washington Irving's "Rip Van Winkle" experienced more shocking changes when he awoke than I did on this return visit. While we both hail from the Catskill Mountains region of New York, he only slept for twenty years, whereas I had been gone for thirty, albeit awake most of the time.

When we spent the afternoon at Cheung Sha beach, we had lovely Mediterranean food at tables set out on the sand under shade trees. Nearby, a windsurfer raced southward over the waves, aided by the precursor winds of an approaching typhoon. Almost as if in counterpoint, a water buffalo ambled northward along the shore.

James had spent his entire adult life in Texas where the prevailing sentiment is to live and let live. You are welcome to choose your own path, and go at your own speed. (Except on the thousands of miles of freeways, of course!) In Mui Wo village, by the ferry pier, there was now a grocery store where we could even buy French wine and German cheeses. This was a vast improvement from the days when we had to lug cartfuls of groceries back from Central Hong Kong on the ferry. James was completing his purchase and had a bewildering array of coins in his hands. (In Hong Kong sometimes $10 is a note; other times it is a coin.) As he was counting out the exact change, the teller grew weary of the slow progress and reached out and grabbed the needed coins from James' outstretched palm, then impatiently hurried him on his way. She obviously was not a Texan.

Late Friday evening when we returned from Macau, we stopped at the cooked food stalls on the pathway leading from the ferry pier at Mui Wo to Silver Mine Bay beach. We each ordered a different Chinese cuisine. James ordered a plate of fried rice along with his main course. In Texas the server would have replied "Anything else?" but not here. "No! That is too much food!" was the curtly delivered verdict. After some negotiation, James was allowed to keep his order intact. Again, James was not back in Texas any more. We did have food left over, which the Ark Eden dogs and Charlie the pig appreciated.

On Saturday it was planned for us to attend a barbeque at the country property of David W. It was our impression that his home was just a stroll away from the main road to Tai O. This was a welcome thought, as we were rather exhausted from a busy week of constant activity. Little did we know that we would be going on a strenuous two-mile hike through the steep mountains to the abandoned village of Lung

Tsai, where nestled in the rugged hills of southern Lantau Island lay hidden the incredible Chinese landscaped garden of Ng Yuen. Built in the 1960's by David's grandfather, Ng Yuen is a fairy-tale setting complete with terraced gardens, statuary, rare Chinese plants, a zig-zag nine angle bridge over a carp pool, gazebos, lotus pond, a stately high-ceiled main house, several smaller guest houses, and cages for peacocks and deer. To do the beauty and uniqueness of this place justice would require a book of its own.

Neglected for decades, but now being restored by David with the help and encouragement of Jenny and the Ark Eden staff, this hidden peaceful Buddhist paradise is simply fantastic. Its sheer size, isolation, and breath-taking views of the surrounding mountains, monasteries and distant sea form a stark contrast to the noisy, crowded, smoggy city of Hong Kong sprawling less than twenty miles away. There our gracious and unassuming host fed us a most sumptuous meal where we dined with a most eclectic gathering of nationalities and personalities.

The Hong Kong I knew of old was peopled mainly by British civil servants or the serious business types. Nowadays Lantau was wonderfully host to a much more colorful range of expatriates. This visit was a completely unanticipated, perfect climax to end a week already filled with great memories. Our tired bodies quickly forgave us for punishing them yet once more, as our senses basked in the myriad sights, sounds and tastes.

The over-riding challenge for me in writing this chapter would be how to fit a cornucopia of experiences into just a few pages. Perhaps there was even enough material for a second book. It seemed only appropriate that I should reflect and begin work on this chapter while seated in the same shady front yard of my old home, now called "Ark Eden" where once I had spent many productive hours writing and editing manuscripts. Junior Flame of the Forest tree was growing nicely where once his massive father had spread his sheltering boughs before the big storm felled that gorgeous giant.

The day before we left Texas on our flight to Hong Kong, it was predicted to rain and thunderstorm every day for that week. As it had been 30 years since my last visit and this was only a week-long visit, this forecast seemed unconducive. I asked my friends that if any of them had good connections with the Almighty, to please intercede on my behalf. During the first five days of our visit to Hong Kong, not a drop of rain fell. Coincidence? You already know my thoughts on that subject. Jenny fretted that her hundreds of sapling trees were never going to get the moisture they needed, as she sensed I had put an embargo on the rain. We arrived at a compromise solution: it could rain at night while I slept.

Thursday we had planned to go to Macau by Jet ferry, but nature added a new factor: Typhoon Linfa ("final" misspelt?) was arriving any moment and the government planned to shut down all transportation that evening. We changed plans and decided to go ahead with Suzy's farewell ceremony a day early. Two Ark Eden staff members spent the morning clearing the long, narrow, steep, winding pathway through the grasses, ferns, shrubs and trees up to the mountaintop which overlooked the lush, green Tung Hang Mei valley where Suzy had happily played as a young child. We climbed the path late that afternoon as the typhoon winds strengthened.

James wore a backpack carrying the beautiful red and gold urn that had protected Suzy's remains on the 8,000 mile journey. Javan carried a sapling tree—a specially beautiful and rare flowering native variety that Jenny the tree expert had selected for us. We also carried shovel, pickax and water as we slowly and laboriously made our way to the summit, where the howling winds greeted us. We stopped and silently took in the panorama: mountains and valleys; harbors and beaches.

I went first. Taking a small handful of ashes from the urn, I tossed them skyward and shouted "Suzy! Be free! Be happy!" Immediately

the winds snatched my words and Suzy's ashes and carried them far aloft. Bravely struggling through his tears, Javan likewise released some ashes into the typhoon winds, bidding farewell to his mom. We took turns holding him while he stood silent in his thoughts. Then Jenny likewise released some ashes. All this time the escort of dogs who had accompanied us on the climb sat silently. James remained faithfully behind the camera. We fell silent again for some time as the winds whipped about wildly. Later, upon reflection, James said that the wild, stormy conditions seemed only appropriate.

Next came time to select the best spot to plant Suzy's tree. After some deliberation, we chose a spot in a protected bend of the pathway, partway down the slope. James carefully carved a hole out of the dry, hard soil. Into this hollow we deposited Suzy's remains, placing her new tree on top. We filled in the space with soil, then watered it, and for some mulch, covered the top with ferns cuttings.

Then we all said our tributes to Suzy. Javan read from her diary. James was mute throughout this whole time; his contribution truly was nevertheless eloquent. Ever the tech savvy facilitator, James had the presence of mind to capture the GPS coordinates with his cell phone to send to Suzy's four siblings in Australia: Joanne, Phil, Andy and Natalie.

Once we had gathered ourselves and made our way safely down the steep pathway as night fell, a gentle rain began to caress the parched hillsides. Later that night the heavens opened and torrential rains, so typical of a passing typhoon, pummeled the valley all night, the heavy drops bouncing noisily off the roofs and patios of the houses while we slept. When we awoke the next morning the rains departed in time for us to have our usual breakfast on the patio table. The frogs croaked ecstatically in their now-soggy homes. The sun smiled down on us and the winds had vanished, leaving the sky scrubbed clear by Linfa's wind and rains. A beautiful new day was dawning.

James and I had done the best we could over the months to comfort and guide Javan, but it was a motherly touch he truly needed at that moment. We were very grateful that Jenny willingly stepped very effectively into that role: hugging and comforting him, mentoring him, asking about his future plans for college and most specially, making a trip back up the mountain with him on our last evening there so he could say another, private goodbye to his mom and place a protective screen around the sapling tree we had planted there.

Late Saturday evening we labored down the two kilometer long pathway through the warm humid blanket settling on the valley. We were leaving the valley for the last time, heading for a taxi in nearby MuiWo village that was waiting to take us to the airport and our midnight flight home. Along the way, Jenny asked Javan how he had enjoyed his visit. Instantly and enthusiastically he replied: "This has been the best week of my life!" That one comment had made all the effort and planning worth it all.

Our flashlights carved narrow tunnels through the darkness. Winding around one turn past the "bus stop" their beams revealed a special goodbye gesture: There on a gate grew a large Dragon Fruit cactus. Once a year, this plant's majestic, huge, ivory and gold blossoms open at night. Despite the fact that Suzy had always hated her given middle name, "Blossom", at that particular moment, the plant had chosen to do just that, and greeted us auspiciously with exactly seven resplendent gems. It had indeed been a very special visit, right till the very end. It had truly been a very memorable, worthwhile detour. Now it was time to return home, our cameras filled with images and our hearts filled with priceless memories. It was time to rest up and prepare for the next adventure...

Lantau Island's farewell gesture

Afterword

Well, I did it! I finally made my journey back to Hong Kong and I wrote my book at long last, finished exactly one year after I began in earnest! I owe many thanks to my family for their patience with me while I was on this latest detour. Thanks to all my friends and family members who helped with suggestions, editing and proofreading.

I sincerely hope you enjoyed it! If you did, please tell others about it! I hope at times this book made you laugh and brightened up your day. I hope that the trivia fans among you found some of the obscure facts interesting and useful for entertaining your friends. I hope that those of you who yearn to travel and to see new horizons will be encouraged to do so, while you still have the opportunity. I especially hope that those of you in Hong Kong, Australia, Austria, Portugal, Poland and Texas will not be offended by my irreverent treatment of the conditions and cultures of your wonderful lands. I hope that the witty ones among you found some good new humor material. [Hopefully those British readers found some "humour" as well.]

Most of all, I hope that my book has kindled your own curiosity to fully explore this wonderful gift we have been given, called life. Some of you who have lived long, full and interesting lives may have been heartened by some fresh nostalgic prods of your own memories. To those creative souls among you who love to express yourselves in words, I leave you with this sound advice: You should write a book!

Sincerely,

Michael J. Hawron,

18th August 2015.

Appendix: British Spelling Conversion Kit

Ianticipate that many of the enthusiastic readers of my new book will hail from Australia, Hong Kong, New Zealand, Canada and the United Kingdom, since I have made many good friends and business acquaintances in all such places during my many years working and travelling overseas. Different countries, of course, have differing cultures; and many who claim a shared language vary greatly in how they use that same language. I will attempt to address these disparities in this chapter. However, I must first offer a caveat: Despite my noblest of intentions, I will undoubtedly be even less successful in bridging cultural gaps than the centuries of diplomacy and commerce and war have been. But in the grand scheme of things, it certainly won't hurt much to have one more effort made at rapprochement.

I lived the first third of my life in Yankee northeastern United States; the next third mainly in some of the other former British colonies of New Zealand, Australia, Canada, and Hong Kong; while the most recent third of my life has been lived in a remote rural corner of Texas. As such, I have the distinct privilege that no matter where I am on this globe, as soon as I open my mouth to utter but a single word, I receive the Universal Reaction: "You are not from around here!"

My first foreign-country culture shock was in Auckland, New Zealand. Auckland in the late 70's was like Main Street America in the early 50's – everything was slow and quaint. The Kiwis good-naturedly struggled to understand what I was saying and likewise I often could not make heads or tails of what they had just said. There were lots of uncomfortable half-smiles and the occasional vacant stares. The problem arose from the misconception that both parties were speaking the same language. Nothing could be further from the truth. In reverse of the maxim "The more things change, the more they remain the same:" The more languages are thought to be similar, the more are their subtle differences and nuances.

Take the fanny for example: In America, that is the useful part of the human anatomy used for sitting upon chairs and other like objects. So it might be quite acceptable for a coach to yell at his bench full of players: "Get off your fannies and get out there and play ball!" However, across the Atlantic the fanny is on the direct opposite side of the anatomy chart, but only that of the female species. So when English novelist John Cleland wrote his racy, controversial and often illegal *Memoirs of a Woman of Pleasure* (aka: *Fanny Hill*) in the mid-1700's, he probably knew exactly what he was doing when he thusly named his eponymous main character.

But my friend Mike (no relation), who had been a tough champion boxer in the US Air Force, didn't know that. He was a fairly decent songwriter and singer, for the ex-military sort, and set out to entertain a roomful of visitors one day at a coffee lounge in Sydney. The Australians, by the way, for the most part were far less likely to be amused with my "accent" and would instead launch the rebuke: "Bloody Yank!" whenever I dared speak. But I soldiered on stoically, considering it to the lesser evil of the two epithets, the other being "Pommy Bastard!" Perhaps you never knew that one popular theory is that the word "Pommy" gets its origin from the acronym POM— Prisoner Of his/her Majesty—which, ironically enough, is what most early Australian settlers were called.

Anyway, back to our visitors: who were not of the prisoner, sailors and drunks variety; they were your garden variety teachers, priests, architects and secretaries. Mike the songwriter had not had the good fortune to read this chapter first and dove into his latest song, which he was certain they would love. The chorus began: "Get off your fannies..." Instead of applause, he was greeted with stunned silence. When one of the braver folks in the crowd offered to explain the reason for their disapproval, our brawny ex-boxer could only blush. Such is the power of language miscommunications, as I well documented in the chapter "Hong Kong Culture Shocks" where my wife Erica was caught saying that she was "buying sex" when she thought she was "going shopping."

If you mispronounce the phrase "cigarette lighter" in Cantonese – due to those nine distinct but not always so clearly distinct tones – you can inadvertently be saying "beat up the waiter" or "go #@%* yourself!" So it really IS important to speak as a Roman when in Rome, and not as a Greek or other Barbarian. Down Under, you don't get "take out" food. You get "take away". A "drug store" would be illegal in many English-speaking lands: you must instead go to the "chemist" shop for your aspirins.

And then there are all those "U"s! Everything takes longer to write when you spell English using English-style because "color" becomes "colour", "flavor" has become "flavour" [my spellcheck editor is going nuts right now], if you are happy you are in good "humour" not "humor" and if you are working you are part of "labour" not "labor." You will watch your behaviour in the splendour of the harbour so as to honour your neighbour, lest he start a rumour about you. That is not to be confused with watching your behavior in the splendor of the harbor so as to honor your neighbor, lest he start a rumor about you.

Then there is the issue of dyslexia, where theater becomes theatre and meter becomes metre and center becomes centre and liter becomes litre and so on. However, as with all rules, there are the inexplicable, illogical, maddening exceptions so that America has glamour magazines, not glamor ones; and the Space Shuttle was Endeavour, not Endeavor and the Party in Australia opposite the Liberal Party is the Labor party, and not Labour, as you might have guessed.

Some Anglo-American conflicts I lack sufficient resources to resolve properly, such as extra syllables: We in the USA have cheap four-syllable aluminum cans, whereas the British struggle with their five-syllable aluminium cans. By the time you finish asking where to recycle your al-u-min-i-um can, most likely the moment has passed. And what about this inconsistent nonsense of insisting on pronouncing the good old basic word "schedule" like it was spelt "shed-ule" yet failing to give the same treatment to "school" so that is sounds like "shool." This inconsistency is beyond my comprehension level of abnormal psychology. I will just leave it paradoxically alone.

After the mid-section years of my life, I had finally mastered the British ways of spelling in my editorial work, only to return to America after an absence of twenty-some years to be greeted with a chorus of "Don't you know how to spell?!" I was also faced with a consumer puzzle the first time I went to the Kroger's grocery: the cashier wanted to know, "paper or plastic?" The last time I went shopping in the USA before my world journeys, all grocery bags were made out of brown paper; all grocery bags in Hong Kong were plastic. I never thought of having a choice in the matter.

So I misunderstood the question: "Paper or plastic?" to mean: "are you paying by cash, or by credit card" since credit cards are basically plastic, and cash is basically paper—except in Australia, where bank notes are plastic, but now I am complicating things unnecessarily. So in answer to the pretty, yet impatient, young Hispanic clerk's question, I replied: "cash." It soon became obvious that she was neither pleased nor amused with my answer, judging from the look on her face. So she repeated the question with an impatient tone: "Paper or plastic!" Now I became tongue tied until the shopper behind me testily clued me in: "she is talking about the bags!" Welcome back to America – the land of consumer choices! Now, to further complicate matters, you have a third option. You can even ask for environmentally-friendly cloth bags, if you really want to slow up the line of shoppers behind you at the check-out counter.

For those of you who are annoyed with the lack of u's in this text, I will hereby offer you an ample supply that you can draw from and add wherever you feel necessary:

uuuuuuuuuuuuuuuuuuuuuuuuuuuuuuuuuuuuuuuuuuuuuuuuu

UUUUUUUUUUUUUUUUUUUUUUUUUUUUUUUU
uuuuuuuuuuuuuuuuuuuuuuuuuuuuuuuuuuuuuuuuuu

And so, my dear Commonwealth readers, I do so hope that you appreciate the favour I have done, in your honour.

Respectfully, Mike

About the Author

Michael J. Hawron studied electrical engineering and behavioral sciences at the Sloan School of Management at MIT before taking a long break from his formal education to travel the world.

Over the next thirty years, Hawron ran various successful small businesses and nonprofits while living in over thirty different countries on five different continents. Along the way, he experienced countless unique adventures, including a close encounter with a group of baboons; surviving near shipwrecks, killer typhoons, earthquakes, and ball lightning; and giving directions to a lost Chinese platoon.

While living in Hong Kong, Hawron worked as a book editor for a PR firm. Having completed his master's degree in higher education at Texas A&M University, he now works as general manager of a digital design firm.

His greatest adventure of all, however, is fathering twelve children. Now a grandfather of fourteen, Hawron lives with his wife, Annette, in Texas.

Made in the USA
San Bernardino, CA
14 October 2015